202
Great Walks

Mark Pickering was born in England but settled in New Zealand, and has wandered around and written about the New Zealand outdoors for the 30 years since, authoring 18 books in all. He lives in Christchurch with his partner and their daughter.

Also by Mark Pickering

Day Walks of Canterbury and Kaikoura
Huts: Untold Stories from Back-country New Zealand
Tramper's Journey: Stories from the Back Country of New Zealand

202
Great Walks

The Best Day Walks in New Zealand

Mark Pickering

RAUPO

Although every effort has been made to ensure the accuracy of information contained within this book, the publisher or author holds no responsibility for any accident of misfortune that may occur during its use. DOC is continually upgrading and altering tracks and should always be consulted before attempting any walk.

A RAUPO BOOK
Published by the Penguin Group
Penguin Group (NZ), 67 Apollo Drive, Rosedale,
Auckland 0632, New Zealand (a division of Pearson New Zealand Ltd)
Penguin Group (USA) Inc., 375 Hudson Street,
New York, New York 10014, USA
Penguin Group (Canada), 90 Eglinton Avenue East, Suite 700, Toronto,
Ontario, M4P 2Y3, Canada (a division of Pearson Penguin Canada Inc.)
Penguin Books Ltd, 80 Strand, London, WC2R 0RL, England
Penguin Ireland, 25 St Stephen's Green,
Dublin 2, Ireland (a division of Penguin Books Ltd)
Penguin Group (Australia), 707 Collins Street, Melbourne,
Victoria 3008, Australia (a division of Pearson Australia Group Pty Ltd)
Penguin Books India Pvt Ltd, 11, Community Centre,
Panchsheel Park, New Delhi – 110 017, India
Penguin Books (South Africa) (Pty) Ltd, Block D, Rosebank Office Park,
181 Jan Smuts Avenue, Parktown North, Gauteng 2193, South Africa

Penguin Books Ltd, Registered Offices: 80 Strand, London, WC2R 0RL, England

Originally published by Reed Publishing (NZ) Ltd, 2003
Revised edition 2006
This revised and updated edition published by Penguin Group (NZ), 2012

Designed and typeset by Jenny Haslimeier and Sarah Healey, © Penguin Group (NZ)
Photograph page 83 by Tony Lilleby, © Crown Copyright, DOC
Photograph page 189 by Sarah Mankelow, © Crown Copyright, DOC
Cover photography: (front) iStockphoto.com: Lake Rotoiti as viewed from the
St Arnaud Range, Nelson Lakes National Park;
(back) Mark Pickering: Cathedral Cove, Coromandel Peninsula
Printed in Australia by Griffin Press

ISBN 978-0-143-56795-0

A catalogue record for this book is available
from the National Library of New Zealand.

www.penguin.co.nz

MIX
Paper from
responsible sources
FSC® C018179

CONTENTS

SOUTH ISLAND

Preface

> 'Above all, do not lose your desire to walk: every day
> I walk myself into a state of well-being and walk away
> from every illness; I have walked myself into my best
> thoughts, and I know of no thought so burdensome that
> one cannot walk away from it . . .'
>
> —Søren Kierkegaard

Why walk? On the face of it, the answer is obvious: to keep fit, to get some fresh air into your lungs, and to stretch your muscles and your curiosity. Human beings are active bipedal creatures and, although this might surprise some teenagers, we are built to move.

Bodies are not well designed for long periods of sitting, either in front of computers or commuting daily in cars. It makes our breathing less generous, our health more fragile. The whole thrust of our technological improvements takes away our natural state of movement and replaces it with inactivity. The car and the dishwasher are wonderful devices, but so are our legs. We have them for life and we need to use them, or lose them.

There are few things more satisfying than a good walk. It requires little in the way of equipment or preparation, and there is a profound pleasure in quietly poking around a corner into a landscape different from your own. And it won't kill you — on the contrary, walking offers a respite from the chronic hurry diseases of modern society and its highly sugared consumerism. It takes us at a slower pace, when society drums on faster. And in a time when many human spaces are noisy and troubling, walking finds quiet and solitude.

Acknowledgements

A big thank you to the various friends who put me up for the night: Kirsty Woods and Peter Williamson in Wellington, Alan Hooker and Beverley Tatham in New Plymouth, Paula Kibblewhite and Bernie Kelly in Hawke's Bay, Lars Brabyn and Ottilie Stolte in Hamilton, and Jean and Roger Gibson way down in Central Otago. It made my many journeys a lot easier.

Especially thanks to my partner, Rachel Barker, and daughter Alex, who put up with my absences but also shared many of my wanderings.

A note on maps

All the maps in this book are from the 1:50,000 LINZ (Land Information New Zealand) database. A scale and north pointer has been overlain on all maps, but it is worth remembering that every map is oriented with north at the top, and the squares shown on the maps are always one kilometre in width.

With some of the longer walks (such as Crater Lake, Mount Ruapehu), there was not enough space on the page to show the full map. In these cases a section of the walk is included instead. A full topographical map is essential for these walks.

Map Disclaimer: Because the printed size of these maps is quite small, they should not be used as a substitute for a full-scale topographical map.

The original maps in *202 Great Walks* were all produced using the TopoMap Pro software (version 2, 250dpi), by Mapworld of Christchurch (www.mapworld.co.nz). Some of the later maps were produced on FreshMap version 3 for Mac. My thanks to Mapworld's owner Neville Jones for being able to utilise these excellent map software packages.

Author's note

This is a completely revised edition of *202 Great Walks*. Great effort has been made to bring the book up to date, refresh the style and content, and include the best day walks in New Zealand. Over 40 new walks have been added.

I revisited 80 percent of these walks. Where I was not able to revisit a walk, I used the web to check Department of Conservation information, and Google Earth was a useful resource for checking changes.

Every effort has been made to keep the information in the book up to date — but nothing stays the same. For example, the Christchurch earthquakes of 2011 may still affect walks such as Godley Head, Halswell Quarry and the Port Hills, so check the city council website for updates.

It is the publisher's intention to update the book on a regular basis. If you do find errors please email the author so these mistakes can be corrected for the next edition.

Mark Pickering
markpickering@clear.net.nz

Introduction

Walk notes

A GOOD START
For every walk, keep your plans modest if you are unfamiliar with the area, or with the exercise. Keep an eye on the weather and tell someone where you are going.

EQUIPMENT
A good parka or raincoat, energy food or a packed lunch, thermos, map, camera, sturdy and comfortable shoes and a sunhat are good things to start with.

There is now a good range of lightweight tramping boots that are impressively comfortable. A raincoat is useful for protection against rain and wind, or for sitting on while taking a break. For some of the alpine walks warm clothing is essential. Walking poles — such as retractable ski poles — are very useful.

CLEAR INTENTIONS
Before you set off, it is important to leave clear intentions of where you are going with friends, family, flatmates or a visitor centre, if applicable (and don't forget to sign out, too). Some walks have logbooks at the start of the track.

TRACKS
No specific gradings are given for these walks, but a general description is supplied, indicating if the track is flat, rolling (up and down) or a hill.

The type of track is also described, such as gravel path, mown grass strip, beach walking, sheep track or four-wheel-drive (4WD) track. The description 'tramping track' indicates a basic track, not necessarily well marked, and where some experience is useful.

The condition of the track is indicated in the description, especially if there is any mud or rock scrambling.

TIMES AND DISTANCES
It is notoriously difficult to suggest walking times that make sense to everyone. The times suggested here are generous, designed for the plodders. Most averagely fit adults could reduce them.

As a rule of thumb the following scale can be used for flat or well graded track travel:

2 km — 30 minutes
4 km — 1 hour
8 km — 2 hours

For hill climbs the actual distance is not as relevant as the amount climbed. On a good track a walker could expect to take the following times:

300 metres — 1 hour
600 metres — 2 hours
1000 metres — 3 hours

SHORTER OPTIONS

Many of the walks in the book have a 1-hour turnaround option. This should suit people with shorter time or shorter legs, or who are short of breath. Usually the turnaround point is at an interesting feature.

WEATHER

New Zealand enjoys a brisk, mild, moist, maritime climate. Long periods of settled weather are unusual, and abrupt changes are the norm. If the weather is not looking favourable, change your plans, for many hill walks are a waste of time if you cannot see the views. It is often windy, so take a windproof jacket that can also serve as a rainjacket. The sunlight can be intense and burn time can be short, so a sunhat and sunblock are useful as well.

WINTER WALKING

The walks in this book are not written for snow conditions; so, for example, the walk to Crater Lake, Mount Ruapehu should only be undertaken in summer or in snow-free conditions.

WALK ACCESS

Basic descriptions of how to get to each walk are included, but a good road atlas is essential. There is usually a carpark with signposts at the start of the walk. Other facilities are indicated.

CITY AND TOWN WALKS

Most of the city and town walks have good bus transport to them, but beyond the city or town your own transport is virtually essential.

WHEELCHAIR AND DISABLED ACCESS

Only a very few of these tracks are suitable for wheelchairs. Many start in visually interesting landscapes, however, so people with disabilities may not need to venture far from the carpark to see some spectacular places.

MOUNTAIN BIKING

Mountain biking has become an enormously popular sport, and a few of these walks are shared with mountain bikes or cross over mountain-bike trails. Unless otherwise stated, or the track is designated multi-use, walkers have priority.

Walk information

INFORMATION CENTRES

Throughout New Zealand there are wonderful information centres in all large and small towns, usually clearly indicated by the big 'i' sign. These centres are usually open seven days a week and are an invaluable starting point in areas you are unfamiliar with.

DEPARTMENT OF CONSERVATION

The Department of Conservation (universally known as DOC) is the government department responsible for the protection and management of wilderness areas in New Zealand. It manages all national parks as well as marine reserves. Something like 25 percent of New Zealand's land area is in wilderness regions of one type or another.

Nearly all the national parks and forests have DOC visitor centres. These are excellent places to start from, providing track advice, pamphlets and maps, weather updates, and information on track closures and upgrades. In some towns DOC has actually combined with the town's information centre to provide a joint information base. A great idea!

DOC has a very good website with a wealth of information on tracks and walks (www.doc.govt.nz).

MAPS

For the more serious walks, always take a topographical map. As indicated in my preface, the maps printed with most walks in this book are extracts from the LINZ 1:50,000 topographical database. You might consider using map software and printing off the relevant walking section before you go. I have also suggested specific topographical maps where appropriate.

Walk courtesy

KEEP TO TRACKS

Please keep to the marked tracks and avoid shortcuts. This is particularly important in fragile wetland areas and in farm parks.

FENCES AND GATES

The farm rule is generally to leave a gate as you find it, whether open or shut. Most fences will have stiles, but if not, climb over the fence by the main strainer posts or where the gate is hinged.

SHEEP AND CATTLE

Sheep are rather nervous beasts and easy to panic, whereas cattle display the opposite trait of excessive curiosity. Walk quietly around stock, and if they are moving away give them time to do so.

LAMBING AND TRACK CLOSURES

A number of tracks pass through rural areas and may be closed from August to October for lambing. Other reasons for closure include fire risk and wildlife management. Please respect these closures.

DOGS

Most dog owners are responsible and careful, and keep their dogs under firm control. This is particularly important in rural areas where stock is present, and in wildlife areas.

For ground-nesting birds, the continual presence of dogs can jeopardise breeding, making it difficult for the birds to re-establish.

Dog fouling is an unpleasant nuisance on walking tracks, and it is the owner's responsibility to remove it. Carry a plastic bag.

FIRES
Many areas have restrictions or a total ban on fires; please observe these. If you see a fire, contact the emergency services.

Walk nuisances

LITTER
Litter is not a major problem on tracks, and mostly occurs in carparks. Do your bit by picking it up and help ensure our beaches and tracks stay litter-free.

INSECTS
The two main problem insects are sandflies and wasps. Any good insect repellent should keep away the small sandfly, a type of black fly that is at its worst on the West Coast of the South Island. Mosquitoes appear mostly at night, so if you are camping a good insect-proof tent is useful.

Wasps are particularly prevalent in the beech forests where there is honeydew, and are at their peak in March and April. They are generally manageable but if you do get stung move quickly, for it usually means you have disturbed the nest and the first sting will quickly be followed by others. If you are allergic, take precautions.

There are no poisonous insects, and the only venomous spider is the increasingly rare katipo — which few New Zealanders have ever seen.

VANDALISM AND GRAFFITI
All walks suffer periodically from vandals and graffiti. If you see evidence of this please contact the track managing authority immediately. If you actually see vandalism, or any suspicious behaviour, and can identify a vehicle involved, take down the licence plate number and report it to the police.

CAR BREAK-INS
It is unlikely your vehicle would be broken into while you are on a day walk, but to avoid becoming a victim don't leave valuables in cars.

WATER QUALITY
A water-borne parasitic protozoa called giardia exists in some freshwater streams and can cause diarrhoea and vomiting. Fortunately it is easily cured and for most people it is a nuisance rather than a threat. Carry your own water if you are doubtful of the local supply, and generally treat any water running through farmland with caution.

It is a pity to have to automatically distrust all freshwater creeks in wilderness areas, and I have no intention of doing so. Recent scientific articles suggest that in order to absorb the 10 giardia cysts necessary to start an infection you need to drink something like 100 litres of water from a stream. Cheers, mate!

Walk appreciation

APPRECIATE WITHOUT POSSESSING

Many of these walks are in fragile areas where if everyone grabbed a chunk of interesting material the consequences of degradation would be obvious very quickly.

People may think 'their small bit' doesn't make a difference, but it does. Interesting stones, driftwood, flowers and so on should be left for others to appreciate. Historic sites should be treated the same way; taking souvenirs of curious bits would soon mean there was nothing left to see.

FOOD GATHERING

The wildlife is usually more dependent on the food sources than you are. Shellfish beds can get depleted very quickly by humans, and people invariably take more than they really need. Collect for yourself and your family, not for all your mates.

WILDLIFE

If you see a wild creature, keep a reasonable distance and be patient. Most birds and animals give warning signals or movements if they feel uncomfortable, so respect their space, and withdraw. Do not come between animals and their escape routes (for example, between seals and the sea). If chicks or young animals are present, be especially discreet.

The Department of Conservation advocates a policy of not feeding wild animals, especially 'friendly' ones like weka and kea. It is usually the wrong sort of food and lures them away from their natural environment. Get expert help for the 'rescue' of injured wildlife.

GUIDEBOOKS TO PLANTS AND BIRDS

New Zealand is rich in unique plant and bird species, and there are many excellent books on New Zealand plants and birds.

For plants, Andrew Crowe has produced a series of attractive books — *Which Native Tree?*, *Which Native Fern?* (both Penguin), and so on — which are full of information on how to identify plants and their uses by Maori.

For birds, *Hand Guide to the Birds of New Zealand* by Hugh Robertson and Barrie Heather (Penguin) is excellent, and lightweight.

CONSERVATION

'Take only photos, leave only footprints' is the best motto. Wilderness is not a replenishable resource, and we cannot buy any more of it if we run out. Nor can we preserve its peaceful and uncluttered environment if we take our noisy, busy culture into it.

Taking care

New Zealand has a relatively harsh climate, with abrupt changes of weather. Rivers can quickly flood and snow can occur in the mountains at any time of the year.

River crossings are common and the mountains are unusually rugged by European and American standards. Tracks and routes are often of differing standards, requiring good observational and map-reading skills.

If you are unfamiliar with the country it is sensible to consult with visitor and information centres for up-to-date weather information and track changes before setting out. The Department of Conservation also has a very good website that lists track and bridge closures, slips and washouts and other issues.

As another precaution, always notify others of your intended movements and when you are likely to return.

NORTH ISLAND

Cape Reinga •
Cape Maria van Diemen •

Dukes Nose •

Waitangi • • Urupukapuka Island

Waiapoua
Forest • • Mimiwhangata Peninsula

South Head • • Tutukaka Head

WHANGAREI ◉ • Mt Manaia
Two city walks

Tawharanui Peninsula •
Kawau Island •
Tiritiri Matangi Island •
Shakespear Park •
Muriwai Gannet Colony • Rangitoto
Kitekite Falls • Island
Cathedral Cove •
Sailors Grave •
Whatipu Beach • **AUCKLAND** The Pinnacles •
Three city walks Broken Hill & Collins Drive •
Otuataua Hunua Miranda The Windows & Karangahake Gorge •
Stonefields Falls Estuary
Orokawa Bay & Pios Beach •
Waikato River • Wairere Butlers Incline •
Falls • **TAURANGA**
HAMILTON ◉ Two city walks
One city Tuahu Track
Mt Karioi • walk **WHAKATANE**
Ruakuri Cavern • Ngahopua Tarawera ◉ Kohi Point
Lakes • Falls •
Omaru Falls • **ROTORUA** ◉
TAUPO One city walk
One town walk Horomanga River •
Mt Pureora • Whirinaki River •
Lake Mt Tauhara • Arahaki • Makorori Point & Pouawa Estuary •
Whitecliffs Taupo Lagoon Lakes Waikareti &
Walkway Ruapani Circuit **GISBORNE**
NEW PLYMOUTH Porere Redoubt • • Lake Rotopounamu Shine Falls •
Two city walks ◉ Tongariro Crossing • Mt Kaweka • Morere Hot Springs •
Te Koru Pa • Waihohonu Huts • Boundary Stream • Mahia Reefs •
Mt Egmont/Taranaki ▲ •The Plateau Taranaki Falls • ▲ Mt Ruapehu Stingray Bay •
Fanthams Peak • York Circuit Crater Lake •
Dawson Falls • Hapuawhenua Viaducts • **NAPIER**
Snapper Rock • Rangiwahia Tops • ◉ Two city walks
WHANGANUI ◉ Sunrise • Cape Kidnappers •
Track Te Mata Peak •
Totara Reserve •

PALMERSTON NORTH ◉
Two city walks

MASTERTON
One city walk
Waikanae River Walk • Castle Point •
Kapiti Island QEII Circuit & • Atiwhakatu River
Wairaka Point Totara Flats •
Mt Kaukau Colonial Knob • Korokoro Stream & Belmont Trig
Makara Headland • Rimutaka Incline
Red Rocks • Boggy Pond & Putangirua Pinnacles •
Somes The Catchpool &
WELLINGTON Island Orongorongo Valley
Two city walks Cape Palliser •
Pencarrow Head •

1. CAPE REINGA & TAPOTUPOTU BAY
A spirited headland track

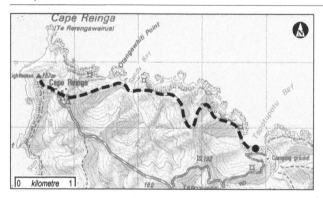

TRACK
A rolling coastal headland path, mostly grass, well signposted.

WALK TIME AND DISTANCE
1.5–2 hours one way Tapotupotu Bay to Cape Reinga; 3–4 hours (7 km) return.

ONE-HOUR WALK
Up onto Tapotupotu headland return.

ACCESS AND FACILITIES
From Kaitaia drive north almost 100 km on Highway 1. Just before Cape Reinga there is a signposted turn-off to Tapotupotu Bay, 2 km, where there is an excellent DOC camping area beside a fine sandy bay. This campground gets packed in summer.

It would be a dreadful letdown to come all the way to the top of New Zealand and be disappointed with the view. Cape Reinga is 450 km from Auckland, but when you arrive at Tapotupotu Bay it is worth it. This rare and remote place has a very fine landscape indeed — swathes of golden sand, windswept heathlands and big cleaving headlands. The walk from Tapotupotu Bay has brilliant views, and overlooks the constant jostling of the seas that meet at Cape Reinga.

From Tapotupotu Bay the track zigzags steeply up onto the grassy headland, marked by red posts. Manuka is the common coastal tree, with an aromatic scent.

The track climbs to the top of the headland, where it turns inland along an old vehicle track, then cuts across the top of a gully onto another headland. You can see the Cape Reinga lighthouse now, as the track descends into the sheltered and unimaginatively named Sandy Bay, which the Maori called Ngatangawhiti Bay. This cove is pretty and secluded, with shady pohutukawa and rock platforms to explore. It is a good place for lunch, and about halfway to Cape Reinga for those who want a 2-hour return walk.

It is a steep climb up the open spur to the Cape Reinga carpark, where there are toilets and information boards.

From the lighthouse there are good views of the Three Kings Islands. Reinga has been translated as 'underworld'; Maori legend says that all souls travel to the pohutukawa tree on the headland at Cape Reinga and descend into the underworld by sliding down a root into the sea. The souls climb out again up onto Ohau, the highest point of the Three Kings Islands, where they bid their last farewell before leaving finally for the world of their ancestors.

Cape Reinga is enormously popular with tourists, and is 'sold' as the most northerly point of New Zealand. In actual fact the northernmost point is North Cape, 30 km away to the east, but let us not quibble, for it is no hardship to swing back along this soaring headland track.

The headland track at Cape Reinga, looking back to Tapotupotu Bay.

2. CAPE MARIA VAN DIEMEN & TE WERAHI BEACH
Beach wilderness and sweeping vistas

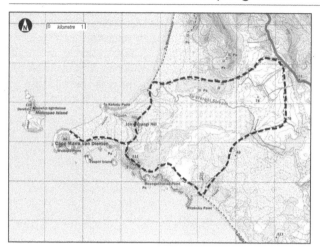

TRACK
Well marked trails, but some soft going in the sand and dunes. The wind can howl here, so pick your day carefully.

WALK TIME AND DISTANCE
3–4 hours (13 km) circuit, but add another 2 hours return if you go to the Cape lighthouse itself.

ACCESS AND FACILITIES
From Kaitaia drive north almost 100 km on Highway 1, and 4 km before Cape Reinga is the signposted carpark. At Cape Reinga itself there is New Zealand's most northerly roundabout, toilets and a Maori archway that plays spooky Maori flute music when you pass through.

Te Werahi Beach and Cape Maria van Diemen together make up a pure wind-blasted wilderness of dunes, ephemeral wetlands and coastal forest. Big skies, big views, strong light. This walk is quite a contrast to the Tapotupotu cliff trail, which is much more intimate in nature, and if you've driven all this way it makes good sense to do both.

The carpark starts at 100 metres altitude, which is almost the highest part of the track. You get a pretty good view here, as the track crosses farmland, then goes through coastal forest and crosses a boggy wetland on a boardwalk.

It's spectacular when you break out onto the beach plain (some Maori shell middens here) and cross Te Werahi Stream. It's the only part of the track where you will get wet feet so it's worth taking your boots off.

From here you start climbing up towards Herangi Hill (159 m), though the track slips around the back and meets a junction in a golden glacier of sand. It's a strange and absorbing landscape of sand sculptures with weirdly rich colours.

It's worth going out to the cape itself, following the lonely marker poles across the sands. A short climb through flax scrub and you reach the automatic beacon, with a good view of Motuopao Island and its desolate lighthouse. This was one of the most remote postings in New Zealand for the lighthousemen.

Back at the junction, the track wanders through coastal shrublands, with good views as it drops down to Twilight Beach. Strange caramel crusts of mudstone cover the crème brulée sands.

There's a track junction just before Twilight Beach, and you turn inland through a miniature desert of sculpted rock outcrops. There are enough orange track lollipops to keep you on target, and at the forest fringe the track edges around a deep wetland, and crosses it on a boardwalk.

At the farmland the markers seem to temporarily disappear, but the trick is to climb the brow of the hill towards the fenceline, and markers intermittently appear as you wander along the fenceline past bemused cattle back to the carpark.

OTHER WALKS AND CAMPSITES

The Tapotupotu and Cape Maria van Diemen walks, as described, are part of a much longer track that goes from Spirits Bay to Ninety Mile Beach. DOC has excellent camping grounds at Tapotupotu Bay, Spirits Bay, and halfway up the Cape Reinga highway at Rarawa Beach.

Looking from Cape Reinga towards Cape Maria van Diemen.

3. URUPUKAPUKA ISLAND

A historic and attractive island for both Maori settlement and European fishermen

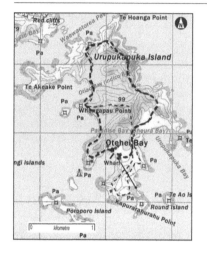

TRACK
Grass and bush tracks, well signposted.

WALK TIME AND DISTANCE
2–3 hours (4 km) circuit.

ACCESS AND FACILITIES
You need a boat to get to this DOC-managed island. Ferry times change all the time, but generally from Russell a cruise runs every day (except Christmas Day) to Urupukapuka Island, and on to Cape Brett and the famous 'hole in the wall' sea arch.

It used to be possible to take the morning ferry to Cape Brett, then be dropped off on Urupukapuka Island by midday. This allowed enough time for a walking circuit of the island if you didn't dilly-dally, and get picked up by the afternoon cruise, about 4-ish.

The Bay of Islands is well named — on the boat from Russell, island after island shifts and slinks out of view: Motuarohia, Moturua, Motukiekie and then Urupukapuka. Each island has its own identity, and for Urupukapuka (the largest island) that is a combination of Maori and European heritage.

There were over eight pa sites on this fertile island. In 1926 the legendary American fisherman Zane Grey established his camp, and wrote a book that made New Zealand famous for big game fishing, *Tales of the Angler's Eldorado: New Zealand*.

The island is now predator-free and DOC has a major programme to upgrade the tracks and historic sites.

The jetty at Otehei Bay is a quiet place. There's a small shop here, and over to the right, the red building is a historic woolshed. The tracks start and finish here, and it's easy walking. Turn left from the jetty and Otehei Bay quickly disappears behind the pohutukawa and scrub forest that has sprung up over the island. Short pretty bays follow in quick sucession.

At Otiao Bay the track turns inland and starts to climb, following the cliff line around the northern coast. Good views but no access to the bays. At Paradise Bay (Oneura) the track meets the coast again, then wanders out over the farm peninsula towards Kapurarahurahu Point. This is a marvellous lookout, both to the mainland and to Otehei Bay.

Time to relax. But when you see the fast bow-wave of the ferry returning from Cape Brett and easing into the harbour, then you know that your little island sojourn has come to an end.

4. WAITANGI MANGROVE WALK

Impressive waterfall and a boardwalk through dense mangrove forest

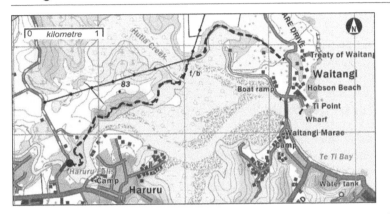

TRACK
Well made paths and boardwalks.

WALK TIME AND DISTANCE
2–3 hours (3 km) one way, 3–4 hours (6 km) return.

TWO-HOUR WALK
To boardwalk return.

ACCESS AND FACILITIES
Paihia in the Bay of Islands is about 60 km north of Whangarei on Highway 1, turn off at Kawakawa The Treaty House is 1 km north of Paihia, and the east end of the mangrove walk starts by the golf course near the Treaty House. For Haruru Falls take Highway 11 (Puketona Road) 3 km and follow the signs to the carpark. This description starts from the Haruru Falls carpark.

Away from the great beaches of Northland, the rest of the coastline is eaten away with saltwater estuaries and mangrove backwaters. It is a shunned landscape, only glimpsed from the road, so this walk is an excellent way to experience the private life of an estuary. The boardwalk is probably about the best mangrove walk there is, with the added attraction of Haruru Falls.

Haruru can be translated as meaning 'roar' or 'thunder'. At the small Haruru Falls carpark it is worth diverting to enjoy this wide, attractive falls.

The mangrove track follows the estuarine coast in a forest mostly of tree ferns, with kanuka, mapou and rangiora Although only second-growth forest it is kiwi habitat — you might hear one if you make a night visit to the carpark.

The forest trail is easy walking past a shag colony, and takes an hour to get to the Hutia Creek inlet, a swathe of mangroves which the 250-metre boardwalk zigzags through with information panels at appropriate sites.

Mangroves are especially adapted to grow in tidal waters. They can secrete salt through their leaf surfaces, and their seeds germinate before leaving the parent tree. Mangroves have distinctive aerial-breathing root systems ('snorkels'), and they also form 'root rafts', which stabilise them against tidal action. The mangrove's sweet-smelling flowers make a distinctive fruity honey. The mangrove is frost-tender and does not usually grow further south than Raglan or Opotiki.

The boardwalks and bridge here are good places to see white-faced herons. Shags are also common, including the little black shag, black shag and pied shag, and so is the bright sound and flight of the kingfisher. The peculiar 'pistol popping' sounds are caused by the snapping shrimp, which has a grossly enlarged special joint for the purpose.

If you don't have transport at the other end, this boardwalk is a good place to turn back.

If you continue, after 30 minutes you come to a good lookout platform where you can see the whole Waitangi estuary. Then the track skirts farmland and a golf course, and pops onto a fairway just before the carpark. It's only a 10-minute walk to the Waitangi Treaty House, which bustles with visitors and ceremony, in contrast to the privacy of the estuary.

Boardwalk across Hutia Creek.

5. DUKES NOSE (KAIRARA ROCK)
A bush walk with mangroves and a rock climb up a pinnacle

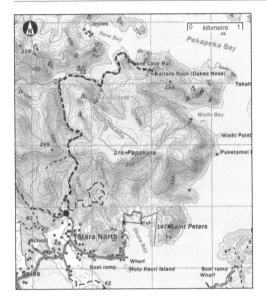

TRACK
Standard bush tramping track, there and back. Dukes Nose (or Kairara Rock) has a chain up the steep rock face, which definitely requires nerve and judgement both to ascend and descend.

WALK TIME AND DISTANCE
4–5 hours (8 km) return.

ACCESS AND FACILITIES
About 30 km north of Kerikeri on Highway 10, turn into Totara North, a historic and charming settlement. After 2 km turn up Campbell Road to the small carpark and DOC sign 'walking track'. The hut at Lane Cove is kept locked, and a booking needs to be made with DOC at Kerikeri to get the key.

Whangaroa Harbour in the far north has a weird, unexpected landscape. Bushy inlets filter down to the sea, and strange rock pinnacles stick up. The place almost resembles Fiordland, if it wasn't for the mangroves and rickety historic towns. It's charming, nostalgic and involving.

The track to Lane Cove initially follows the old bridleway over the bush saddle, a 200-metre climb, then down into Shermans Stream till it merges with Waiarakau Stream.

Rock bluffs loom over this flat river valley, and you are almost immediately beside mangrove forest. There's no sign of the sea, but the track wanders along a tidal waterway that feels untouched by the outside world.

The track reaches the inlet, and pops over a low saddle to Lane Cove Hut. The 16-bunk hut is barely a metre above the high-tide line. A blissful place, where you can look out across the lapping waters of Pekapeka Bay, and gaze at the strange rock outcrops around the harbour.

One of these is called Kairara Rock or Dukes Nose. A steep side-track leads to the base of the bluffs, and a chain has been bolted in place. It gives moral support as you pant and sweat up the greasy rocks.

There are bluffs at every edge of this pinnacle, so on top it's like a little lost world, with panoramic views of Whangaroa Harbour. Getting off Dukes Nose is actually harder than getting up, so take care.

6. SOUTH HEAD HOKIANGA HARBOUR
Seascape and signal station

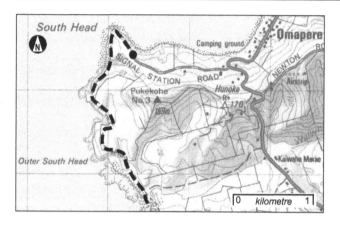

TRACK
Grassy paths and low-tide beach walking, some clambering.

WALK TIME AND DISTANCE
1 hour on headland and beach, 2 hours (3 km) return to Waiwhatawhata Stream Bay and point, 3–4 hours (8 km) return to Waimamaku River mouth. A low or mid-tide is definitely best.

ACCESS AND FACILITIES
From Omapere on Highway 12, drive south for 1 km then follow Signal Hill Road 2 km to the well situated carpark.

South Head commands the entrance to Hokianga Harbour. In 1838 John Martin erected a signal mast to help boats cross the dangerous bar, and he acted as pilot once vessels had entered the harbour. Martin also built a small cottage and boatshed at the waterside. Following the decline of the timber trade, the signal station's long period of service was brought to a close in 1951.

There is a good view from the carpark, but it is even better from the short walking track to the old signal site, with the huge, barren sand dunes on the North Head of Hokianga Harbour gleaming white in the sun.

There's a short historic trail around the headland (10 minutes), and plenty of opportunity to explore the coast at low tide, where the cleared path for the historic pilot boat ramp can still be seen.

A graded track goes down to the main beach, but to continue south you need to climb up onto the next headland and follow the track around a recessed rock cove. The track then follows a fenceline around farmland before dropping through sand dunes into Waiwhatawhata Stream Bay.

There are extensive tidal platforms here, and the track continues around to the point at the south end of the bay. If you wish, you can continue along this wild and remote shoreline for 4 km to the Waimamaku River mouth. It is certainly tempting.

OTHER WALKS

South Head is at the top end of the Waipoua Coastal Track, a three-day tramp that travels past Waipoua Forest then over Maunganui Bluff to the Kai Iwi Lakes. There is also a low-tide route from South Head to Omapere settlement.

Fishing from South Head.

7. WAIPOUA FOREST
King kauri

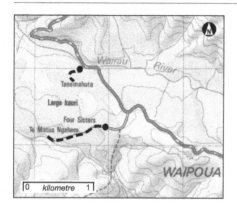

TRACK
Flat and easy walking on good forest paths.

WALK TIME AND DISTANCE
Tane Mahuta is 10 minutes return; Four Sisters 5 minutes return; Te Matua Ngahere 30 minutes return.

ACCESS AND FACILITIES
Waipoua Forest is on Highway 12, about 30 km south of Opononi and 60 km north of Dargaville. The signposted forest lookout, just south of the forest headquarters, is worth a side trip. The Trounson Kauri Park is the closest DOC campground, about 15 km south of Waipoua.

These walks are short but unique, for the Waipoua Forest is one of the last places in New Zealand where you can see big kauri in a pristine forest. These huge trees never fail to impress, and when you consider that they were part of the era of the great moa and the giant eagle, then in the pre-human history of New Zealand, a biblical quotation seems apt — 'there were giants in the earth in those days'.

Everything about kauri is larger than life. They can live up to 1000 years, and a tree the size of Tane Mahuta could be milled to make 10 houses. Waipoua is the kauri's most important sanctuary, 2600 hectares of mature kauri that was preserved only as late as 1952.

Kauri is a conifer, and starts life as a normal-looking tree in a nursery forest like manuka, grows through a teenage or 'ricker' stage, then thickens into middle age and swells into a vast cylinder while the crown gets thin. The bark flakes off in pieces the size of dinner plates, which prevents epiphytes establishing a hold.

The Tane Mahuta walk goes to the largest kauri in existence, quite awesome, with a 13-metre girth and 17 metres to the first branch. The Four Sisters walk follows an elegant boardwalk around four 'sisterly' kauri.

The Matua Ngahere ('father of the forest') walk is the most impressive of the three, mainly because you have time to become absorbed by the forest as you head deeper into it. The silence is deafening, and big trees slide by in a splendid parade until you reach the second biggest kauri in existence.

8. MIMIWHANGATA PENINSULA
A right royal coastline of beaches and birdlife

TRACK
Mostly open farmland and scattered bush reserves. The signposting is adequate but discreet, and a map pamphlet is helpful in navigating around this peninsula. In general you can walk anywhere, but use the stiles and don't disturb the stock.

WALK TIME AND DISTANCE
2–3 hours (3–4 km) return, walking the peninsula circuit *or* the coastal lookout and Waikahoa Bay. For the whole lot allow 4–5 hours (7–8 km) return.

ONE-HOUR WALK
Okupe Beach to Taukawau Point return.

ACCESS AND FACILITIES
Mimiwhangata is about 50 km north of Whangarei. Turn off Highway 1 at Whakapara and follow the sealed road to Helena Bay and Teal Bay, then a narrow, winding, unsealed road over a bush saddle to the coastal carpark. There is another access via the Kaiikanui Road, but this is tortuous. Carpark, information board, toilet and ranger station here. Strictly no dogs.

Even by Northland's high standards, Mimiwhangata has a ridiculously perfect beach landscape, remote and relaxed, with sandy bays ending in headlands covered with pohutukawa. Offshore islands hang around the coast and the coastal fishing boats that chug languidly by are the only reminder that there is another world, somewhere. It's so good even Queen Elizabeth and Prince Philip stopped by for a picnic on the beach in 1955.

If you stroll south from Okupe Beach you round an attractive headland into another long and gorgeous beach. Which in turn leads onto other headlands, and other beaches . . . However, most visitors turn north along Okupe Beach, past the lodge to the headland, where you can pick up a vehicle track over to Kaituna Bay. The eastern rosellas are often making a colourful racket in the pohutukawa, and kaka sometimes come in from the offshore islands.

Follow the vehicle track as it circles the wetland and you might spot the rare brown teal, along with the nosy pukeko. The spotless crake and bittern are much shyer. There are excellent views along the coast, and welcome swallows flit about the headlands, as well as pipits.

Another vehicle track leads down to the wide Mimiwhangata Bay. About halfway along a gravel road leads over the saddle back to the ranger station and carpark. Mimiwhangata is both a marine park and a farm park, and you can sense that the sheep are smugly aware that they are on to a good thing.

From Mimiwhangata Bay it's a good walk over the next headland to the sheltered Waikahoa Bay, where camping is permitted. Paradise ducks raise their chicks here, and seem quite happy dabbling in the sea.

Following the shoreline a bush track is signposted which clambers up a kanuka-covered spur to a lookout point. A ridge track offers an alternative exit through bush and farmland (and past some massive pohutukawa trees) down to the road saddle and back to the ranger station.

A very satisfying day, and back up the dusty road out of Mimiwhangata, you might catch a last regretful glimpse in the rearview mirror of an island-sprinkled sea.

Tidal platforms and islets at Mimiwhangata.

9. TUTUKAKA HEAD
Interesting islets and curious coves

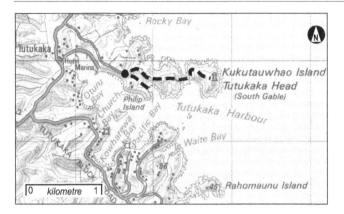

TRACK
Grass footpath and stairs, some beach walking and a short bush track. You need a mid- or low tide.

WALK TIME AND DISTANCE
1 hour (2 km) return.

ACCESS AND FACILITIES
Access has currently become complicated due to a dispute between landowners and the council. The old Tutukaka Reserve Road (just north of Tutukaka itself) is now called 'Landowners Lane' and signposted as private. There is an access track from the Tutukaka marina, which leads up to Landowners Lane, that you can walk along to the headland carpark. It is hoped that the land dispute can be resolved quickly as this is a very special piece of coastal scenery.

Tutukaka Head is a succession of islets with tiny jewel-like bays on either side, where the sea sweeps right through when it wants to. Surf scours the tide platforms, and Kukutauwhao Island anchors the whole fragile assemblage of islands together.

The main track from the carpark leads over the grassy headland, then sharply down a staircase to the beach. The little sandy bays are perfect, and so are the rock platforms that skirt both sides of the peninsula.

Kids will love to play hide-and-seek among the rock stacks and sea-sculpted rocks. If they get bored, the final part of the walk clambers up a bush track onto Kukutauwhao Island. At the high point a lighthouse watches over the Poor Knights Islands, with views everywhere.

There is an alternative track from the carpark, which goes down to an unnamed bay where there is nothing more than sand, grass and solitude.

10. WHANGAREI CITY WALKS — A.H. REED MEMORIAL KAURI PARK & WAIMAHANGA WALKWAY
Urban kauri forest and coastal causeway

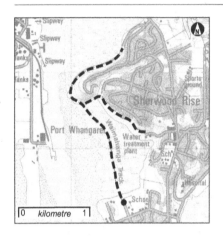

TRACK
A.H. Reed Memorial Kauri Park: excellent boardwalk from the middle carpark, suitable for wheelchairs. Other bush tracks are more basic.

Waimahanga Walkway: good flat gravel-led track, on causeway, bush track to Waverley Street.

WALK TIME AND DISTANCE
A.H. Reed Memorial Kauri Park: middle boardwalk 10-minute circuit; full walkway 30 minutes (1 km) one way. Waimahanga Walkway: 1–2 hours (5 km) return; circuit 1 hour 15 minutes (Cockburn Street, causeway, Waverley Street, Raurimu Avenue).

ACCESS AND FACILITIES
A.H. Reed Memorial Kauri Park: from the city take Mill Road and Whareora Road to either of three carparks: top waterfall, middle boardwalk, or lower.

Waimahanga Walkway has several access points. Onerahi Road leads to: Old Onerahi Road and Waimahanga Road; Waverley Street (this has the best carparking); and Raurimu Avenue to Cockburn Street.

A.H. REED MEMORIAL KAURI PARK
This splendid walk can fit into most people's schedules. There is a spectacular short boardwalk around several thick-waisted kauri and a waterfall higher up.

To do the best walk in this park, get dropped off at the top carpark and walk down to the lower carpark. First you descend past the sudden 24-metre waterfall (although there seems to be no decent lookout onto it), then the track wanders through lush forest to the middle boardwalk.

At times the canopy walkway platforms are a giddy 10 metres above the valley floor, and the gentle stream underneath is softened by deep-green, moss-encrusted boulders. The track then winds down easily to the bottom footbridge at the lower carpark.

WAIMAHANGA WALKWAY
Good exercise for flat walkers, as the causeway follows an old port railway line built in 1911. The views are a bit scant, blocked by the luxuriant mangrove forest, but there are two bridges where you can watch the estuary gurgle in and out through the mud.

From the Cockburn Street carpark follow the causeway to the first wooden truss bridge, then it is another 10 minutes to the George Point footbridge. There are some views of the port here, and the main track continues on to Waimahanga Road carpark, but it is a good idea to take the side-track. This leads past a footbridge and into a fine remnant of coastal forest with totara trees and lush ferns. This track exits onto Waverley Street opposite the sewage treatment works and kindergarten. It's not a bad circuit to go up onto Onerahi Road and down Raurimu Avenue to the Cockburn Street carpark again.

A boardwalk section of the A.H. Reed Memorial Kauri Park walk.

An old bridge on the Waimahanga Walkway.

11. MOUNT MANAIA
Volcanic rock plugs and spectacular views

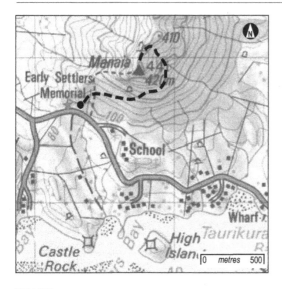

TRACK
A steep hill walk on a well shingled track — and I counted 1088 steps on the way up! The old alternative track down has been closed.

WALK TIME AND DISTANCE
2–3 hours (3 km) return.

ONE-HOUR WALK
Bluff lookout return.

ACCESS AND FACILITIES
From Whangarei follow the airport road then the coast road to Whangarei Heads and Urquharts Bay, then take Ocean Beach Road 1 km to a carpark and information sign. At McLeod Bay (1 km before Mount Manaia) there are toilets, picnic tables and a children's play area.

This striking mountain can be seen from many points around Whangarei Harbour and Bream Bay. Fingers of volcanic rock stretch up from a coastal forest, and DOC has built a viewing platform that is spectacular and nerve-racking.

The andesite rock is the remains of a volcano that erupted 20 million years ago, and the peak is of important cultural and spiritual significance to Ngati Manaia and Ngati Wai.

From the large carpark beside the pub, follow the track past the sculptures and picnic table. At first the track sidles gently, but this quickly changes as it climbs up through dense bush with some impressive puriri trees. The track lurches upwards around the base of Mount Manaia to the bluff lookout (not signposted but an obvious worn trail), where there are good views of Bream Head and the Hen and Chicken Islands. No handrails here!

The track steepens past fine specimen trees of totara and kauri, then reaches the main ridge, wriggling past increasingly forbidding rock pinnacles. It's an exciting place as you reach the steps leading up to the top viewing rock. No handrails at all, and it's a bit dizzying looking out over the bluffs to the Marsden Point oil refinery.

From the top you can see the isolated trigged summit of Mount Manaia. According to Maori lore, the local tribes used to take the remains of their dead warriors and chiefs to the top of these peaks, though I cannot imagine how they did it.

OTHER WALKS IN THE AREA
At Bream Head there are several excellent tracks. Circuit to Smugglers Bay and Home Point 2 hours return.

The pinnacles of Mount Manaia.

12. TAWHARANUI REGIONAL PARK
Peninsula of promise

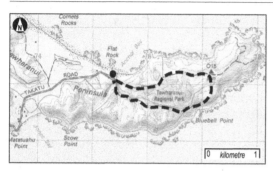

TRACK
An easy rolling walk on farmland, with bush groves and some mud.

WALK TIME AND DISTANCE
1–2 hours (4 km) return, but if including Takatu Point add another hour.

ACCESS AND FACILITIES
From Highway 1 at Warkworth, follow the road through Matakana to Omaha Flats Road, then turn right at the roundabout onto Takatu Road, through to Anchor Bay in Tawharanui Regional Park. Tawharanui Peninsula is now a predator-free reserve, and you drive through large automated gates to get to Anchor Bay. Here, there are toilets, a picnic area and excellent camping reserves. Anchor Bay is also a marine reserve.

Northland seems to have a baffling surplus of coastal scenery, and each twist and turn of the road to Tawharanui reveals another magical indentation. Matronly peninsulas shepherd close-knit groups of islands, and each bay is a golden slice of summer all year round.

Anchor Bay is an open, sandy beach broken with tidal platforms, offshore reefs and headlands with sea caves. Large pohutukawa trees rustle on the beach edge. It is hard to walk away from all this, but if you choose to do so, there is an excellent walking circuit around the peninsula.

From Anchor Bay follow the farm road up onto the broad tops of the peninsula, crossing the Ecology Trail. There are good views along the farmland past grazing Hereford cattle and Romney sheep.

After about 2 km you reach a track junction that is about 90 metres above sea level, where you have the option of following the peninsula out to Takatu Point. You can see cloud-capped Little Barrier Island in the distance, and Kawau Island nearby to the south.Follow the track along the south coast and turn onto the side-track that drops through a shady stream with stands of manuka and puriri, then follows alongside a dam, meeting the Ecology Trail again on the way. Shortly you exit out to Anchor Bay again and that stunning stretch of sand.

OTHER WALKS
South Coast Track, Ecology Trail and sand dune circuit.

13. KAWAU ISLAND
Time out on a timeless island

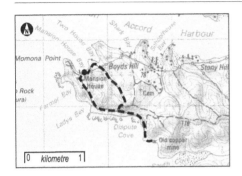

TRACK
Well graded bush track, or rock-hopping at low tide to get to the old copper-mine engine house.

WALK TIME AND DISTANCE
1 hour (2 km) return to copper mine, 2 hours (3 km) for full circuit and additional wandering.

ACCESS AND FACILITIES
Daily ferry service (Kawau Water Taxis) from Sandspit, a wharf about 10 km from Warkworth. There is a DOC charge to go inside the Mansion House. There are toilets and tearooms, and plenty of places to picnic outside.

As Te Kawau-tu-Maro, 'island of the motionless shag', Kawau Island was a prime fishing ground for Maori, but when Samuel Marsden landed in 1820 it was deserted. Manganese was discovered here in New Zealand's second underground mine, then copper in 1844.

Cornish miners were brought in, with some 300 miners and their families at the height of the industry; the 'Mansion House' began life as the mine manager's house, built in 1847.

In 1862 Governor George Grey bought the island. He owned it for 25 years, during which time he enlarged the house and established a cultured paradise of exotic birds, plants and conversation. From 1888 onwards a succession of owners ran the Mansion House as a guest house, holiday camp and watering hole for boaties. Restoration started in 1976 and the renovated Mansion House was officially opened in 1979.

From the wharf, walk past the Mansion House, persistent peacocks and exotic plants, onto the Coach Road that leads to Ladys Bay, a small, discreet cove. The track continues on to a lookout on a grassy clearing, and from here you take the Miners Track down to Dispute Cove — a nice snoozing spot.

Either take the inland track to the copper mine or, if it is a mid- to low tide, wander on the tidal platform to the massive ruin of the engine house. The rich colours of copper stain the rocks and the stillness is broken only by scavenging gulls.

On the return you can explore the broad tidal platforms around to Ladys Bay, or follow the Redwood Track down to Two House Bay and around the point to the Mansion House. Of course, you have to allow some time to explore the grand Mansion House, and by then you will be scampering to catch the return ferry. You quickly run out of time on Kawau.

14. SHAKESPEAR PARK (WHANGAPARAOA PENINSULA)
A happy alchemy

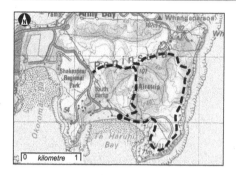

TRACK
Rolling farmland and short bush tracks. Some mud and small hill climbs.

WALK TIME AND DISTANCE
2–3 hour (6 km) return circuit.

ONE-HOUR WALK
Headland return.

ACCESS AND FACILITIES
Turn off Highway 1 onto Whangaparaoa Road, which leads to a carpark. There are picnic facilities, pukeko, peacocks, toilets and a camping area at the far end of Te Haruhi Bay. This park is now guarded by a predator-proof fence.

At the end of the Whangaparaoa Peninsula is Shakespear Park, named not after the bard but after one W.H. Shakespear, who purchased the land in 1883. A shrewd buy, most people would think, for it included a glorious beach at Te Haruhi Bay, wide swathes of tidal platforms, some pockets of bush reserves and excellent views along the sea-eaten coastline.

In 1967 another shrewd buyer came along: the Auckland Regional Authority purchased the land for a park. And the public have not been slow to enjoy this gorgeous park, which is alive with choices for the lazy or the walker.

The best circuit walk starts from Te Haruhi Bay and follows the Tiri Tiri track up onto the headland, then swings along the easy farmland tops, displacing the well fed sheep and passing a short side-track down to Pink Beach.

Platoons of perambulating pukeko peck in the paddocks, but the main track climbs up to a farm road and wanders around to the lookout platform, with the Hauraki Gulf spread out before you. The main poled track continues down a spur to Te Haruhi Bay — where the peacocks are still prowling on the foreshore.

OTHER WALKS
The Heritage Trail features forest, wetland and Maori sites, 1–2 hours return.

15. TIRITIRI MATANGI ISLAND
New Zealand's rarest birds in abundance on an island with stunning sea views

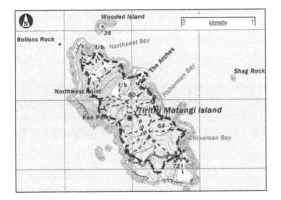

TRACK
Easy bush and grass trails, and boardwalks, throughout the island, but make sure you grab a pamphlet map, for the network of tracks can be confusing, and makes the 220-hectare island seem bigger than it really is.

WALK TIME AND DISTANCE
You could spend all day here, but the ferry timetable will dictate the time allowed. Minimum needed for wharf return circuit is 2–3 hours (5 km).

ONE-HOUR WALK
From wharf up the Wattle Track to lighthouse return.

ACCESS AND FACILITIES
360 Discovery Ferries run regular trips to the island leaving from Auckland and Gulf Harbour Wednesday–Sunday and on most public holidays. Bookings essential. It gives you about 5 hours on the island. Toilets are located at the wharf, Hobbs Beach and at the visitor's centre. Guided walks are available.

The last resort. That's how the islands around New Zealand have been described. Tiritiri Matangi Island is arguably one of New Zealand's finest open sanctuaries, and New Zealanders cannot claim to have seen their country until they have been to 'Tiri'. They are seeing New Zealand as it was 1000 years ago, an avian paradise, free of predators such as rats, stoats and humans. And this magical island is only 30 km from downtown Auckland. It is effectively a zoo, but nowhere else in New Zealand can you readily walk amongst so many bird species in such significant numbers.

At the wharf visitors are met and given a brief introductory talk on the island and its significance, and then sent off to explore the island. The description covered here will follow the Hobbs Beach, Kawerau and Ridge tracks to the lighthouse, returning to the wharf via the Wattle Track.

From the wharf turn left along the track to Hobbs Beach, passing nesting boxes for little blue penguins (lift the lid and have a look). Already you should have seen and heard the raucous saddlebacks and parakeets as they chase each other noisily through the canopy, as well as busy fantails and bellbirds. Much of the forest on Tiri has been planted by volunteers in the last 30 years.

Along the pretty Hobbs Beach you may see tui feeding on the flax nectar and getting coated with orange flax pollen. At the end of the beach the Kawerau Track climbs under the huge pohutukawa into a bush gully where brown quail often scurry along the track ahead of you. Near the top of the Kawerau Track are stitchbird feeding trays, and early in the morning these areas can be a flurry of hungry stitchbird beaks and feathers — they take little notice of humans.

On the main Ridge Track the views are excellent, and usually whiteheads can be seen feeding along the bush margins. The track wanders along the crest all the way to the historic lighthouse, visitor's centre and shop, where friendly takahe poke about.

It's likely you are running out of time now. A good return to the wharf is down the Wattle Track. There are several seating areas beside water troughs, and if you sit quietly for a while birds such as the North Island robin will appear. Kokako are often heard and spotted on this track.

The Wattle Track crosses the road once, and reaches a small pond where brown teal can often be found. Then it's a couple of minutes to the wharf, and as on Prospero's island, the magic will cease:

> . . . the isle is full of noises,
> Sounds, and sweet airs, that give delight and hurt not.
> Sometimes a thousand twangling instruments
> Will hum about mine ears; and sometimes voices
> That, if I then had waked after long sleep,
> Will make me sleep again . . .
> —Caliban, in Shakespeare, *The Tempest*, 3:2

Wharf at Tiritiri Matangi.

16. MURIWAI GANNET COLONY
Soaring by sea cliffs

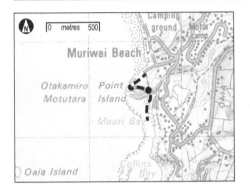

TRACK
Easy, well made walking tracks.

WALK TIME AND DISTANCE
30 minutes return gannet colony; 1 hour return via Flat Rock. Add 30 minutes for visiting Maori Bay.

ACCESS AND FACILITIES
From Auckland follow Highway 16 towards Helensville for 25 km, then turn off at Waimauku, some 12 km from Muriwai. The last stretch of road down to Muriwai is steep and narrow; watch out for walkers. The closest access to the gannet colony is at the Maori Bay carpark, where there are toilets and superb information panels. There is also extensive carparking and a general store by the main beach.

A short walk to an amazing sight: a squabbling, jostling, cackling, thriving gannet city. There are a thousand nesting pairs of gannets at Muriwai. The viewing platforms are only metres away, and give a marvellous bird's-eye view of what it is like to be a gannet. When they are not fighting for their space on the cliff edge they are whooshing overhead, bringing back food for their young or effortlessly soaring over the Pacific.

The headland updraughts make it easy for the gannets to get to and from the nesting sites; and the abundance of food has enabled the colony to expand. It started on the offshore Oaia Island, then moved onto Motutara ('island of seabirds'), and when this rock stack became overpopulated the gannets started a mainland colony.

The Muriwai gannet colony.

You can also walk past the viewing platform and down to Flat Rock, which is a popular fishing spot, despite being both slippery and dangerous with a surf breaking. From the beach it is a short walk past the main carpark and up Maori Bay track to the main carpark again.

You can also follow a locked access road from the carpark down to Maori Bay itself — a dark volcanic rock cove, dotted with the corpses of gannets that didn't make the grade.

17. AUCKLAND CITY WALK — ONEPOTO BASIN & KAURI GLEN

Hidden city craters, bush glens and coastal parks

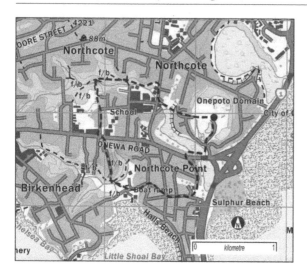

TRACK
Gravel paths, boardwalks, bush tracks and grass swales, some short climbs.

WALK TIME AND DISTANCE
2–3 hour circuit (4 km return).

ACCESS AND FACILITIES
Onepoto Domain is on the North Shore and can be reached off Highway 1 at the Onewa Road exit, straight through into Sylvan Avenue, then immediately left into Tarahanga Street, and immediately right into the Onepoto Domain road. Head to the end of the road where there are plenty of carparks, picnic areas and toilets.

Old volcanic basins and bush reserves intertwine discreetly throughout Northcote. There are track links from Onepoto Basin into the Kauri Glen Scenic Reserve, and then on to Le Roys Bush and then Little Shoal Bay and . . . well, you get the idea.

You need to have a good map and sharp eyes to find the track signs, and you might get lost. Blame me. But this is splendid backyard discovery stuff that kids would really enjoy. Cafés on the way round. There are three busy roads to cross.

From Onepoto Domain, cross the broad grass fields directly into Puawai Place. Go up past Tarahanga Street and keep a sharp lookout for the sign to Rotary Reserve, and this pleasant bush track meets a junction. Turn right and you walk upstream out of the bush and end up beside the busy tennis courts.

Cross Lake Road and walk north 50 metres and around the back of the buildings on the left is a grass reserve, and a track starts here that leads into Kauri Glen. At first it is narrow and follows the stream closely to Woodside/ Fowler Avenue, where it changes sides and gets onto a much better track.

Kauri Glen Park is an unexpectedly dense reserve of impressive kauri trees in the heart of Auckland. Take the first left track option. There are good steps and stairs out of the glen, leading onto Gladstone Road.

Follow the south stretch of Gladstone to busy Onewa Road (there's a good crossing point at St Mary's School), and veer into Seaview Avenue. There's a lovely line of houses along this road and a sharp bush track that drops down to Le Roys Bush, then into Little Shoal Bay.

This is a pretty seaside bay with picnic tables and toilets. By the Scout den, steps lead up to Clarence Road, then cross directly into Vincent Road, and walk down past the café and wine bar onto Stafford Road and down to Stafford Park. From here a concrete path leads up to Waimana Avenue, then you have to dodge across Onewa Road again.

Now you are on a sophisticated cycleway with elegant leaf seats and a frond-styled footbridge that leads you back into Onepoto Domain. A neat way to finish.

18. AUCKLAND CITY WALK — HARBOURVIEW
Great space, great place

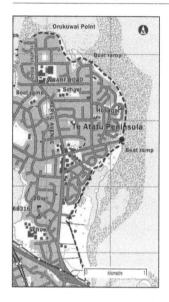

TRACK
Flat, easy paths on gravel and boardwalks.

WALK TIME AND DISTANCE
1–2 hours (5 km) return.

ACCESS AND FACILITIES
Off Te Atatu Road, right into Harbour View Road and drive to the carpark at the end.

Walks at Opanuku Walkway, Paremuka Lakeside, Henderson Creek and Waipareira are stunning examples of what can be done to provide urban walkways in the heart of the city.

Harbourview just about tops them all, with its view across the glittering Waitemata Harbour to the tall, metallic skyscrapers downtown. The walkways start by a carpark and a totally useless but utterly stylish picnic platform, on the site of a historic homestead that burnt down.

You can go north or south.

If you head north from Harbourview Beach, a good track wanders along the coast and reaches Kelvin Strand park, about 2 km away. It then continues around the tip of Te Atatu Peninsula to Te Atatu Road and Chapman Road close by Henderson Creek.

Head south from Harbourview, and a short boardwalk circles the pond, but the main track wanders along the shoreline, where shorebirds dabble among the ponds and creeks. There is a handsome historic brick homestead along the track, and several exit points to Te Atatu suburban roads, with a good carpark at Gloria Avenue.

The walk crosses wide open spaces before it ends too soon by hitting the Northwestern Motorway, but it is a lovely return.

Picnic platform and pampas, Harbourview.

19. RANGITOTO ISLAND
Easy access to a volcanic icon

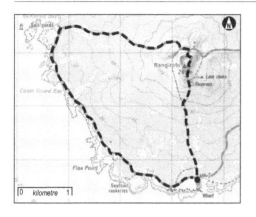

TRACK
Good gravel tracks and paths up a steady 259-metre hill.

WALK TIME AND DISTANCE
2–3 hours (6 km) to summit and return; 4–5 hours (12 km) summit and McKenzie Bay return. Take drinking water.

ONE-HOUR WALK
Kidney Fern Glen walk.

ACCESS AND FACILITIES
Fullers ferries leave from Auckland and Devonport wharves, which gives you about 5–6 hours on the island. Remember to check the ferry pick-up time before you leave the wharf. There are toilets, a barbecue area, a summer ice-cream shop, a saltwater swimming pool and an information shelter at the wharf.

There is a 4WD 'road train' operated by Fullers, which takes you almost to the summit.

Rangitoto's shallow volcanic cone is an icon for Auckland and a great escape from the city. It has New Zealand's largest pohutukawa forest, extensive lava fields, mangrove swamps, and a fine walking network. There are no cars, and the only hustle and bustle is the rush of walkers off the ferry. A good day out in any weather, rain or fine.

From the wharf take the popular and broad summit trail, with its many excellent information panels on the way. The scoria rock and rustling pohutukawa create a strange landscape, and on a hot day you can feel the heat radiating off the black rocks.

You pass two track junctions, to Wilson's Park walk and the lava caves walk (take a torch), then the track steepens slightly to the summit and a splendid panorama of the Hauraki Gulf.

For the full circuit, from the summit take the track to the west and follow this down to pretty McKenzie Bay. Then follow the coastal road, which passes a side-track to a lookout over the black-backed gull colony at Flax Point.

The main track continues over a mangrove inlet, past the historic baches, back to the wharf and that tempting ice-cream shop.

20. KITEKITE FALLS & USSHER CROSS
Waterfall wander in the Waitakeres

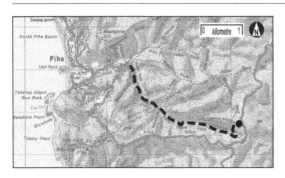

TRACK
This track description starts off Piha Road and goes down past the falls to Piha An easier and shorter walk to Kitekite Falls is from Piha and Glen Esk Road, up the south side of Glen Esk Stream. There are many track junctions and choices, which can be confusing, even with all the signposting. On some maps it is called Kitakita Falls.

The Auckland Council produces several maps detailing all the different track options thoughout Waitakere Ranges Regional Park. The full series is available from Arataki Information Centre on Scenic Drive. Don't walk in the Waitakeres without them.

WALK TIME AND DISTANCE
Kauri Grove, Ussher Cross, Kitekite Falls: 2 hours (5 km) one way.

ACCESS AND FACILITIES
Access to Ussher Cross–Kitekite Falls: on the road to Piha look out for the carpark at the Cowan Track.
Access from Piha: drive to Piha and along Glenesk Road to the carpark.

This walk gives you a smorgasbord of what the Waitakeres have to offer. Superb forest on the higher slopes, a clear cascading stream, then the sudden leap into nothingness as a waterfall appears under your feet. Finally a rich coastal belt of nikau palms, opening up to the definitive beach.

The best walk option is to get dropped off at the Cowan Track carpark on the Piha Road, and walk down to Kitekite Falls and Piha The Cowan is a short rough track that drops steeply and links to the Kauri Grove Track. This sidles easily alongside the Stockwell Stream and Glen Esk Stream to the four-way junction of Ussher Cross.

Keep going on the Kauri Grove Track a short way further to the top of Kitekite Falls, then follow the Connect Track down steeply to meet the main Kitekite Track.

For the falls themselves, walk back uphill a short way — it is worth it, a graceful gusher and the pool is deep enough for a bracing swim. You can keep going on this track, climbing a little then sidling easily around the valley and down to the forest floor. Then it is a broad track past several junctions and attractive bridges down to the carpark at Glenesk Road and a justly famous beach.

*Top: Manukau Heads, Whatipu coast
(see following page).
Above: Kitekite Falls.*

21. WHATIPU COAST
A wildness of wind and shore

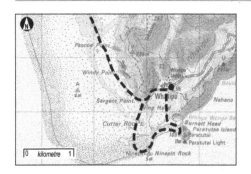

TRACK
All flat beach and coastal walking. The headland walk to Karekare beach may involve a scramble and is best at low tide. Sands along this stretch of coastline can come and go, and some people find easy walking to Karekare on wide sands.

WALK TIME AND DISTANCE
2–3 hours (10 km) return to Tunnel Point; 4–5 hours (14 km) return to Karekare beach.

ONE-HOUR WALK
A circuit can be made from the carpark to include Signal Hill, Paratutae Island and Cutter Rock.

ACCESS AND FACILITIES
From downtown Auckland drive to Titirangi and follow the coastal road past Huia to the north head of Manukau Harbour at Whatipu carpark, about 25 km. There are toilets and an information board.

Sticking out on the north edge of the Manukau Harbour, Whatipu is one of the truly great beaches — wild and stinging on windy days, haunting on calm mornings. There is an abundance of coastal scenery here, with a huge beach plain, headlands, islets, tidal platforms, ephemeral dune ponds and swathes of jointed rushes waving in the equally abundant wind.

Historic features include the old wharf on Paratutae Island, the wreck of HMS *Orpheus* (New Zealand's biggest shipwreck, in 1863, with the loss of 167 lives), the caves used by Maori for shelter, and the tunnel and timber tramway that can be traced all the way to Karekare beach.

From the Whatipu carpark follow the track to the sea caves; the largest is called Te Ana Ru. A 4WD road leads past dune lakes, and once around the corner it is not far to the distinctive prominence of Pararaha Point, about 4 km from the Whatipu carpark.

Continue along the beach to a spur, then head up through the dunes to the cliffs and the historic tunnel and tramway, which was built in the 1870s to carry kauri timber from Karekare to a wharf at Whatipu.

Once through the tunnel it is easy walking to Cowan Point and the bluff at Karekare Point.

From here it is barely a kilometre to Karekare but depending on the sands you might need a low tide to cross the tidal platforms, then follow the scrambly track. You pass remnants of the old tramway, then round the corner and reach the magic of Karekare.

22. OTUATAUA STONEFIELDS
An ancient place

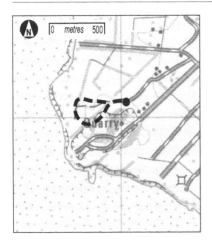

TRACK
No formed tracks, but marked trails over the pastureland and stone mounds.

WALK TIME AND DISTANCE
1–2 hours (2–4 km) return.

ACCESS AND FACILITIES
Very near Auckland airport but not as well signposted as you would expect. From Highway 20A (just before the first airport roundabout) turn onto Ihumatao Road for 3 km, then go down Oruarangi Road and into Ihumatao Quarry Road. There are signboards and a carpark at the end of the road.

Some 800 to 1000 years ago Polynesians landed in New Zealand, bringing with them the seeds and tubers of their island homes. Essentially tropical crops like kumara need careful maintenance, and they struggled to grow in this unfamiliar land.

The gardeners learnt that by manipulating stone mounds to create microclimates they could warm the soil, protect the crops from winds, reduce moisture loss and make their kumara flourish.

Every stone in these coastal fields has been shifted, first by the Maori, then by Europeans, who criss-crossed the land with drystone walls. The result is an ancient matrix of agriculture that was later discarded and left to the sweeping winds off the Manukau estuary.

The three self-guiding trails — historical, botanical and geological — all become muddled up with each other, and people just seem to wander off on their own personal explorations and discover all sorts of things — a Moreton Bay fig tree, 800-year-old storage pits, a barberry hedge, a saucer-shaped volcanic cone, a karaka grove.

Or else visitors sit by the shimmering coastal edge, gazing out to the Manukau Heads and wondering what it must have been like to come to an empty land where your crops wouldn't grow.

Old stone fences and a Moreton Bay fig tree in the Otuataua Stonefields.

23. HUNUA FALLS & COSSEYS DAM
Just the ticket on a hot Auckland day

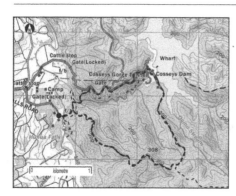

TRACK
Mostly well graded and well sign-posted bush tracks.

WALK TIME AND DISTANCE
2–3 hours (4 km) return.

ONE HOUR WALK
Cosseys Dam return.

ACCESS AND FACILITIES
From Papakura on Highway 1 take the Hunua Road to Hunua settlement, then Falls Road to carpark. Pleasant picnic area and toilets.

The Auckland Regional Council erected a picture frame to capture the live image of Hunua Falls, and this attractive area is just the ticket on a hot Auckland day. There's an easy bush trail to the waterfall, and an interesting circuit goes up to the placid dam lake and back. A good day out for the family.

From the carpark cross the footbridge, with a good view of Hunua Falls, turn left and after a few minutes you meet the main track junction. The Cossey Gorge track heads upvalley before dropping down to the stream, and stepping stones across Cossey Creek.

A bit of ambling along the streamside, then the track gets steep as it climbs up a bush spur and meets another track junction, just before the dam road. You could take the road, or it's better to stroll along the bush-sidle track as it reaches the dam and pops out into the dam carpark.

The road is locked so there are no cars, and it is a pleasant stroll across the dam to the picnic seats at the far end. The lake is well sheltered and usually ringing with bird calls.

Carry on up the signposted bush track as it reaches a platform lookout — tui seem to be everywhere. The track undulates along the ridge, climbing slowly for 20 minutes to another track junction.

Take the right-hand track (don't go through the gate), and this sidles easily through the forest, past a short side-track to a group of kauri. Once the track reaches the actual spur, it drops sharply back down to Hunua Falls. A great wee circuit.

24. MIRANDA WETLANDS
The margin of the land

TRACK
Old farm track, stopbank, shellbanks and mudflats.

WALK TIME AND DISTANCE
1 hour (2 km) return.

ACCESS AND FACILITIES
Miranda is at the lower end of the Firth of Thames, along the coastal road from Clevedon to Waitakaruru. Alternatively you can access Miranda off Highway 25 some 10 km from Waitakaruru.

There are several access points to the Miranda foreshore, including opposite the Miranda Shorebird Centre and from rest areas along the highway. The best access is about 800 metres south past the Miranda Shorebird Centre, where there is a stile and signpost, and a bird-watching hide a short distance from the road.

There is a picnic and camping area for self-contained campervans about 2 km north of the Miranda Shorebird Centre. Shop at Kaiaua.

Early mornings at Miranda spill washes of gentle colour over the flat horizon. The sea turns from black to silver and then blue, and the shellbanks reflect the first glitter of the morning sun.

This is one of the best sites for wading birds in the country, birds with exotic and faraway names that reek of Asia Minor — red-necked stint, Terek sandpiper, lesser knot, whimbrel, eastern curlew, turnstone, bar-tailed godwit and Pacific golden plover.

Miranda does not involve much walking. The best times to visit are at dawn and dusk. High tides bring the birds closer, while low tides reveal the slither of the tidal streams as they trickle through the exposed mudflats. From the stile a vehicle track wanders through the Robert Findlay Wildlife Area to the bird-hide.

Keen birders will need a good pair of binoculars, but anyone can enjoy the open, pure expanses of Miranda, and the occasional buzzing car on the coastal highway does not disturb the peacefulness. It is 100 km from Auckland — a world away.

25. WAIRERE FALLS
Graceful waterfall and historic Maori trail

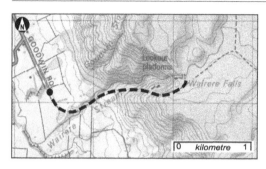

TRACK
An easy walking track that turns into a steep tramping track. Several footbridges

WALK TIME AND DISTANCE
2 hours (3 km) return to lower waterfall lookout; 3–4 hours (4 km) return to top of waterfall.

ONE-HOUR WALK
To second bridge return.

ACCESS AND FACILITIES
From Te Aroha drive south beside the bushy escarpment of the Kaimai Range along the straight Te Aroha–Gordon Road–Okauia Road, some 25 km to a right-angle corner. The Wairere Falls carpark is signposted 1 km down the unsealed Goodwin Road.

A showpiece waterfall that, if you are game enough, you can admire from both the graceful foot and the stomach-heaving top. There are boulders like giant's marbles, attractive footbridges, and a scary route up to the Kaimai escarpment.

The track starts by wandering up the Wairere Stream in a regenerating forest of kawakawa, then crosses a bridge, skirts some farmland, and drops back beside the stream. The stream is attractive, with rich mosses on the big boulders, and there are two more bridges to cross with boardwalks.

The track then climbs to the foot of a steep 40-metre (126-step!) staircase, with a number of landings to pause on. After another 100 steps there's a side-trail to a lookout platform, where you can admire the splendid waterfall framed by bush, as it tumbles down in two leaps of 73 and 80 metres. It is about 2 hours return to here.

The bush track continues to zigzag steeply up to the top of the escarpment. Because Wairere Falls is a natural break in the mountain defences, the Maori used the route for hundreds of years. At the top, the old Maori trail is followed for 15 minutes to a side-track that takes you to the dizzying lookout platform at the top of the waterfall.

The views of the Waikato are amazing, and on a clear day you can see the distant peaks of the Tongariro plateau.

26. BUTLERS INCLINE
Historic tramlines and a super steep climb

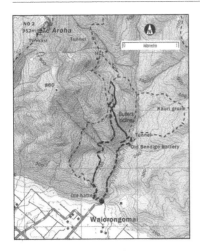

TRACK

Well marked bush tracks with easy stream crossings. Take the pamphlet and map, as the maze of interconnecting trails can get confusing.

Te Aroha information centre has pamphlets on the Wairongomai mining history and plenty of other information on the historic town. Good information boards on the tracks, and a significant restoration of the Fern Hill incline is underway. This is a great area for families to explore with enough to keep the kids interested.

WALK TIME AND DISTANCE

2–3 hours (3 km) return.

ONE-HOUR WALK

Stroll along the mid-level tramway (the main Piako County Tramway) to the foot of Butlers Incline, and return.

ACCESS AND FACILITIES

From Te Aroha drive 3 km south on the Te Aroha–Gordon Road to Wairongomai turn-off, then 2 km to carpark and old battery site. Toilets and information board.

Wairongomai goldfield in the Wairongomai Stream was a great and glorious failure. The rush started in 1882–83 and the local council was so excited at the rich prospects that they financed the building of the massive Piako County Tramway, including the Butlers Incline.

You start to appreciate the huge mine workings as you walk up the low-level track, and it's hard to realise that most of this bush was cleared for the mine operations. The low-level track is easy walking and then turns uphill and pops out at the foot of the Butlers Incline on the mid-level track.

An alternative way to get to Butlers Incline is via the mid-level track, or main Piako tramway, from the carpark.

Are you ready for the Butlers Incline challenge? It's a 400-metre climb at a 25-degree angle. DOC encourages people only to walk up the incline, which still has its rails in place. As you toil up you can see where the lines split to allow the wagons to pass. The principle of the incline is that the full wagons pull up the empties, and there are three self-acting inclines all told at Wairongomai.

Some people resort to hand-over-hand work and you will be totally stuffed by the time you pass under a small footbridge to reach the top.

Did I mention there's an easier way round? Take the low-level, New Era Branch track as it crosses the stream twice before climbing a spur up to the tramway just before the May Queen Incline. Walk back along the tramway to reach the head of the incline. This is a good spot for a cup of tea, and to appreciate the impressive reconstruction of the original pulley system.

From here it's all downhill to the carpark. Take the high-level packtrack as it first twists back across the small footbridge, and then wanders past two pretty waterfalls with glimpses of Buck Rock. Just before the Fern Hill incline, take the direct track (still on the high level) down to the fenceline and carpark.

OTHER WALKS

Wairongomai would take a few weekends to explore, with tracks linking up to the ruins of Hardies Hut, and all the way onto Mount Te Aroha itself. You can no longer drive up the road to the peak.

Old railway tracks at Wairongomai.

27. HAMILTON CITY WALK — HAMMOND PARK
Some silence in the city

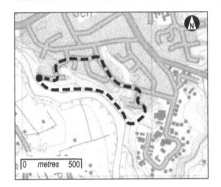

TRACK
Boardwalk and quiet road footpaths. Accessible to baby buggies, and to wheelchairs part of the way.

WALK TIME AND DISTANCE
1 hour (3 km) return.

ACCESS AND FACILITIES
Rather complex access, so take a road map. From Cobham Drive turn down Howell Avenue, then Louise Place and right into Malcolm Street, and right again when Malcolm Street forks down a road to a pretty riverside picnic and car-turning area.

This is an unexpected gem that even many Hamiltonians do not seem to know about. It is an easy, friendly little circuit that you could safely take your grandmother on.

From the clipped and tidy river park, turn upstream and you will reach an architect-designed boardwalk. This zigzags amiably along with good views of the river (as well as people's backyards) until it reaches Hammond Park. With all the native bush and birds, this stretch of boardwalk really seems a long way away from busy city life.

Across the grassland of Hammond Park there is a steep access path (you may have to push granny at this point) up onto Balfour Crescent. To complete the circuit continue up to Hudson Street, then left along to Malcolm Street. Short, but very sweet.

OTHER WALKS
The Hamilton Public Gardens are spectacular and quite close to Hammond Park. They have many detailed and lovingly recreated gardens, such as the Japanese Scholar garden, the Maori garden, the Indian garden, the Renaissance garden etc. There's also an information centre and café.

A boardwalk along the Waikato River, Hammond Park.

28. MOUNT KARIOI
Weird and wonderful

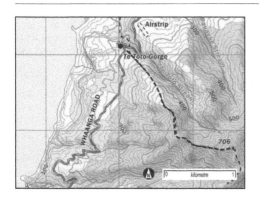

TRACK
A steep tramping track, demanding some rock scrambles with ladders and mud. Map: Raglan R14.

WALK TIME AND DISTANCE
3–4 hours (4 km) return to rock lookout; 4–5 hours (7 km) return to summit. Total climb to lookout 420 metres.

ONE-HOUR WALK
Fenceline return; good views.

ACCESS AND FACILITIES
From Raglan take the Whaanga Road, which becomes increasingly narrow, dusty and dramatic, until you reach the carpark overlooking the sea.

There is something odd about Mount Karioi, but it is hard to put your finger on it. Maybe it is the peculiar assemblage of forest types, or the white-scalped trees that look as if the wind has gnawed at them. The coastline is black and bleak.

Raglan seems perfectly normal, with busy cafés and grooving surfers, but the tortuous road to Karioi leaves all that abruptly behind and the landscape becomes harsh and embattled, with no soft corners.

At the carpark there is a short grass track down to a lookout platform, with impressive views over the black escarpment down to the rough coastline.

Te Toto track to the Mount Karioi summit starts climbing through kanuka and lancewood forest, then gets out into open grasslands that must have been burnt over. Twisted, whitened trees are a testament to the constant wind, and out to sea you can see one good-sized island that does not show up on any maps.

Along the track there are a couple of rocky outcrops to negotiate, with wires bolted on and a ladder to help on a tricky bit. You encounter some good views here, though if it is windy (it is always windy) you will be concentrating on holding on.

The track dips down to a thickly forested saddle and climbs up to the foot of a rock bluff, then sidles sharply left. There is a very steep scramble up through a dirty gully with big tree roots and a wire to help, then you reach a flattish point where the side-track goes on to a rock lookout with a brilliant view.

Is the true summit worth it? Probably optional — the views are a bit better, but there is still an hour to go, including several rock outcrops with wires and ladders, before the summit is reached.

29. RUAKURI NATURAL TUNNEL & MANGAPOHUE NATURAL BRIDGE
A labyrinth of limestone

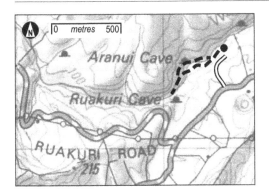

TRACK
A well made gravel track with directional arrows (Ruakuri Tunnel), and a farm track with some mud (Mangapohue Natural Bridge).

WALK TIME AND DISTANCE
1 hour (2 km) return Ruakuri Tunnel; 30 minutes (1 km) return Mangapohue Natural Bridge.

ACCESS AND FACILITIES
From Highway 3 drive 8 km to Waitomo resort, 1 km to Tumutumu Road, and 2 km along this to a signposted side-road down to a large carpark beside the Waitomo Stream. There is a shelter, picnic tables, toilets and information boards here. A pleasant spot for lunch.

For Mangapohue Natural Bridge, continue from Waitomo along the Marokopa Road some 20 km to the signposted carpark; toilet, information boards.

Note: The commercial aspects of Waitomo are rather overwhelming the natural landscape, with numerous options from glowworms to blackwater rafting. DOC oddly calls the Ruakuri tunnel walk the 'Ruakuri Bush Walk', but it's much more than that, and it's free.

Water on limestone creates peculiar landscapes, and some of the oddest of these lie in a band of rock from Waitomo to the Marokopa coast. Here you can find caves, tunnels, archways, tomo (the Maori word for sinkholes), 'disappearances' where water runs underground, and the attractive 'karren', water-sculpted rocks. Both these walks are short, but splendid.

RUAKURI NATURAL TUNNEL
This walk wanders easily from the carpark around a gantry over the moist and dark Waitomo Stream gorge. At the downstream entrance of the tunnel the track dives through a 'squeeze' then over the top of a natural 'bridge' and down

to several spectacular lookout points. It is somewhat baffling, but imagine the track doing a convoluted figure of eight. One spectacular viewpoint is from a platform right inside the natural tunnel itself. Back in the daylight there is a lookout at the upstream end of the tunnel, then the track returns to the carpark by a devilish route.

It crosses the natural bridge again, drops down steps and platforms, and twists underneath these in a spiral through another limestone 'squeeze'. At last the track settles down to a calm run back over the footbridge onto the main track and back to the carpark.

MANGAPOHUE NATURAL BRIDGE

From the dusty, scrubby carpark you get little warning of what's ahead. Cross the bridge and walk easily into the archway, where there is a lookout platform on top of the inner arch.

The archway is 17 metres high, and a grandiose remnant of an old underground waterway. There are clusters of stalactites on the roof and a smaller archway inside the main one.

The track continues through the tunnel to the farmland, then climbs up past strangely shaped rocks (one with giant oysters fossilised in it) and eventually descends back to the carpark.

30. MOUNT PUREORA
Mountain at the heart of the North Island

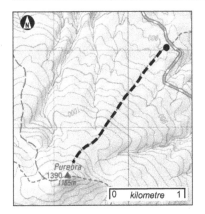

TRACK
A tramping track on a steady climb, with boardwalks in places. Sometimes muddy. You need a fine day to make the climb of 300 metres worthwhile.

WALK TIME AND DISTANCE
2–3 hours (4 km) return.

ONE-HOUR WALK
Forest tower return.

ACCESS AND FACILITIES
A good road map is important. From Highway 32 it is about 15 km along Link Road through the Pureora Forest Park to the saddle summit and the start of the Link Track to Mount Pureora. The road is winding, gravelled, but not too narrow, unsuited to people in a hurry, though there are always a few forestry workers who are. There is a large picnic and camping area at Kakaho, 5 km from the highway.

Link Road continues right through the forest park to Barryville Road; left is the park headquarters, right is to Barryville on Highway 30. There is an information shelter, a carpark and toilets opposite the park headquarters.

For the forest tower follow the signs from Barryville Road to Pikiariki Road, then past the Buried Forest turn-off to a signposted junction after 4 km. It is then 500 metres down a side-road to the carpark.

Mount Pureora is not quite the dead heart of the North Island, which lies some 5 km to the northeast, but it feels like it. From the soft summit you can look out over the vast sweep of the central highlands, as far as the snowy peaks of Mount Egmont/Taranaki and Mount Ruapehu.

From the carpark saddle the track climbs steadily through beautiful bush, with occasional streams tinkling. There are several boardwalked sections, but no views at all until almost the very top.

As you scramble up the last eroded sections of track you enter a tiny fragment of alpine herbfield. Mount Pureora, at 1165 metres, is just high enough to allow this alpine ecosystem, and of course it provides superb views.

FOREST LOOKOUT TOWER
A short walk through the forest leads to the lookout tower, where ladders zigzag past platforms up four storeys to high up in the bush canopy. Kaka, parakeets and bellbirds are all commonly heard, and there is an early morning chance of hearing the rare kokako.

31. CATHEDRAL COVE
A 'truly romantick' archway

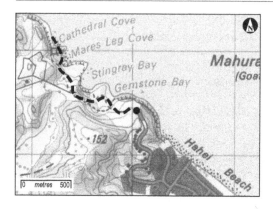

TRACK
A well graded gravel track, with most of the climbing on the return. Currently it is not permitted to walk through the archway itself as it is considered a rockfall danger.

WALK TIME AND DISTANCE
1 hour (2 km) return.

ACCESS AND FACILITIES
From Tairua take Highway 25 and drive 15 km north to Whenuakite Junction, then follow the signs a further 10 km to the settlement of Hahei. The Cathedral Cove road climbs above Hahei and on to a fine lookout at the large carpark. Viewing platforms, toilets, information boards. Also discreetly hidden toilets at Cathedral Cove itself.

James Cook observed the transit of Mercury here in 1769, and Joseph Banks enthusiastically noted a 'truly romantick' archway. Maori lived along this coast for centuries and there was once a fortified pa site right above the archway itself. It is a short, eye-catching walk, massively popular in summer, so get in early.

From the carpark the track wanders in and out of bushy gullies and past a side-track through a puriri grove, which is well worth taking. These puriri are immense trees, famous for the hardness of their wood.

A smidgin further there is another short side-track down to Gemstone Bay, and still further on another side-track to Stingray Bay. Both these secluded bays are good for snorkelling in summer, with crystal-clear water.

The main track continues with occasional good views of Mercury Bay, then zigzags down a flight of steps to Mare's Leg Cove. This delightful bay was named for an unusual offshore rock formation shaped like a horse's hind leg, but this has since collapsed.

The archway is on your left. Twenty metres high and 10 metres wide, it leads through to Cathedral Cove itself, which is dominated by Te Hoho or Sail Rock. On a hot day the lapping water, sculpted rocks and sparkling views over Mercury Bay are so overwhelming you just have to lie down and take a nap in preparation for the long hot slog uphill.

Cathedral Cove archway.

32. THE SAILORS GRAVE COAST

Lonely grave on a lovely coast

TRACK
Well marked bush tracks over headlands with beach walking in between and some rockhopping. A low tide is important.

WALK TIME AND DISTANCE
Te Karo Bay to Lynch Bay 2 hours (4 km) return; Lynch Stream track to Highway 25 2–3 hours (5.5 km) one way.

ONE-HOUR WALK
From Te Karo Bay over the first bush headland, and return via the rocks at low tide.

ACCESS AND FACILITIES
From Tairua drive 3 km north on Highway 25 to Sailors Grave Road, then down to big carpark (with toilet) overlooking Te Karo Bay. For Lynch Stream track, continue north on main highway 3 km to Whenuakite Kauri Grove track and carpark.

Coromandel has many beautiful beaches, but the Sailors Grave coast is a rare example of a shoreline unspoiled by too much housing development. The local Tairua community fought hard for this benefit. Apart from a few discreet baches, the bush coast looks pristine and inviting from the lonely carpark. A coast begging to be explored.

From the carpark walk down to Te Karo Bay and just across the stream, tucked under the bush, is the sailor's grave.

Land graves for sailors were rare, as they were usually buried at sea. In May 1842, 22-year-old William Simpson from the British Navy ship HMS *Tortoise* was accidentally killed while loading kauri spars onto the ship in Te Karo Bay. The headstone and white picket fence are well maintained and the grave is surprisingly serene.

Stroll along the shore till a well marked track climbs over the headland into Otarara Bay. This is even prettier than Te Karo, and at the far end is marked a second headland track which climbs a bit higher and leads over to Lynch Stream bay.

A charming way to return to the carpark is at low tide, scrambling around the headlands and admiring the rich yellow and red oxides that taint the rocks in rainbow colours.

Offshore islands and islets sprinkle the azure sea, which just dazzles in the morning sunlight. Magical spot.

OTHER WALKS

The reasonably well marked Lynch Stream bush track takes 2–3 hours one way from Highway 25 to the coast. It's best done in that direction. The first part of the track is well graded and leads to some impressive kauri, but from then on it's an up and down tramping trail, with quite a lot of stream crossings. Suits experienced walkers.

Low tide at Te Karo Bay.

33. THE PINNACLES

Historic packhorse trail to kauri dam and spectacular volcanic rock plugs

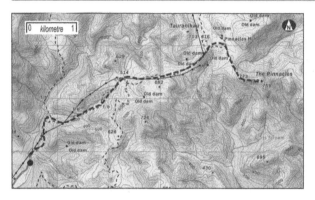

TRACK
All tracks are well marked, but the stone and mud surfaces can get slippery after rain.

WALK TIME AND DISTANCE
7–9 hours (12 km) return.

ONE-HOUR WALK
Hydro Camp return (4 km).

ACCESS AND FACILITIES
From Thames drive south 2 km to the Kauaeranga Valley Road, and follow the attractive valley 13 km to the smart visitor centre and carpark. The park headquarters has a nature walk, historical artefacts, good information panels and toilets. Book and pay for your campsite here.

It is another 6 km on a winding unsealed road to the road-end and the start of the Kauaeranga Kauri Trail. There are several excellent camping grounds along the roadside.

This is a great day tramp that climbs through the twisted volcanic plugs and plateaus of the Coromandel landscape up to the high point of 773 metres at The Pinnacles. It's not as much of a slog as you might think, and there are plenty of rewards along the way, including nikau palms, waterfalls, historic stone staircases, original kauri dams, and amazing views.

From the carpark take the main track as it crosses the Kauaeranga River on a long footbridge and follows the river at an easy grade through groves of nikau palms. At the junction, take the Webb Creek/Pinnacles/Kauaeranga Kauri track as it climbs steeply up this attractive and narrow stream.

There are several waterfalls in this tight valley, as well as three footbridges, and the original hand-cut stone staircases that were built to assist the packhorses up this steep grade. It's almost a 300-metre climb to the Hydro Camp, and after rain these steps can get greasy.

Bluffs lean over the track as it reaches the track junction at the Hydro Camp. During the late 1940s workers camped here when establishing the 'hydro-line' (powerline) over to the east coast, and the lines are still there.

Easier in grade now, the Pinnacles track sidles past the gloomy plug of Tauranikau, and the views become more general as the track winds through stunted scrub forest to a track junction. A side-branch drops down to the spacious Pinnacles Hut (40 bunks, gas cookers and a warden in season).

There's also a side-track to a kauri log dam, which is impressive, but sadly the bare stripped hillsides around testify to the awesome effectiveness of the loggers' simple methods.

The well marked track to The Pinnacles begins gently enough, then gets steeper as it approaches the rock outcrops. It has to twist up and around severe rock and scrub gullies, and needs the assistance of several ladders before it reaches the final top, a total 200-metre climb from hut to the first and highest pinnacle.

Much of the Coromandel is visible, especially the immediate foreground of contorted rock outcrops and white-stumped hillsides. Sea on both sides and the Hauraki Plains fade into haze. Not a bad idea to bring some sustenance, and slowly digest lunch and the view.

The ladder leading to The Pinnacles.

34. BROKEN HILLS & COLLINS DRIVE
Wandering water races and tenacious tunnellers

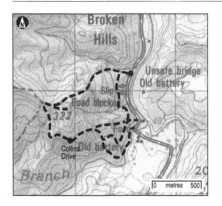

TRACK

Steep, narrow, well worn tracks, with quite a bit of hill work. You will need a torch for the big tunnel, and should expect to get wet feet.

WALK TIME AND DISTANCE

2–3 hours (3 km) return for the Collins Drive circuit. Not all the tracks are shown on the map boards at the road-end, which can be confusing.

ONE-HOUR WALK

Water race return.

ACCESS AND FACILITIES

The area is known as Broken Hills, or sometimes Golden Hills, and the main access is off Highway 25 at Hikuai, then some 6 km up the Puketui Valley Road to a carpark and an extensive (and exceedingly attractive) camping area. The Tairua River pauses here in several gorgeous pools, so take the tent and the kids, and make a weekend of it. The old through-road on to Puketui Road and Highway 25A is closed.

Adits, drives and tunnels are all the same thing — artificaly dug holes in the ground. The Collins Drive is a spectacular 500-metre-long tunnel, and part of a track circuit that also includes three craftily chiselled water-race tunnels and a complicated network of mining ruins. If goldmining history is your thing you will love this place. Even if it is not, you will still be impressed.

From the carpark follow the old road over the footbridge and turn uphill on the signposted track. It is a hard climb through bush past the Water Race Track junction and up to a saddle. Here a side-track climbs steeply to a sort of lookout, with good views towards The Pinnacles of the Coromandel Range.

Down from the saddle the track reaches the entrance of Collins Drive, and you squelch in. A third of the way along the drive has a short side-tunnel with glowworms. Halfway through there is a kink in the tunnel's length, and just before the end there are two boarded-up side-passages with very good glowworms.

Phew, you're out. Take the steep steps down from the 'aerial hopper' sign to the Water Race Track, then turn right (upstream) and go through three elegant tunnels, which were driven to take the water at an even gradient.

Beyond the last tunnel there is another track junction; take all the downhill options back to the old road, and follow this back downriver to the carpark.

OTHER WALKS

There are many short walks in this area, including Gem of the Boom, Golden Hills Battery and Broken Hills Battery.

35. THE WINDOWS & WAITAWHETA GORGE
Magnificent tunnel and gorge walkway

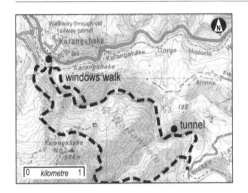

TRACK

Well graded and gravelled up the gorge, and well marked over the hill, with some climbs.

WALK TIME AND DISTANCE

The Windows 1 hour return (2 km); hill circuit 3–4 hours (6–8 km return).

ACCESS AND FACILITIES

Off Highway 2 at Karangahake carpark, there are information panels, toilets, and a café across the road. Watch out for speeding traffic 'cause they sure as hell ain't looking for you! Access to the far end of the Waitawheta Gorge is via Dickey Flat Road and a small campground with toilets.

This is a superb walking area for familes, with sheer-sided gorge walls stained with the peculiar red and yellow oxides of minerals. Tunnels, tramways, 'windows', and other old mining relics give a tremendous sense of the past.

The Windows is a short spectacular circuit, ideal for families and small children. It can be combined with the short gorge walk or the much longer hill walk.

The first footbridge over the Karangahake River is an old-fashioned beauty. For the Windows walk, cross the second footbridge and climb up onto a higher level tramline track. This pierces the rock walls, with various 'holes' or 'windows' overlooking the Waitawheta Gorge along the way. A torch is handy but you can get away without one.

Shortly the track goes down a staircase back to the main gorge track. For the easy walkers, wander back down the gorge, exploring some spooky side-tunnels as you go (you'll need a torch for these), and back to the carpark.

For the hill walkers, from the upper Windows track junction, the gorge opens a little and a good track leads for 30 minutes further to a 100-metre straight tunnel, which you can sneak through without a torch (keep your head low!).

Just before the tunnel is an excellent picnic spot on rocks beside the river, and another man-made tunnel used to divert part of the stream.

Shortly after the tunnel, the track crosses a footbridge and reaches a junction. Straight on, the track goes over another footbridge to Dickey Flat Road end.

Otherwise, turn up the Dubbo 96 bush track. It climbs steadily, crosses a side-creek, then climbs again up to a junction with the County Road Track (the other route goes up onto Karangahake Hill itself at 544 metres).

Follow the easy County Road Track around richly coloured mineral bluffs, and go down the road 10 minutes to Scotsmans Gully. Follow this short, pretty track for 15 minutes back to the main carpark on Highway 2.

36. OROKAWA BAY

A lonely, lovely bay

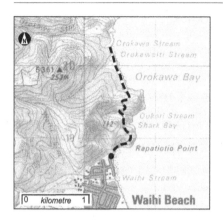

TRACK
A well graded and rolling coastal path along an old bridleway.

WALK TIME AND DISTANCE
2 hours (4 km) return.

ONE-HOUR WALK
Second headland return.

ACCESS AND FACILITIES
From Waihi Beach settlement make your way to the far north end of the beach by the large carpark. The first part of the walk may get blocked at high tide (or you need to wade), though an hour either side should be fine.

This pleasing track starts from the north end of Waihi Beach, with old shaggy pohutukawa trees shading some interesting rock formations. The track climbs to the first headland corner at Rapatiotio Point, and turns into a much quieter world. Orokawa Bay has no roads leading to it.

The track ambles along about 200 metres above the sea, slipping through attractive bush gullies and wandering around headlands with good views back over the coast. You can see Mayor Island and White Island, occasionally gushing white smoke.

The first view of Orokawa Bay is seen through waving toetoe and there is a seat from where you can appreciate it. Then it is a quick descent to an untrammelled piece of coast with a white and glorious beach, backed by rustling pohutukawa.

There is plenty to explore here, including the fishing rocks, and there is a roughish track up Orokawa Stream. This crisscrosses the stream to William Wright Falls, dropping over a band of rock. The coastal forest is lush, tropical and silent.

Orokawa Bay from the headland track.

37. PIOS BEACH & BOWENTOWN HEADS
Short walks to headland views and sheltered beaches

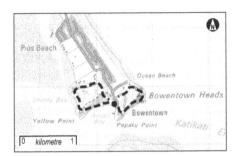

TRACK
Grass and gravel paths, sometimes muddy.

WALK TIME AND DISTANCE
1 hour return to headland summit; 1 hour return to Shelly Bay; 1 hour Anzac/summit circuit. All 3 km return.

ACCESS AND FACILITIES
From Highway 2 take the Athenree Road, then Steele Road and Emerton Road to the main beach on Seaforth Road. Alternatively drive from Waihi Beach to Seaforth Road and follow this all the way to Anzac Bay where there is a carpark, toilets and an extensive picnic area.

There are popular campgrounds at both Athenree (with hot pools) and Bowentown, and the entire area, with its sandy beaches, pohutukawa coast, estuaries and general facilities, is perfect for a family weekend.

The Tauranga Harbour is a huge inland lagoon, stretching from Mount Maunganui in the south to Pios Beach in the north. The headland is a relaxed and miniature version of the more famous Mount Maunganui hump, with short, easy walks to a terraced pa site, fishing beaches and a marvellous outlook over the Bay of Plenty.

None of the walks take more than an hour, but if you include the summit, the pa and a beach swim, the time just flies away.

From Anzac Bay (which is part of Bowentown Domain) walk up onto the rocky headland and pa site. There are fine views of the entrance, and the pa Te Kura a Maia is magnificent, with lines of terraces sloping down to the sea. The track goes on up to the top carpark and wanders past a side-track to Cave Bay, a popular fishing spot.

There are good views from the summit and a track that circles underneath and goes down the other side to sidle above the motor camp back down to the access road and Anzac Bay.

The track to Shelly Bay leaves from Anzac Bay and follows a well benched (if muddy) path up through pohutukawa forest and over a grass clearing down to Shelly Bay. There seem to be trails all over the place, either up onto the summit or down to prime coastal fishing spots. Yet despite its popularity, it seems to be quite easy to find a cosy corner of your own on this lovely headland.

38. TAURANGA CITY WALK — WAIKAREAO WALKWAY
Gentle urban track around a fine estuary

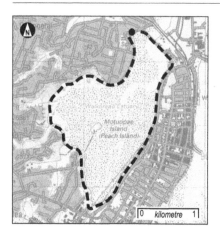

TRACK
Flat gravel paths and boardwalks.

WALK TIME AND DISTANCE
2 hours (7 km) one way for the whole Waikareao circuit.

ONE-HOUR WALK
Maxwell Road to Coach Road carpark return.

ACCESS AND FACILITIES
The Waikareao estuary is in the heart of Tauranga. A good starting point is the carpark area at Maxwell Road, off Chapel Street, but there are many other access points.

This is an intimate and interesting estuary walk alongside urban reserves and mangrove inlets. There are no roads to cross and plenty of unhurried places along the way, with linking tracks into other parts of the city.

At the attractive carpark and picnic area by Maxwell Road, take the well signposted track along the Daisy Hardwick section of track around to the Goods Road carpark. The track travels between the sparkling estuary and a profusion of urban plants spilling over from people's backyards.

At Goods Road there is a patch of coastal forest, then the botany changes character as the track winds along a mangrove inlet. Just near the Coach Road carpark there is a boardwalk out into the estuary, with an information panel and a lookout platform with seats.

The main track follows a beautiful boardwalk, cutting across the mangroves, then goes around the point and passes the low-tide road to Motuopae Island.

This is a good return point if you want to stay on the quieter sections of track.

The next part of the walkway wriggles along coastal mangroves till it reaches the busy Waihi Road, then turns along the even busier Waikareao expressway. This is still a good track though, popular with runners, with footbridges linking to Graham Park and Tauranga Domain. The last section of track follows Chapel Street back to Maxwell Road.

The mangrove estuary and boardwalk to the lookout on the Waikareao Walkway.

39. TAURANGA CITY WALK — MOUNT MAUNGANUI
An easy walk round (and up) a landscape icon

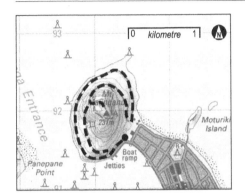

TRACK
Well graded tracks through coastal forest, and hill climb to summit.

WALK TIME AND DISTANCE
1–2 (3 km) circuit return from Pilot Bay.

ONE-HOUR WALK
1 hour return round the coast; 1 hour return to the summit.

ACCESS AND FACILITIES
From Tauranga cross the bridge, drive 2 km to Mount Maunganui beach and then to Pilot Bay. Toilets and carparking.

'The Mount' is the emotional and cultural icon of the Bay of Plenty, and it sticks up at more than its mere 230-metre height would suggest. The Maori knew the Mount as 'Mauao', and used the hill as habitation, lookout and pa refuge. It provides good easy walking and plenty of views, and the cafés and bars of the town are not far away.

From Pilot Bay head south along the coastal track, which stays 50 metres or so above the shore. A short side-trail goes down to a pretty, sandy beach where you get good views of the harbour entrance and the Tangaroa statue. This stretch of coast and reef is also an important scientific reserve.

The coast track rounds Stoney Point, with views of the dead-flat Rabbit Island, and the pohutukawa providing shade. North West Rock is a popular surf-fishers' hang-out, and at low tide you can scramble about the reef platform. Round the corner there are several attractive sandy coves at low tide.

The track climbs slightly to a track junction. Here, climb up the historic 1860 stone steps and join the Oruahine Track as it continues up onto a plateau and turns steeply uphill to the Waikorere Track junction.

Follow the Waikorere Track as it climbs steadily through regrowth forest, past a side-track to a lookout, then on to the beacon on the summit of the Mount.

There are excellent views, of course, particularly of the beach, township and Mayor Island. It is then easy walking down the old vehicle track as it winds down through scrub and farm country, passing a large reservoir, before reaching Pilot Bay.

40. TUAHU TRACK
Ancient Maori trail into the Kaimai Range

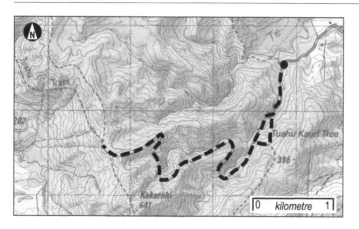

TRACK
A good benched track that climbs steadily through forest to the ridgeline.

WALK TIME AND DISTANCE
4–5 hours (12 km) return. 40-minute kauri tree loop track return.

ACCESS AND FACILITIES
Turn off Highway 2 onto the Hot Springs Road and follow this 5 km past the Sapphire Springs motor camp to the road-end carpark and toilets. The motor camp has a large swimming pool, freshwater pools and a food store.

The Tuahu Track is a long, easy climb to the crest of the Kaimai Range. Originally it was a Maori trail, but it was widened to a bridle path in the late 1890s. Although the total climb is 400 metres, it is so gentle and genial that it does not seem like it, and the eventual view is a reward for the effort.

About 10 minutes after leaving the carpark you reach a side-track that goes up to a large kauri — well worth the deviation. This side-track then continues and regains the main Tuahu Track. Note also a bit further on the side-track to Sentinel Rock.

The main Tuahu trail wanders in and out of stream gullies, climbing very steadily, and with little in the way of views until you are nearly at the top. Eventually the track reaches the crest of the ridge at a four-way track junction.

Follow the Tuahu Track for another 5 minutes to get broad views of the Waikato, or turn up the track towards Te Rereatukahia Hut to find an immediate flax and tussock clearing with a panorama of the Bay of Plenty and Mayor Island. A great munch spot, safe in the knowledge that the downhill return on the Tuahu Track is a romp.

41. TARAWERA FALLS

Magical meeting of escarpments, disappearances and waterfalls

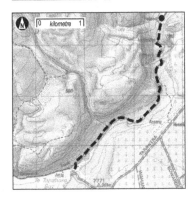

TRACK
Bush track with a short hill and some clambering.

WALK TIME AND DISTANCE
2 hours (4 km) one way to lake.

ONE-HOUR WALK
Waterfall return.

ACCESS AND FACILITIES
The road to Tarawera Falls is a public access easement but the gates by the forest headquarters are closed every night. In theory you need a $5 access permit bought on the day, purchased from the Kawerau Information Centre. However, I notice the locals don't seem to pay, and it's not clear whether the gate is locked at night. Note any fire and logging operation restrictions.

From Kawerau take River Road then Waterhouse Street across the bridge and past the forestry headquarters to a T-junction. Tarawera camping area and Tarawera Falls are signposted, about 20 km to either carpark from Kawerau.

Beside Lake Tarawera there is a superb camping area, with toilets and a resident caretaker in season. It's a good idea to base yourself at the Lake Tarawera camping area, and get a lift down to the start of the Falls track, and walk back to the lake.

In the midst of the bland uniformity of pine forest around Kawerau are the energetic and quirky Tarawera Falls — bluffs, tomo, waterfalls, swimming holes, a wonderland of surprises and variety, tinged with a touch of Tolkien in the thick forest interior.

The track from the lower carpark goes through kanuka forest to an elegant footbridge, then through tawa and rewarewa forest with silver fern underneath. The Tarawera Falls thunder out from a natural fissure halfway up a rock face. Many people do not go beyond here, but they miss half the fun.

The track climbs cleverly and steeply up through the bluff walls, and once on top it divides. The left-hand track goes in a spectacular loop directly above the Tarawera Falls, winding past bridges and streams to the tomo where the Tarawera River disappears into a narrow rock cavern.

The loop track joins the main track again, and continues upriver through a deep, dense bush of moss and unlikely boulders. It soon reaches another waterfall, then a cascade and, in the reflective river, reaches a deep swimming hole with a platform.

From here on the walk is more sedate as it goes through second-growth forest towards the swampy margins of Lake Tarawera. Finally, there is a grand swingbridge across the Tarawera River to the carpark, camping and picnic area on the other side.

42. KOHI POINT
A circuit of ancient pa, bush bays and tidal platforms

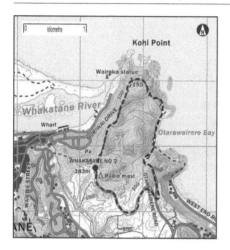

TRACK
Good bush tracks, and some beach walking. Low tide is essential!

WALK TIME AND DISTANCE
2–3 hours circuit from hilltop pa down to Otarawairere Bay and up road (3.5 km).

ONE-HOUR WALK
From the carpark walk down spur to coastal lookouts.

ACCESS AND FACILITIES
From Whakatane take the road to Ohope Beach to the turn-off at Otarawairere Road, then veer left at the next junction to the lookout and carpark on the hilltop. About 4 km.

Kohi Point is heavy with history. There are at least eight pa sites along the ridge from the carpark to the end of the point, and a further four pa along the rugged coastline between Kohi Point and Ohope Beach. Kaputerangi is claimed to be New Zealand's oldest pa site, founded between AD 1070 and 1210.

The carpark has magnificent views of the coast, Motuhora Island, and distant White Island. As you walk down the open grass slopes into the bush escarpment track, you can see typical features of the pa — ditches, terraces and storage pits.

Much of this history is overgrown by the shrub forest of pohutukawa, manuka, kawakawa, kanuka, rangiora and notably the rewarewa, with its splendid and almost alien-looking dark red flowers.

The track plunges down the spur (600 steps in all) with fine views over the turbulent Kohi Point itself. Then it sidles around to the staircase down to Otarawairere Bay. This is where the low tide is crucial.

It is an attractive bay, with 'sand' that on closer inspection seems to be composed of zillions of tiny shells. Pohutukawa shade the beach, and there's a picnic area and toilet halfway along. Here the track to Otarawairere village starts, but before climbing up it, it's well worth fossicking to the south end of the bay.

At low tide you can scramble around the rocky islet point where there are some dramatic geological strata, twisted in quite bizarre shapes. You cannot get round to Ohope Beach because a sea-channel cuts right in against the rock.

The track up to Otarawairere village is actually an old road put in by a film company many years ago. The Otarawairere village was constructed as a company village by the Tasman Pulp and Paper Company in the affluent 1960s, and boasts some of the best views in the Bay of Plenty. Follow the scenic road back up to the lookout and carpark.

OTHER WALKS

Kohi Point is part of a much longer 8–9 hour walk (10 km) to Ohope Beach and through bush reserves back to Whakatane. Well worth doing.

The view from Kohi Point carpark.

43. NGAHOPUA — CRATER LAKES
Mysterious lakes and virgin forest

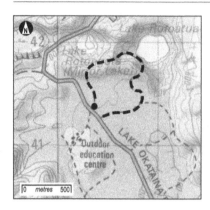

TRACK
Forest trail in hilly bush country.

WALK TIME AND DISTANCE
1 hour (3 km) return.

ACCESS AND FACILITIES
From Highway 30 turn off at Ruato down the Lake Okataina Road. The Ngahopua/ Crater Lakes track starts just opposite the short road to the Outdoor Education Centre, where there is good carparking.

The Maori word ngahopua means 'depressions' or 'bowls', and these old volcanic craters have filled to form lakes — Rotongata and Rotoatua. Because the track does not go down to the lakeside, but peers at them at a distance from the thick bush rim, they seem remote and mysterious — like sacred places you are not allowed to reach.

The track is straightforward and climbs from the road through beautiful bush, with big tawa and rimu dominating the canopy. Epiphytes fill every niche in the lush forest.

At some point you become aware that you are on the rim of a large crater, with all the land falling away, and shortly you see Lake Rotongata, silent and girdled with reeds.

The track then continues along the well defined rim, with several lookouts on the way, and at the last lookout there is a fine view into Lake Rotoatua. The lake is deep, with sheer walls. It was formed 3500 years ago but seems somehow timeless.

After this point you descend quite quickly to a junction with the Anaha Track, and then onto the road, where the spell is broken.

OTHER WALKS
At the end of Lake Okataina Road there is the Eastern Lake Okataina Walkway, a good walk, 3 hours one way.

Lake Rotoatua.

44. ROTORUA CITY WALK — LAKE FRONT & SULPHUR FLATS
A hot steamy walk!

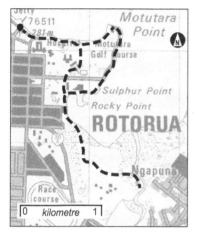

TRACK
Footpaths, forest trails and boardwalks. Well signposted, but do not venture off the boardwalks onto the sulphur plain itself.

WALK TIME AND DISTANCE
1–2 hours (4 km) return.

ACCESS AND FACILITIES
Off Highway 5 (driving south into Rotorua) turn onto Lake Road and stay on Lake Road to Lakefront Drive. Good carparking by sound shell and jetty area, with café, toilets and children's play equipment.

The city of Rotorua sits precariously on top of a thermal field, and you sometimes wonder if by banging your foot down too hard you might start another geyser. The place reeks (literally) of thermal action, and the city walkway around this little peninsula and across Sulphur Point is an immediate and exciting way to enjoy it. You can finish the circuit by cutting across the base of the peninsula.

This attractive urban walkway starts from the busy jetty area on the waterfront, and circles the peninsula and golf course at Motutara Point. There are good views over the lake, plenty of birdlife including scaup, shags and swans, and many interesting lakeside corners to explore. It is not a dull walk.

The track then meanders through fringes of manuka and passes close by the

historic Tudor-style Bath House, then around to the thermal area by Sulphur Point. Hot steam seeps out of holes and weird colours stain the grey plain. After rain the place can really steam.

The boardwalk crosses the thermal area crisply, as if in a hurry to get across, but there are information panels on the way to slow the visitor. Sulphur Flats is a good turnaround point.

On the return, pick up Hatupatu Drive and walk in front of the Bath House, then cross the base of the peninsula via the rose gardens back to the jetty area.

Sulphur Flats, Rotorua.

45. WHIRINAKI RIVER
Simply the best

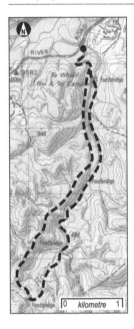

TRACK
Well benched and mostly flat bush pathway.

WALK TIME AND DISTANCE
2 hours (8 km) waterfall circuit.

40-MINUTE WALK
Moerangi junction return.

ACCESS AND FACILITIES
From Highway 38 turn right towards the Minginui turn-off, then turn right over the Whirinaki River bridge to meet River Road. There is a DOC camping area 2 km downvalley of this road junction. Follow River Road upvalley for about 7 km to the carpark and signboard. It is useful to have Te Urewera National Park map.

Until I receive word to the contrary, I am prepared to state that Whirinaki is the best forest in New Zealand.

Statuesque and dense, it is a forest of exceptional quality and calibre. Trees like rimu, kahikatea, matai and miro grow to extraordinary heights at Whirinaki and have a profound effect on the visitor.

The Whirinaki track starts by passing through the Oriuwaka Ecological Area, a scientific reserve where there are outstanding podocarp trees, then crosses the Whirinaki River at Te Whaiti-nui-a-Toi Canyon. This is a deep, attractive slot in the rockbed.

After the canyon the track settles into an easy, well benched grade along the river terrace, passing the side-track to Moerangi. The birdlife can be thick, with robins, shining and long-tailed cuckoos, parakeets, kaka, songthrush, blackbirds, tui and bellbirds.

The Whirinaki River.

There is a footbridge over the Mangamate Stream and not long afterwards a side-track goes down to the Whirinaki waterfall. This is a thundering leap, with a viewing platform from where you can take it all in.

A bridge crosses the top of the waterfall to other vantage points, and this track can be followed back to the carpark. It travels along an old logging road on the other side of the Whirinaki River, and makes the visual point that this magnificent forest came within a few hundred metres of being eradicated.

46. ARAHAKI LAGOON
Lagoon in the heart of the forest

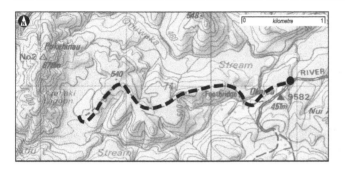

TRACK
A bush-walking track, benched at first, with some small climbs. After rain the lagoon can be quite large, but much of the time it is a grassy swamp with a worn trail around it.

WALK TIME AND DISTANCE
2 hours (4 km) return.

ACCESS AND FACILITIES
From Highway 38 turn right towards Minginui, then just before Minginui itself turn right over the Whirinaki River bridge to meet River Road. There is a DOC camping area 2 km downvalley of this road junction, but follow River Road upvalley to the Whirinaki Track carpark, then continue on a much rougher road some 2 km to the carpark.

This is an ancient place that smothers your thoughts with the quiet of centuries — a lonely lagoon in the midst of an encircling rim of kahikatea trees. The thick silence is broken only by the calls of kaka, robins and bellbirds.

The track starts unexceptionally, wandering through an old logging area with manuka and lancewoods, then it descends to a footbridge to cross the Waiatiu Stream.

A short, steepish climb brings you into dense tawa forest with the occasional massive rimu, and the track softens onto a ridge, passing through groves of perfect tree ferns. There is little windfall, and the forest seems undisturbed by the outside world.

The descent is hardly anything at all and quite suddenly you arrive at the lagoon. I was there after a wet summer and the lagoon was full, almost touching the stately kahikatea. The frogs sounded like an orchestra of didgeridoos, and large black shags and kaka flapped melodiously across the empty marsh. Little else disturbed this pond of tranquillity.

It truly is an otherworldly place.

47. LAKE WAIKAREITI & LAKE RUAPANI CIRCUIT
Beautiful lakes, secret ponds and silent swamps

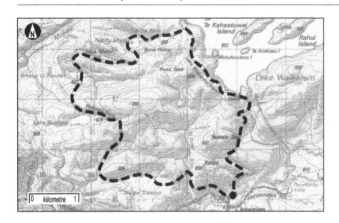

TRACK
A garden path to Lake Waikareiti, then a standard and rolling bush track.

WALK TIME AND DISTANCE
4–5 hours (11 km) Lake Waikareiti–Lake Ruapani circuit.

ONE- TO TWO-HOUR WALK
Lake Waikareiti return.

ACCESS AND FACILITIES
Highway 38 is an unsealed, tortuous and narrow road that passes through Te Urewera National Park to the visitor centre and carpark for Lake Waikareiti. There are toilets here. Rumour has it that this road is going to be sealed soon, but do not hold your breath.

Enjoy a fulsome forest day walk, visiting in a slow circuit Lake Waikareiti, isolated ponds and strange silted-up lakes, with their own 'tundra' of wetland plants and subalpine species. You feel psychologically displaced in this remote landscape, and the views across the dry ponds seem positively Jurassic — you fully expect to see a moa strolling across the meadow.

The track to Lake Waikareiti is as smooth as a garden path and climbs effortlessly past a fern forest with red beech dominating the canopy. The path reaches a low saddle where there is a toilet and shortly afterwards a lakeside shelter. This is a useful place for a breather, out of sandfly habitat.

A more ordinary bush track approximately follows the shores of Lake Waikareiti for 2 km to the junction with the Lake Ruapani track.

Soon there is the eerie tranquillity of Puna Hokoi, a clearing and wetland, followed by two small ponds, Hine Rere and Ngutu Manu. The track follows a stream that disappears, then climbs a small saddle to Whano o Ruapani, a larger lakelet.

It is 1 km over a bigger hill to Lake Ruapani itself. Orchids are often found on the wetland margins of the lake and, surprisingly, black-backed gulls and spur-winged plovers can also be seen.

After this the track goes over another short hill and down a streamside to the Waipai Swamp and a respite from the engulfing bush, then it is 2 km back to the carpark and out of the woods.

Crown fern, Ruapani Track.

48. MAKORORI POINT & POUAWA ESTUARY
Coastal rock formations and New Zealand dotterels

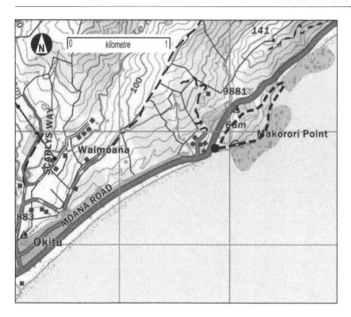

TRACK
Well maintained tracks on Makorori point, tidal platforms at Pouawa estuary.

WALK TIME AND DISTANCE
Makarori headland and return via low tide route 1 hour (1 km), Pouawa estuary 1–2 hours (2 km) exploring. Both walks are best at mid- to low tide.

ACCESS AND FACILITIES
From Gisborne take Highway 35 about 10 km to rest area at the south end of Makorori Point. Toilets and shelter. Pouawa is over the hill another 8 km and down a side-road to a carpark and camping area by the sand dunes.

There's a shortage of decent public walking tracks in the East Cape area, which is such a pity, because every part of this coastline is charged full of drama and sunlight. These two short coastal walks prove the point.

From the rest area and carpark at the beach it is an easy walk up onto the Makorori Point headland. There are good views all around, before the track descends back to the beach, and close to a group of pine trees where pied shags roost.

Assuming you have a low tide it is an easy scramble around the coastal headland, where there is an impressive array of different rock formations. Strata in deeply etched layers, rocks shaped like bollards and sea-pebbles the size of dinosaur eggs. On the tidal platform the more active of the shags wait patiently for something to happen.

Back at the carpark it is worth strolling along to the whale cemetery, where the plaque details the story of how many blue whales were stranded and buried in this large mound. Okitu Bay beach is a fine long sandy straight, and much of the way there's a trail through the sand dunes.

POUAWA RIVER ESTUARY

Pouawa estuary is 8 km further along the road, and is a gorgeous wee spot. There are extensive reef platforms, and on any good low tide you can see the locals hunting for kina in the exposed rocks. Small sea-channels run through the rocks and seaweed clings like fine hair.

From the carpark it is a shortish walk around Pariokonohi Point and another huge beach stretches out, running all the way to Whangara Island.

There's no shortage of space here, which is where the rare New Zealand dotterels make a kind of living. In August and September, if their courtship survives the endless disturbance of quad bikes, they will make a small nest or 'scrape' on the frail sandy spit. The chicks will be out by October, about two or three in number, and are brilliantly camouflaged, the adults luring away humans with broken-wing behaviour.

For six weeks the chicks fossick amongst the sand, driftwood and Coke cans, and fledge sometime in November and December, fortunately just before the Christmas onslaught of holidaymakers.

OTHER WALKS

Okitu bush walk, 15 minutes return, starts opposite southern Makorori Point carpark.

49. MAHIA REEFS
Tidal platforms on a long murmuring shore

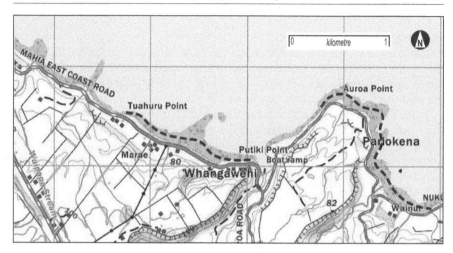

TRACK
Tidal platforms and sandy beaches. Low tide important.

WALK TIME AND DISTANCE
1–2 hours for exploring, sunbathing, meditating, etc.

ACCESS AND FACILITIES
From Wairoa it is about 40 km to Mahia Beach, and another 10 km across the peninsula to Mahia village and Auroa Point. From Mahia onwards there are many rest and pull-off areas along the shoreline. Mahia village had a coffee shop up the hill in 2011, a good place for a gossip with the locals.

There's not much of a walk here really, and Mahia is more of a place to wander, explore and daydream. Like all peninsulas, you can feel a tangible isolation, and one romantic translation of Mahia is 'indistinct sounds', which explains the atmosphere exactly.

The main sandy bay at Mahia Beach is backed with hundreds of sometimes lavish summer houses, but if you drive over to the other side of the peninsula at Oraka, the baches are more homely. Mahia village sits on top of a headland, and after here the road winds around the shoreline to a romantic if dodgy fishing wharf at Whangawehi Stream.

Just along from here is the Whangawehi Reserve, notable for the hollowed-out stone which reputedly was used as a baptismal font by the early missionaries in 1842. There are also several small Maori cemeteries enjoying an unrivalled outlook over the sea to the distant Young Nick's Head.

The seal ends but the road edges around Auroa Point and quite unexpectedly runs out onto a sandy beach. Pohutukawa and ngaio provide some shade on the foreshore.

All along this coast at low tide the sea reveals a virtual rock-desert of sea-reefs and tidal platforms. Long furrows of rock run from the sandy coves out to sea, as if some mad ploughman had decided to have a go at bringing the seabed to pasture. These 'tramlines' come in many unusual permutations of style and colour.

While humans stroll about in bemusement at the geological spectacle, the seabirds get to work. White-faced herons carefully probe the channels of water, and even mynahs come down to the waterline looking for small crabs. Black-backed gulls and black shags tend to be solitary feeders, and you might see a sleek gannet do a spectacular dive for fish just offshore.

If you sit in the sun at Mahia you are bound to nod off, as the foreshore tussock rustle in the sea breeze and the pied shag spreads its wings to dry. When you wake up the sea has returned.

The Mahia Reefs' unusual rocky furrows.

50. MORERE HOT SPRINGS
Natural hot pools and dense nikau palm forest

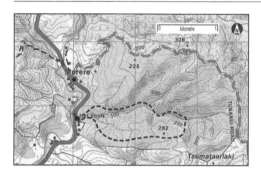

TRACK
Good paths around the main hot pools, but rougher walking tracks higher up in the reserve.

WALK TIME AND DISTANCE
2-3 hours return (4 km) for the Mangakawa hot pools circuit.

ACCESS AND FACILITIES
From Wairoa on Highway 2 it is about 40 km to Morere; or 60 km south of Gisborne. There is a café and shop, and a charge for use of the hot pools, which in practice means that you have to pay to gain access to walk in this reserve. Since most people are keen for a bathe anyway this is not a difficulty, but if you object to paying for walking there is a free alternative entrance to the reserve off Tunanui Road via the Ridge Track.

Morere is an attractive bush reserve, full of nikau palms, and dissected with small gurgling moss streams. It's a good spot for 2-3 hours to break a long car journey. The hot pools are in two parts: the lower baths are the biggest, with a swimming pool and attractive glades for picnicking; the upper pools are hotter, smaller and surrounded by deep bush.

From the office and rest areas, follow the signs to the Mangakawa Track Junction, and start to wander up this gentle spur. The nikau forest is profuse — rimu, totara, tawa, kohekohe are all present, as is the twisting kiekie vine higher up.

All through the Morere bush you will hear the persistent trill of the grey warbler, as well as the distinctive rising call of the shining cuckoo. The cuckoo migrates to New Zealand from the Pacific Islands in spring, a journey of 6000 km. The female deposits her egg in the grey warbler's nest. The cuckoo chick hatches first, and by autumn it is flying back to the islands.

Meanwhile, the track crosses to the top of another spur, and descends very steeply — you will need your hands here — eventually easing into a moist series of gullies where mosses and lichens cram every available niche. The track crosses the elegant creek in a small series of bridges and steps, and you will pass several small cascades. The whole streambed seems alive with greenery, as well as several slimy 'hot spots' in the bush.

Where the creek slightly opens out you pass a track junction with Ridge Track and reach the Nikau Pools. There are two hot pools and a cold plunge pool, as well as changing sheds and toilet. The hot pools vary in temperature from 32 to 40°C, and after the bush walk are eminently satisfying.

People emerge fairly enervated from the hot pools, but fortunately it is only a short stroll through the nikau groves down to the main pool and carpark.

51. TAUPO TOWN WALK — CRATERS OF THE MOON & HUKA FALLS
Simply steaming

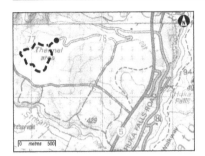

TRACK
Flat boardwalks and gravel paths. The warnings to keep to the track are serious.

WALK TIME AND DISTANCE
Craters of the Moon 1 hour (3 km) return. Huka Falls 30 minutes.

ACCESS AND FACILITIES
Craters of the Moon is off Highway 1, signposted about 4 km north of Taupo, and down a short 1-km side-road to a carpark, toilets and information shop. There is a charge. Huka Falls is on Highway 1, almost opposite Craters of the Moon, well signposted, with large carpark.

Two great short walks, next door to each other. Huka Falls is a tremendous torrent of water in a narrow canyon. Craters of the Moon is a thermal steamfield that is growing.

From the Craters of the Moon carpark the easy track goes into the thermal area where large craters give vent to clouds of white steam, which after rain are sometimes so thick it is like walking through a hot fog.

Everywhere the surface is alive with little vents between the big craters and wafts of sulphur, creating an alien outpost. Plants struggle in this area, and those that succeed can be suddenly blighted when a steam vent opens unexpectedly underneath them.

The track does a circuit through the steamfield, with lookouts and information panels at appropriate places, demonstrating the finer points of steam vents, fumaroles, mud craters and the like. Changes in the activity of steam vents can occur daily. A truly alive place.

HUKA FALLS (AND TRACK TO TAUPO)
Probably the most popular tourist site in the North Island, but it's still a tremendous sight. If you are keen there's a track from the falls, all the way back to Taupo (about 1 hour, 4 km) that includes a natural riverside hot pool on the way.

Steamfields and umbrellas, Craters of the Moon.

52. MOUNT TAUHARA
A grunty bush climb to a high peak

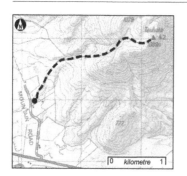

TRACK
A tramping track up a steepish hill, with mud and a trench and some clambering in places.

WALK TIME AND DISTANCE
3–4 hours (5 km) return.

ONE-HOUR WALK
Water tank return.

ACCESS AND FACILITIES
From Highway 5 take Mountain Road to the carpark and signpost. Permission to cross the land and use the track is given by the Maori trustees.

This is a strenuous track leading to a 1088-metre volcanic peak overlooking Lake Taupo, and it is surprisingly popular considering the going is quite rough in places. On any weekend day there might be 20 to 30 people winding up through the dense bush to the rock lookouts. Take a lunch, for the view is superb.

From the carpark the track crosses a farm paddock, then follows up an easy grass spur and along a fenceline to a water tank on the bush edge. There are fine views here.

The track twists through the thick bush of kamahi and manuka, climbing erratically as it passes a seat. Higher up it passes quite close to a good-sized stream (I found it drinkable), and gets easier as it wanders onto a 'saddle'.

There are some short stretches of track along deep earth trenches, then the bush becomes more alpine as you walk up the final slopes to the beacon, where there is an excellent panorama

A side-trail turns along a ridge to more rock outcrops, and (if you find it) a worn trail cuts down to the main track again.

Climbing towards Mount Tauhara.

53. LAKE ROTOPOUNAMU

Serene lake with tall podocarp trees and pumice beaches

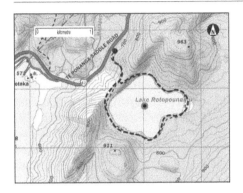

TRACK
Well maintained bush track.

WALK TIME AND DISTANCE
1–2 hours (3 km) return.

ACCESS AND FACILITIES
From Turangi travel 3 km west to the junction of Highway 47 and 41, and follow Highway 47 over the saddle 6 km to the roadside carparks. Traffic can blat along this road so take care when crossing to the track entrance.

Rotopounamu means 'greenstone lake', a poetic reference to the clear emerald-coloured water. Different lights create different lake colours, and Rotopounamu can just as easily look a steel blue or a dull grey. It was formed by a landslide some 10,000 years ago, and is about 1 km across and 9 metres deep.

The bush is dense and tall, with massive examples of rimu, red beech and matai, and the birdlife is almost a who's who of New Zealand bush birds: kaka, parakeet, tomtit, bellbird, long-tailed cuckoo, whitehead, rifleman, blackbird, chaffinch, robin, native pigeon, shining cuckoo and grey warbler. In the morning you can get a real blast of dawn chorus, such as might have been heard before humans arrived in New Zealand.

From the road the track follows an easy grade to a track junction. A step along the right-hand branch brings you to a great viewpoint overlooking Lake Rotoaira. Seats for the already weary.

The track goes down into the dense podocarp forest and onto Five Minute Beach, the first of several white pumice beaches. On a hot day some people try a swim but the water rarely gets above freezing.

From here on the track starts its slow circumnavigation of the lake through an array of different forest types. Around Five Minute Beach the bush is mostly kamahi, with lemonwood (tarata) fairly thick, and a side-track investigates a large matai. Known as 'black pine' by the early settlers, these podocarps have distinctive hammer-dent bark.

Then the track finds itself in tall red beech forest, with here and there large kahikatea looming up, and rimu 'weeping' in dignified groves. At Long Beach you get a break from the bush and this is an excellent spot for a rest or a 'little something' to get you round the rest of the lake. The grey ducks are also interested in your little something, but dabchicks and shags tend to remain aloof.

Kidney ferns become much more prominent on the shadier side of the lake and occupy wide areas, and kamahi forest starts to dominate again at Ten Minute Beach and back to the track junction again. A truly great piece of forest.

54. PORERE REDOUBT
The last battleground

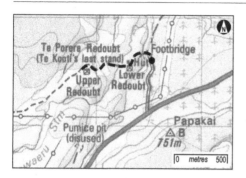

TRACK
Gravel track.

WALK TIME AND DISTANCE
1 hour (1 km) return.

ACCESS AND FACILITIES
From the township of National Park, drive east on Highway 47, past the turn-off to Whakapapa, some 18 km. Porere is signposted and a gravel road leads to a small carpark and info signs.

Not a big walk, but a powerful return to the past, and the site of the last pitched battle in the New Zealand Wars. In 1869 Te Kooti Arikirangi Te Turuki led about 300 men and women here, and built a redoubt that was attacked by a mixed government force of Armed Constabulary and Maori warriors from Whanganui, Taupo and Hawke's Bay, perhaps about 500 men in all. This place was immortalised as Te Kooti's last stand.

The track crosses a bridge over the small Whanganui River, and climbs up to the lower redoubt. A platform gives you a view of the layout of the trenches, but this redoubt was quickly overrun. The attackers would have continued along the line of the track now, up to the high redoubt, with its network of slit trenches, rifle loopholes and fiercesome 4-metre-high walls that stood out boldly on the brow of the ridge.

Te Kooti's men had seen the government forces crossing the open tussock grasslands, but they had the bush at their back to escape into. The final attack was swift, and Te Kooti's defenders killed only four of the attackers before becoming overwhelmed, losing 37 in the bloody engagement. Many of Te Kooti's men fired on the attackers from outside the redoubt, and then melted into the bush. The battle was won, and lost.

Te Kooti was defeated, but gave the government forces the slip. However, he was never again the same threat. He later founded the Ringatu Church, was eventually pardoned in 1883 and died in 1893. Porere Redoubt is now a peaceful scene, calmed by the silence, but by no means forgotten. At the end of one of the slit trenches there is a small plaque in remembrance of 'Te Kooti's men'.

55. TONGARIRO CROSSING
Venture into the interior

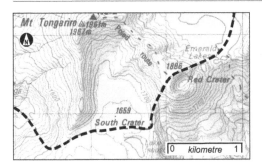

TRACK
A well marked track with some steep climbs and loose scoria. Do not attempt this in poor weather since you will not see a thing, and will have a miserable time. Take plenty of water, food and warm clothing. Even in summer the temperature can drop quickly.

WALK TIME AND DISTANCE
One-way crossing 7–8 hours, 18 km. This is a long, full-day tramp.

ONE-HOUR WALK
Mangatepopo Hut return (or if starting from Ketetahi 1.5 hours return to bush edge).

ACCESS AND FACILITIES
From National Park take Highway 47 and turn onto the unsealed Mangatepopo Road, travelling some 6 km to the carpark. The Ketetahi Springs side-road is off Highway 47A, and leads to information boards, a shelter and toilets. The springs are on Maori land and access is not necessarily permanent or permitted, so check with DOC first.

In summer, several companies arrange transport pick-ups for either end of the track. See DOC at Whakapapa.

This is dubbed the finest one-day walk in New Zealand, and perhaps it is. A volcanic heartland of steaming hot springs, lakes daubed with unearthly colours, barren volcanic craters and the grey, brooding cinder cone of Ngauruhoe.

It is popular, and busloads of people are dropped off at Mangatepopo and sent scurrying into this god-forsaken wilderness with scant idea of what they are in for. They mostly survive, but if you want to beat the crowds start early.

From the bleak Mangatepopo carpark the track hurries past the junction to Whakapapa and a side-track to Mangatepopo Hut and up the gradually confining valley. You can smell the soda springs (but they are not hot), and then you start up the first serious climb, nicknamed The Giant's Staircase, to the South Crater.

It is breathtaking on top, with good fast travel across the plateau as you blithely slip by Tongariro on the left and Ngauruhoe on the right. The sharpest climb is now 200 metres up the ridge onto Red Crater itself, at 1886 metres the highest point in the crossing.

So many places to explore but little time, so bounce past the two Emerald Lakes, looking like green serpent's eyes, and wander over the vast plain past Blue Lake to the far lip of Central Crater. At this saddle the track leads down a zigzag trail to Ketetahi Hut, then on to the hot springs, distinguished by the permanent puff of cloud that hangs over the flank of the mountain.

An easy trail goes down over tussock and sweet-smelling turpentine scrub to the bush edge. Enjoy the final views of Lake Rotoaira and Mount Pihanga, and follow the track through the totara forest over the undrinkable stream and on to the carpark.

Lunch by the Emerald Lakes, Tongariro Crossing.   *Taranaki Falls (see facing page).*

56. TARANAKI FALLS
Across a volcanic plateau to a 20-metre waterfall

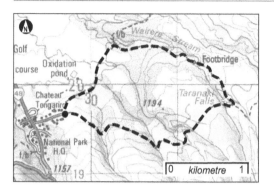

TRACK
Generally well gravelled or boardwalked, but can get muddy.

WALK TIME AND DISTANCE
2 hours (5 km) return.

ACCESS AND FACILITIES
From Highway 48, at the Chateau turn down Ngauruhoe Place to the carpark. The Chateau area has the Tongariro information centre, toilets and café.

This is a justly popular walk on the pumice plateau, with unrivalled views of the twin volcanoes of Ruapehu and Ngauruhoe, plus a streamside beech forest and a fine waterfall. The air is keen and sharp, and the starting altitude of this walk is 1140 metres. Take warm clothes, some scroggin and a camera.

From the carpark you weave along a well made trail through fields of tussock and scoria. There are numerous small gullies to cross, with bridges and mountain streams, and at one point you climb up onto the edge of an old andesite lava flow, formed about 15,000 years ago.

You quickly reach the edge of the Taranaki Falls, which roar over the lava rock. There are lookout points near the waterfall, though the track soon meets a junction, and turning left there is a quick, sharp drop through mountain totara down to the base of the waterfall.

There are plenty of lunch or picnic rocks here and on a hot Tongariro summer's day it is a great place for an afternoon siesta. The track now closely follows the Wairere Stream, first over tussock, then into cool mountain beech forest.

After the footbridge the stream runs down many cascades, and there is a short side-track to one of them. Turn left at the track junction and you quickly break out of the bush and onto the tussock plain again. A few more gullies to cross and you are back at the carpark.

57. CRATER LAKE
Hard yakka, but what a view!

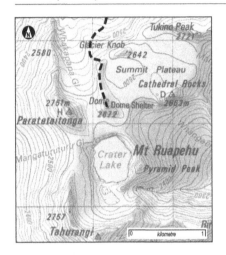

TRACK
An ambitious day tramp to the volcanic crater lake of Mount Ruapehu. The chairlift runs through the summer holiday season, but beyond the chairlift there is no real track, just a steady climb over rocks following boot-trails and a confusing array of cairns. In the future, DOC may provide a marked route during summer.

Note: This is a day tramp for the experienced and well equipped; take a map and compass. Tongariro National Park 273-04 map is especially good as it has a highly detailed 1:12,500 map of the whole crater lake walk. You need good clear weather: in the mist the potential to get lost is considerable. This description assumes there is no snow on the route, usually implying a January–March walk.

WALK TIME AND DISTANCE
6–7 hours (9 km) return, 1000 metres total climb (utilising chairlift). If walking from the Top o' the Bruce carpark add 2 hours.

30-MINUTE WALK
From the top chairlift a summer nature trail is laid out.

ACCESS AND FACILITIES
From the end of Highway 48 beside the Chateau, follow the road up to the Top o' the Bruce and Iwikau village, where there is a carpark, toilets and many ski huts. The chairlift operates during the summer period and saves 300 metres in height. It operates between 8.30 a.m. and 4 p.m.

Mount Ruapehu sits like a massive, grumpy grandaddy in the middle of the North Island, sometimes fuming to itself, occasionally erupting, but usually placid. Ruapehu is not as inaccessible as it looks, courtesy of a skifield road to 1600 metres and a chairlift beyond that. This is a formidable walk, but immensely satisfying, looking down upon the grey-green crater lake and standing almost on the top of the North Island.

From the Top o' the Bruce the unmarked route weaves up through the skifield huts, keeping the main chairlifts on your left. It takes 1 hour to plod up to the New Zealand Alpine Club Hut, the highest private hut on the mountain, with a fine view of the Pinnacles Ridge.

Descend to the nature trail at what is marked on the maps as Delta Corner.

You are now on the standard route, as if you caught the chairlift.

Follow up the worn boot-trails under The Cirque bluffs onto Restful Ridge, a somewhat ironic name, I feel. To avoid a non-negotiable bluff, the worn trail slips off the ridge into a feature called The Trough, then sidles back onto Restful Ridge again.

The last of the chairlift pylons has petered out, and the large, smooth rocks of Restful Ridge are coloured orange, with occasional old snow patches. There are plenty of cairns to guide you. This is good walking, and you are out on an open mountain with your destination well in sight. Near the crater rim the boot-trail becomes very distinct and zigzags sharply up onto the crater wall.

The summit plateau looks magnificent, and in summer this large, flat plain is mostly free of snow. The rugged Te Heuheu peak is to the left and Cathedral Rocks are straight ahead — but where is the lake?

The trail continues along the crater wall onto the significant bump of Dome at 2672 metres, and the ungainly Dome Shelter. Note the entry via the 'chimney'. The crater lake lies sullenly, and silkily, below you. The Tahurangi high peak of Ruapehu (2797 metres) is on the other side, with multicoloured and writhing strata bluffs surrounding the lake. The North Island is like a mirage. Pretty good, eh?

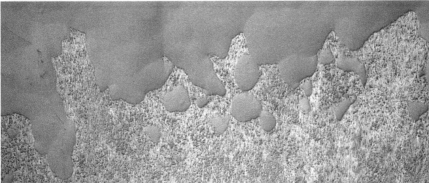

Top: Crater Lake, Mount Ruapehu.
Above: Cliff and seaweed on the Whitecliffs Walkway (see page 101).

58. HAPUAWHENUA VIADUCTS
Historic coach road through forest to a splendid old railway viaduct

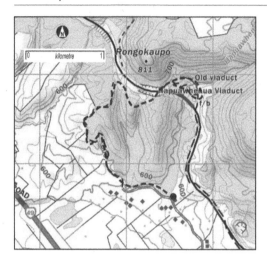

TRACK
Good condition and easy walking, track also shared with mountain bikes.

WALK TIME AND DISTANCE
2 hours (4 km) return.

ONE-HOUR WALK
To lookout on edge of farmland.

ACCESS AND FACILITIES
From Ohakune and Highway 49 take Marshalls Road some 3 km to the carpark.

You don't have to be a railway buff to enjoy this magnificent walk, which is a welcome addition to walks in the Ohakune area. You can visit winter or summer, and it's interesting enough for most kids, with two viaducts, a tunnel and many well produced display boards that make the history of this area come alive.

It is also a mountain-bike trail, and people regularly cycle through to Horopito on Highway 4. It is generally uphill to the viaducts, so it's a good downhill run back to the Marshalls Road carpark.

The first stretch of walk follows the original coach road, and in places you can still see the cobblestones (setts) in place. The road gradually rises past farmland and reaches a good lookout, before turning into some lovely native forest.

The track drops down to an old railway tunnel (but you can't walk through it unfortunately), then climbs up through more thick fern forest before dropping down to the historic viaduct.

It's an amazing piece of engineering, built in 1908 — curving, built on four steel lattice towers and 13 concrete towers, with a length of 284 metres and a maximum height of 45 metres. It's quite freaky looking down through the gaps of the railway sleepers.

On the far side there's a picnic area, with excellent historic information, and you can follow the gravel road in a loop down across the stream and up back to the main track again. The modern viaduct is rather elegant as well, and it's quite a sight if a modern train rumbles and clatters past.

59. WAIHOHONU HUTS
Volcanic panorama and a historic hut

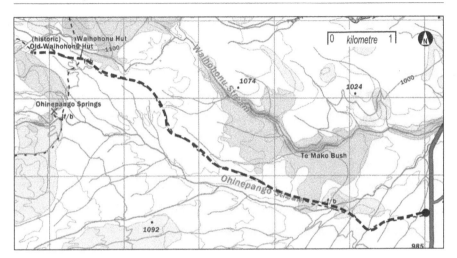

TRACK
Generally well marked but sometimes highly eroded tracks. You are already at an altitude of 1000 metres when you get out of the car, and even though this is an easy alpine walk, take warm clothes and a windjacket.

WALK TIME AND DISTANCE
2–3 hours (12 km) return from historic hut.

ONE-HOUR WALK
Te Mako Bush (3 km) return.

ACCESS AND FACILITIES
On Highway 1 (known here as the Desert Road) the turn-off and carpark for Waihohonu is about 25 km north of Waiouru. Keep a sharp lookout for it.

The winds can howl across the spacious tussock plains of the Tongariro plateau, and can bring snow in the middle of summer, so this is definitely a fine weather trip. It's also a great walk among volcanoes, leading to a genuine piece of New Zealand history.

From the carpark follow an old vehicle track to Te Mako Bush, an attractive copse of trees beside the Ohinepango Stream. The water runs clean and fresh, which indeed it should because it is bubbling out of the ground from the Ohinepango Springs some 4 km away.

A short walk through the mountain beech, then you are out into the tussock again. After a while you can see a patch of bush in the distance and this resolves itself into a track junction, where the right-hand choice goes across the footbridge and on to a camping area.

Go left and suddenly you are beside the 40-bunk Waihohonu Hut. Built in 2011, with gas rings, solar lights, and even a wetback for hot water, the hut is palatial, and cost more than most average homes.

The views are stupendous: Ngauruhoe through one window and Mount Te Heuheu (2720 metres), a side-peak of Mount Ruapehu, through the other.

From the hut the track almost immediately splits. The left branch travels about 10 minutes in and out of a large scoria gully and across the Ohinepango Stream to the natural springs. They are nestled in a bush grotto, usually loudly occupied by a pair of paradise ducks.

The straight-ahead track leads 15 minutes to the old Waihohonu Hut, painted a bright red and well sheltered in a glade of beech forest.

This vintage hut was once on the tourist coach road and is listed by the Historic Places Trust as a category 1 hut, one of the few mountain huts that are designated. It was built in 1901 and it has an unusual construction, for pumice was used as insulation between the double wooden walls. The walls are covered in graffiti, some of it going back to the 1920s.

As you head back to the carpark across the tussock plain, it's hard not to keep looking backwards at the tremendous mountain views.

View of Mount Ngauruhoe.

60. WHITECLIFFS WALKWAY
Dramatic cliffs on a historic coastal walk

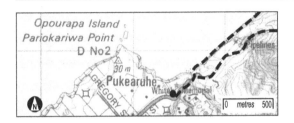

TRACK
Beach walking, then steep steps, a bush trail and rolling farm tracks. A low tide is essential as the cliffs are steep, with no escape routes. The inland track is closed for lambing between July and September.

WALK TIME AND DISTANCE
3–4 hours (8 km) Waipingao Stream and 'pipe' track circuit. Add 2 hours to visit the historic stock tunnel, though it seemed to be closed at the time of writing. The Whitecliffs Walkway continues on to the Tongaporutu River.

ONE-HOUR WALK
Along the beach to the natural archway and return.

ACCESS AND FACILITIES
From New Plymouth it is 36 km north to the turn-off into Pukearuhe Road and 11 km to the end of this road. Carparking at the actual road-end is non-existent, so park up alongside the fenceline by the farmland (there is a rough sign there) and walk the last 500 metres down to the beach.

Here on this magnificent coast is a walk of great drama. Pukearuhe was one of the finest defensive and fighting pa in the country, and it overlooks a rollercoaster beach and formidable sea cliffs. There is unique history here, with the pa site, a European redoubt, and a military tunnel that was built in 1880 to assist the garrison, but later employed as a humble stock tunnel.

First walk down the road ramp to the coast, where at low tide you wander past a graceful sea arch and tidal platforms onto the Waipingao Stream. After rain, waterfalls slip-slide over the sea cliffs.

From Waipingao Stream it is a good side trip, again with a low tide, along the shoreline to look at the historic tunnel.

The main track picks its way up Waipingao Stream along an old vehicle track, and the valley is full of nikau palms, tawa and rewarewa. At the junction you are faced with the prospect of 670 steps up the spur to the Mount Davidson saddle.

This track follows a public easement along the top of the 200-mm Kapuni gas pipeline, and after the sweat uphill the views are excellent from the 250-metre-high Mount Davidson saddle.

All the hard work is over now, and it is easy walking on a poled route down through the sheep paddocks and along the vehicle track back to the carpark. You can see Mount Egmont/Taranaki on a clear day.

61. NEW PLYMOUTH CITY WALK — TE HENUI
A subtle city walkway — sea, cemetery and stream

TRACK
A mixture of gravel paths, bush trails, footpaths and grass paths, with a steady climb up a stream, then a descent. Generally well marked, though a town map is useful.

WALK TIME AND DISTANCE
1.5–2 hours (6 km) return.

ACCESS AND FACILITIES
In New Plymouth start from East End Reserve, off Buller Street. There is a carpark, picnic place, toilets and a children's play area. There are many other access points to Te Henui Walkway.

New Plymouth has an outstanding network of urban walkways, utilising both the beachfront and the bush gullies that trickle through the town. Te Henui Walkway has something of everything: coast, an intimate bush stream, a historic pa site and a cemetery — what more could you want?

From the Buller Street carpark cross the outlet of Te Henui Stream beside the sea, and negotiate the signposts around the first bend and across another footbridge. The track settles into a streamside bush walk, passing obliviously under the busy Devon Street East bridge and wandering up a quiet dell.

Under Northgate Road the track passes plantings of camellias and magnolias, and Te Henui cemetery. It then crosses another footbridge and, keeping close to the stream, winds past small reserves and residential backyards up to Cumberland Street.

Turn down the other side of Te Henui Stream here, and follow the signposts down past small bush and grass reserves then up to Timandra Street. The walk is quite high above the stream now, and goes through the open parkland of Avery Reserve and Puketara Pa then on to Te Henui cemetery.

The signposts somewhat desert you here, and you have to pick your own way through the headstones to find one of several tracks that lead down to Te Henui Stream again, and back to the living shoreline.

OTHER WALKS IN NEW PLYMOUTH
Barrett Domain (1 hour return) and Huatoki Walkway (3 hours return).

62. NEW PLYMOUTH CITY WALK — COASTAL WALKWAY
Surf and city intermingle

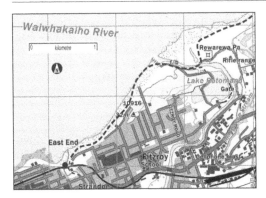

TRACK
A good concrete path all the way to the Te Rewa Rewa footbridge.

WALK TIME AND DISTANCE
1.5–2 hours (6 km) return.

ACCESS AND FACILITIES
In New Plymouth start from East End Reserve, off Buller Street. Access to the northern part of East End Reserve can be reached from Devon Street East and Nobs Line. The reserve has carpark, picnic places, toilets and a children's play area. A mobile café was there in 2011.

This coastal track is all about waves: the tree-trunk-littered shoreline with its big Tasman Sea rollers, the famous new 'wave' bridge, and the quirky 'wave' mobile café. New Plymouth's 10-km coastal walkway stretches along the entire length of the city, and beyond, but this northern section embraces its wilder side. All of it is worth walking, probably one of the best urban walkways in New Zealand.

Cross the elegant 'lightning bolt' footbridge over Te Henui Stream, then the broad track wanders along the coastal fringe. Great views back to the silhouetted power-station chimney and offshore islands, with an occasional big ship looming on the horizon.

The track swings past the Fitzroy Beach Holiday Camp, and then suddenly into coastal dunes with the golf course on your right. The views are quite uncluttered now, as Mount Egmont/Taranaki gets more obvious.

The Waiwhakaiho River is busy with whitebaiters in season, and is now spanned by the 83-metre Te Rewa Rewa footbridge (opened in 2010), likened to a Tasman Sea wave. This is a good return point, but you can go all the way to Bell Block.

OTHER WALKS IN NEW PLYMOUTH
Huatoki Walkway (3 hours return).

63. TE KORU PA
A sacred and silent pa site

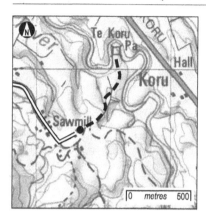

TRACK
Farm vehicle track down to the pa site, then bush trails.

WALK TIME AND DISTANCE
1 hour (2 km) return.

ACCESS AND FACILITIES
From Highway 45 at Oakura turn down Wairau Road and Surrey Hill Road to parking at the end of the road by the sign. Well signposted.

Many Maori pa sites are little more than grassy paddocks with a few nondescript humps and hollows, but Te Koru Pa is different. It is secluded, down in the soft loop of the Oakura River valley, and covered with bush that conceals an extensive and spooky network of trenches and embankments.

From the road follow the poles down the farm track, then across a paddock to the edge of the reserve. The pa is covered with regrowth forest, so at a distance it looks like a bushy hump. It is only when you are walking on the bush paths that you realise the hill is actually substantial earthworks, terraced with defensive walls. Some of these walls are supported by the original stonework.

As you wander about you discover old kumara storage pits (rua) and a complex network of paths, some of which lead down to the river with its smooth grey boulders like dinosaur eggs. The silence is intense, and you cannot help but feel the presence of the early Maori who lived and loved in this once great pa.

The distinctive boulders by the Oakura River, Te Koru Pa.

64. THE PLATEAU
Traversing the high slopes of Mount Egmont/Taranaki

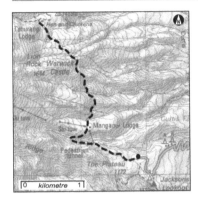

TRACK
Good gravelled track above the bushline, climbing slowly to Tahurangi.

WALK TIME AND DISTANCE
To Tahurangi Lodge 3–4 hours (6 km) return. An alpine walk, suitable as a summer walk only; you need to be well equipped and pick your day. A map is useful: Egmont National Park 273-09, or Egmont P20.

ONE-HOUR WALK
Skifield return.

ACCESS AND FACILITIES
From Stratford and Highway 3 take the Stratford Mountain House road up the zigzag to a huge skifield carpark simply called The Plateau. There is a lookout platform and toilets here.

On a fine summer's day this walk cannot be beaten. It starts at 1100 metres, and traverses steadily up and around the side of Mount Egmont/Taranaki. It trawls under impressive rock formations and through a tussock landscape with shy alpine flowers, and offers extensive views across the tidy plains to Ruapehu and Ngauruhoe on the horizon.

From the carpark the track is easy and well graded as it passes through a shrub belt of leatherwood and koromiko. After you pass the flying fox the track angles into a narrow gorge.

You often get old avalanche snow lingering in the valley but there will usually be footsteps to follow. A short climb out of the gorge and you are at the desolate skifield, where there is a large public shelter with toilets.

The track sidles out of the skifield and across various mountain streams and alpine gullies filled with buttercups and daisies in spring. The views are marvellous, the gradient gentle, and the track well poled as it sidles under the volcanic outcrop of Warwick Castle in expansive slopes of tussock.

It is not long before the television pylon and Tahurangi Lodge come into view. There is a small, unlocked emergency shelter underneath the lodge. The return to the Plateau carpark is an easy and pleasant downhill task.

65. YORK HISTORIC CIRCUIT
Railway ruins in the bush

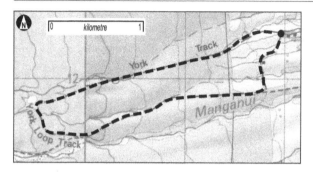

TRACK
Generally flat and easy paths following old tramways, railway lines and access roads. Sometimes a bit overgrown, with a smidgin of rockhopping along a stream.

WALK TIME AND DISTANCE
2–2.5 hours (6 km) return.

ONE-HOUR WALK
Sand trap return.

ACCESS AND FACILITIES
From Highway 3 turn down York Road and go right to the road-end; and carpark. Good interpretation sign.

The York track is one of those obscure places that are immensely interesting once you have discovered them, making you wonder why you did not go before. The track follows old railway lines into a huge crusher site, now buried in the bush, and the walk does a circuit, with remnants of industrial history all the way round. There is enough to keep the kids interested and a good place for a snack-stop halfway round.

Through the gate the track is immediately in thick, luxuriant regrowth forest and quickly reaches a track junction. Turn left to the crusher site, where large concrete structures look appropriately Byzantine in the thick bush.

Rock was crushed on this site in the 1940s and railed out to help build the Wellington–New Plymouth railway line. Fifteen minutes or so further along the track (and waterpipe) is the strange concrete sand trap, near the Manganui River.

The track continues on an old tramline and along a pretty stream to a footbridge, which makes a pleasing picnic or halfway resting area. A tad further is the small clearing known as the 'foot station', then it is a dead straight line back to the carpark — a fine downward romp on the old service road.

66. DAWSON FALLS
Through goblin forest to a waterfall

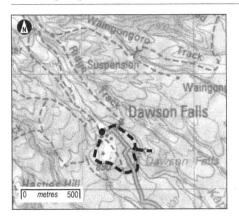

TRACK

Good bush tracks with some up and down. Study the map boards at the carpark or visitor centre carefully, for there are numerous track options in this area

WALK TIME AND DISTANCE

1–2 hours (1.5 km) Dawson Falls circuit on the Kapuni Loop Track.

ACCESS AND FACILITIES

From Stratford and Highway 3 drive south and take the Opunake Road some 12 km, then follow the narrow and sealed Manaia Road 8 km to the top carpark. Visitor centre, public shelter, lookout platform, information boards, toilets. The historic power station is well worth a visit.

Dawson Falls is a popular scenic walk to a dashing waterfall, and can be made into a circuit from the carpark. The forest is thickly crusted with lichens and mosses, giving the trees a fairytale look, hence the local name 'goblin forest'. In rain or mist this forest can look even more mysterious.

Walk back down the road a short distance and pick up the start of the track. It passes one footbridge, with a view of Kapuni Stream, then the track drops down on a river terrace above Kapuni Stream.

There is another footbridge right above the falls themselves, and just around from here an excellent lookout for people who do not want to drop down to the base of the falls themselves. However, the signposted side-track is worth taking; the 18-metre-high falls look better from below, and on a hot day you might fancy a bracing shower.

The Kapuni Track circuit now continues uphill, crosses the road and climbs slowly back up to the public shelter and carpark.

OTHER WALKS

Wilkies Pools Loop Track (1 hour), Konini Dell Loop Track (1 hour) and Ridge Loop Track (1–1.5 hours).

67. FANTHAMS PEAK
Soaring views on the way to a high peak

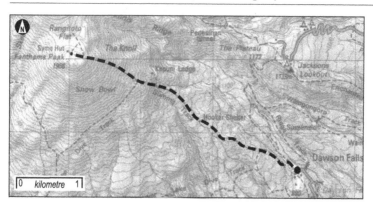

TRACK
A well marked bush track up steps to boardwalk through tussock, then soft, pluggy scoria following poles to Fanthams Peak, climbing all the way. Take a map: Egmont National Park 273-09, or Egmont P20.

Despite the ease of access, this can be tough country in bad weather, and Mount Egmont/Taranaki has a notoriously fickle climate. This walk is suited to the experienced and well equipped, and there is no point in going unless you can see the views, so wait until you get a good forecast. It will be worth the wait.

WALK TIME AND DISTANCE
5–6 hours (7 km) return. 1.5-hour walk Hillary Seat return.

ACCESS AND FACILITIES
From Stratford and Highway 3 drive south and take the Opunake Road some 12 km, then follow the narrow and sealed Manaia Road 8 km to the top carpark. Visitor centre, public shelter, lookout platform, information boards, toilets.

Mount Egmont/Taranaki is not perfectly symmetrical: there is an odd subsidiary pimple on one side, called Fanthams Peak (1966 metres). The walk to it is steep, starting from the goblin forest (see previous page) and up to a volcanic plain, with views right over the heart of the North Island to the volcanoes of Ruapehu and Ngauruhoe.

The summit track is well marked as it crosses a footbridge and climbs steadily through a heavy and mossy forest. After passing a couple of junctions the track reaches the Hillary Seat, and the first good view of Mount Egmont/Taranaki.

The track now eases somewhat and pulls up more gradually to the Hooker Shelter, which roughly marks the edge of the bush and the start of the subalpine belt. Good views now, and a steady, stepped walk up towards the junction to Kapuni Hut. These steps can be a bit of a curse, but they are a feature of tramping on Taranaki.

The Kapuni Hut verandah is the last sheltered spot, then the track cuts through the last of the alpine scrub and reaches the upper rock slopes — puggy going in the porridge-like scoria.

The route is well poled, but there are trails everywhere, which in misty weather can cause some confusion. At last you reach the edge of Rangitoto Flat, a volcanic plain with crusty scoria and bright-stained rocks. Stick to the poled route as it climbs a little above Rangitoto Flat and sidles directly to the glinting iron sides of Syme Hut.

Plenty to see and do up here, and the hut sits in a commanding position. The return should be straightforward, but make sure you stay on the poled route if the weather closes in.

68. RANGIWAHIA TOPS
Mountain cedar forest and tussock tops

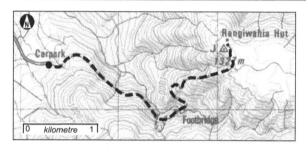

TRACK
A graded packtrack (a nineteenth-century road for packhorses or stock, wide enough to take the horse and its panniers) that climbs steadily to the tops. An active slip about halfway up has caused problems for walkers, and there is a 30–40 minute steep detour around the slip. DOC signs state this is 'no longer an easy walk'.

WALK TIME AND DISTANCE
3–4 hours (5 km) return to hut. Allow another 1–2 hours to get to the main ridge and back.

ACCESS AND FACILITIES
From Highway 1 at Mangaweka township turn off to Rangiwahia. It is about 15 km to the turn-off onto Te Para Para Road and a further 4 km to Renfrew Road, then 4 km to a gate and DOC sign 'Ruahine Forest Park'. More basic road for 1 km up through another gate and cow paddock to carpark at a surprising altitude of 810 metres. Information boards and toilet.

This well graded track was put in by early runholders to take sheep up onto the tussock tops, and the first Rangiwahia Hut was a shepherd's hut. Later Rangiwahia became the second skifield in New Zealand.

Today, Rangiwahia is a stunning escape from the urban rat-race where you can see the triptych of North Island volcanoes — Mount Egmont/Taranaki, Mount Ruapehu and Mount Ngauruhoe.

From the carpark the track wanders up through some attractive rimu forest with peppertree (horopito), rangiora and wineberry (makomako) underneath. The new slip requires an hour-long detour. Then there is a grove of red beech and an elegant footbridge over a gorge.

You enter mountain cedar (kaikawaka) forest — a distinctive pyramid-like tree with a rich red straight trunk. The track keeps its easy grade, and zigzags up through the subalpine leatherwood (tupare) forest to the tussock grasslands.

The 12-bunk hut has a verandah on which to eat lunch and take in the views, and beside it on the small hilltop there is an even better lookout. There is a worn tussock track a short way above the hut, but it is more than 3 km to Mangahuia, the 1583-metre-high summit. If you have the time, go there.

69. TOTARA RESERVE
Several walks in a splendid forest reserve

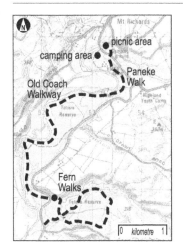

TRACK
Bush tracks with some mud.

WALK TIME AND DISTANCE
1 hour (1 km) nature walk.

ACCESS AND FACILITIES
From Ashhurst take the Pohangina Road almost 20 km to the reserve, which is well signposted, and is now called the Totara Regional Park Reserve.

On the north side of the reserve is the gorgeous picnic area, and power points for campervans. On the south, there is a spacious camping area, new ablutions block, and new plantings. Predator traps have been extensively laid. Track work is ongoing and signage may change in the next few years.

The Totara Reserve has some of the best lowland totara trees left in the district, and part of the pleasure of being here is just enjoying this ancient forest. There's a highly scenic picnicking and camping area beside the Pohangina River, and it is a good place for a weekend family camp, with plenty of interest in the river and several walks.

The nature walk has been upgraded considerably and is the best short walk in the reserve. It would suit anyone of any age and inclination.

The walk starts at the picnic area, wanders through a stunning assemblage of totara trees, and reaches the road beside the largest totara tree of all. Then it crosses the road and continues through forest, past a wetland area, and around the back of Camp Rangi Woods. Here, you can follow the main camping access road back to the picnic area.

OTHER WALKS
Kahikatea Walk (30 minutes return) is up the Pohangina Valley East Road, just past the pretty St Bartholomew's church. Pettifar and Gilchrist Loop tracks are 1 km south of the Totara Reserve and include parts of the old Coach Road, 1–2 hours each. The Fern Walk is 2 km south of Totara Reserve and is a 3–4 hour circuit through kahikatea, rimu and totara.

70. SNAPPER ROCK

Tidal platforms, coastal sand cliffs and strange ventifacts.

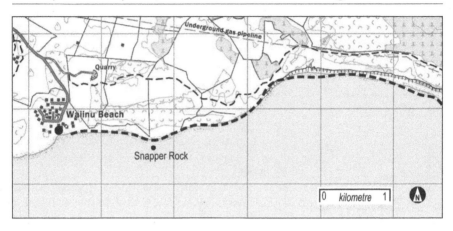

TRACK

Easy beach walking, but important to aim for a low tide at Snapper Rock for this walk, particularly if you intend to go right through. The coastal cliffs are interrupted by gullies and streams so there are escape routes if you misjudge the tides.

WALK TIME AND DISTANCE

From Ototoka Beach to Waiinu Beach is 2–3 hours one way (8 km), and having transport arranged at the other end is probably the most attractive way to do this walk. From Waiinu Beach, Snapper Rock return is about 1–2 hours (3 km).

ACCESS AND FACILITIES

From Whanganui drive on Highway 3 about 15 km to Kai Iwi and 5 km almost to Kai Iwi Beach settlement. Take the signposted Maxwell Road about 4 km to the Ototoka Beach Road, then 4 km to the carpark on the cliff. Locally this is known as Maxwell's Beach. There is a toilet here.

From Whanganui to New Plymouth there is a narrow margin of wilderness between the turbulent Tasman and the prim quilted farmland. It's a bracing and frequently stormy shore of sand cliffs and reef platforms, and it's a wonderful place to explore.

The carpark at Ototoka sits on top of a cliff with fine views up and down the coast, and you can see Whanganui city in the distance. A walking track crosses a smart bridge over a waterfall, and drops down to the wide open beach sands.

Scattered here are numerous boulders that seem entirely made of sea shells. You can almost break off chunks in your hand.

Walking north you quickly reach a headland where boulders have made a jumble of interesting shapes. Flax and marram grass secure the dune cliffs behind. Ahead of you is the long sweep of Ototoka Beach, some 4 km of open beach plain.

There is no vehicle access at Ototoka Point, and the black rock pile at Snapper Rock prevents most vehicles from getting past, except at very low tide. In consequence this beach is usually free from the pesky quad bikes that roar along much of the eastern coast.

Snapper Rock (Nukumaru Rock) itself is a jumble of large, flat rocks, which are a bit of a scramble to get over. At low tide there are various sand channels that enable you to walk around and underneath the rocks. But if the tide is wrong you may have to bash through the sand dunes. This area is popular with fisherfolk, hence the name.

It's 2 km around several subtle headlands to Waiinu Beach, which has a large carpark, picnic area and camping area. A sign states that the gathering of ventifacts is illegal. What, you might ask, is a ventifact?

They are any wind-sculpted stones, worn into shapes variously described as 'triangles', 'brazil nuts' and 'Chinese hats'. Ventifact is a latin word meaning 'wind-made', and on this coast they have resulted from the stones of older beaches becoming exposed as the top layers of geologically young sand are blown away and 'sand-blasted' against the resisting pebbles. If you find one, please leave it for others to enjoy.

The long Ototoka beach.

71. PALMERSTON NORTH CITY WALK — TURITEA WALKWAY

Varied and interesting urban walkway

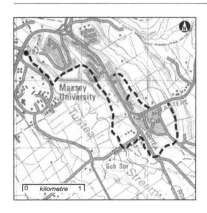

TRACK

All sorts, including footpaths, bush tracks, gravel paths and grass trails. Rolling country but very well signposted. This description is for the full walk circuit but there are numerous variations. A town street map is useful.

WALK TIME AND DISTANCE

2–3 hours (7 km) return.

ONE-HOUR WALK

Bledisloe Park to Atawhai Park is about 1 hour return.

ACCESS AND FACILITIES

Turn off Tennent Drive, just before Massey University, into the carpark, which is very easy to miss. Watch for signposts, otherwise there are various other access points off the campus itself, or Springdale Grove, Old West Road, and so on.

A real hidden gem of a walkway, craftily designed to follow the tinkling Turitea Stream around the university and through the new southern suburbs. The track negotiates parks and gardens, urban streets, streamsides, pockets of bush, farmland and ponds — a little bit of everything.

From the carpark turn into Bledisloe Park, an attractive area of native trees, flowering shrubs and footbridges beside the Turitea Stream. The track is sheltered and private here as it crosses the stream a couple of times then turns uphill to Atawhai Park and a narrow gully to Springdale Grove.

Across the road the track nips through a pleasant pocket of bush known as Barbers Bush, then climbs through pine trees and farm paddocks to the Old West Road. There is a short stretch along this road and Turitea Road, then across more farmland to Pacific Drive; excellent views here.

The walkway crosses the road to a lovely stretch of track in Addershore Reserve beside a small lake and around to Aokautere Drive. Walk down busy Aokautere Drive to the Poutoa Walkway (just beyond the shopping mall), which follows through pleasant reserves to come out on Summerhill Drive, almost opposite Springdale Grove. Return to Bledisloe Park.

72. KAPITI ISLAND
Outstanding wildlife refuge and important Maori and
European historic sites

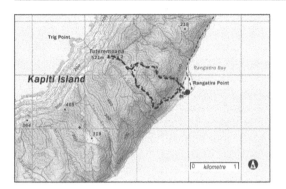

TRACK
Well marked tracks and paths in foreshore areas, but more like a tramping track
to Trig Lookout. No fires, no smoking.

WALK TIME AND DISTANCE
To Trig Lookout and back 2–3 hours (3 km) return. Okupe Lagoon 2–3 hours
(6 km) return.

ONE-HOUR WALK
Walks around Rangatira Point and The Whare.

ACCESS AND FACILITIES
You can only visit the island via a licensed operator, and these can be contacted
through DOC in Wellington, or check the web. Kapiti Island is getting popular
and the number of visitors is restricted, so you may have to book some months
ahead.

Kapiti Island looms large on the coastline north of Wellington. Steep-sided,
dark-faced with a line of breaking surf whitening the rocky edges, it hardly
looks welcoming. Yet the island has been a refuge for Maori, a haven for sealers
and whalers and latterly a wildlife reserve of outstanding importance for New
Zealand.

The little spotted kiwi is extinct on the mainland but survives here, and
Kapiti also houses rare populations of tieke (saddleback), kokako, takahe,
brown kiwi and stitchbirds. The kaka are gregarious and memorable, and there
is a rich variety of bush birds and shorebirds.

The history of Kapiti Island would make a good novel. 'Ko te Waewae Kapiti
o Tara raua ko Rangitane' refers to the island as the meeting place between
two relatives, Tara and Rangitane. Kapiti has been occupied sporadically and
peacefully from 1200 by the Muaupoko and then later Ngati Kahungunu, till

Ngati Toa led by the warrior chief Te Rauparaha invaded in 1822. Te Rauparaha then made Kapiti his base and fended off other tribal attacks.

He seized the opportunities presented by the arrival of the Europeans and their new technology, swapped the shrunken heads of his rivals for European guns, and conducted raiding parties as far south as Christchurch. His activities became notorious and he was arrested in 1846 and died in 1849.

The whalers knew Kapiti as Entry Island (after Captain Cook's chart) and had up to seven shore-based whaling stations there. By the late 1840s the whales were largely gone, and farmers arrived. Three-quarters of Kapiti's virgin forest was destroyed, and goats, possums, pigs, cats, rats and dogs were introduced. By the turn of the century Kapiti was a mess.

In 1897 a Reserve Act was passed, and one of the first caretakers was Richard Henry, the famous custodian of Resolution Island. He had failed to save the kakapo there and was disheartened about the difficulties of maintaining a nature reserve on Kapiti. Yet history will treat him more kindly, and Henry's house on Kapiti is the historic whare, which he repaired and lived in for 20 years. It has become a sort of memorial to this pioneering conservationist.

Being in a boat hauled by tractor across the beach and out into the rolling surf may sound romantic, but the short channel crossing can be stormy. Much of the sea channel between Waikanae and the island is now a marine reserve.

The boats land at Rangatira Point, where the DOC ranger will give an introductory talk on Kapiti and conservation projects.

After the talk you are left to wander around, and the birds are the main attraction. Weka and takahe will be mooching about and the North Island kaka will make a dramatic appearance. Although wild, these birds have become friendly to humans, though feeding them is no longer permitted.

Saddlebacks may also visit. These striking orange and black birds have a harsh 'machine-gun' rattle, and dance around the branches in an agitated display.

Most people look around Rangatira Point first, visit the historic whare, then take the Trig Track up the steep hillside and onto the Trig Lookout. Then return via the Wilkinson Track to Rangatira Point.

The Trig Track up to the lookout is steep, and joins Wilkinson Track near the top before reaching the lookout tower at Tuteremoana peak at 521 metres. The spectacular west coast is a fortress of cliffs and you are perched on its top battlement. Excellent place for lunch.

On the bumpy boat trip back the formidable bulk of Kapiti will look less sinister, more like a refuge than a prison.

Facing page: A handsome footbridge over the Waikanae River.

73. WAIKANAE RIVER WALKWAY
River path meandering and dune lagoons

TRACK
Flat riverbank paths and stopbanks, urban footpaths and beach walking.

WALK TIME AND DISTANCE
2–3 hours (8 km) from river mouth to Highway 1 and return.

ONE-HOUR WALK
To Otaihanga Reserve footbridge.

ACCESS AND FACILITIES
From Highway 1 turn onto the road to Waikanae Beach, and to the carpark beside the riverbank. There are many other entrances and exits onto the river walkway.

This is a pretty little pathway through willows and native sedges beside the Waikanae River, as it makes its unhurried progress to the sea. Quite private, and Waikanae residents have had the pleasure of this footpath all to themselves for too long.

The Waikanae river mouth is a good starting point, and you can follow the track north along the river past the Waimanu Lagoons. After a kilometre you reach an impressive footbridge that leads to the Otaihanga Reserve area. This has a carpark and toilets.

Staying on the north bank the good track leads upriver, and links various reserves along the riverbank for the next 3 km, including Edgewater Park, Jim Cooke and Memorial Park.

There's another impressive footbridge at Te Arawai leading to the Karu Reserve. Then you can wander in peace and quiet all the way until you reach the fairly frantic Highway 1.

74. STINGRAY BAY
Casual surfers' track to a popular bay

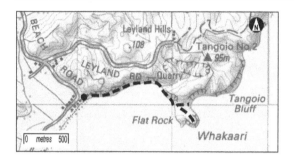

TRACK
A roughish coastal path, slippery when wet, with some beach walking. Recent rock fall and slips have damaged sections of this rough track, and people should take care to heed any warning signs.

WALK TIME AND DISTANCE
1–2 hours (3 km) return.

ONE-HOUR WALK
Old hut bay.

ACCESS AND FACILITIES
Off Highway 2 and down Tangoio Beach Road 2 km. Carparking on the grass verge, next to the surfers' cars.

A rough and ready coast with battered baches, sea cliffs and stony coves — two grass hillocks make ideal coastal lookouts, and there are dark swathes of tidal platforms to explore.

Surfers have made this trail their personal highway, pattering on bare feet as they cart their boards towards the singing surf of Stingray Bay.

From the Tangoio Beach baches pick up the well worn coastal path, which wanders north along pebbled coves under big cliffs. There are some interesting rocks here, and an old hut halfway, before the track goes on to the flat grass sward of a small peninsula, which the Maori call Whakaari.

On the far side is the wild Stingray Bay, and there are trails up through the thick grass onto both little hills. Alternatively, at low tide you can follow the tidal platforms and rough trails right around the peninsula itself and watch the surfers swinging on the wave breaks. A great little spot.

Coastline on the way to Stingray Bay.

75. BOUNDARY STREAM & SHINE FALLS
Abundant bush birds and a truly shining waterfall

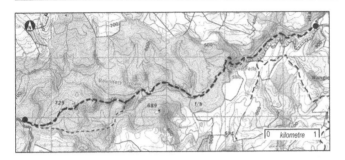

TRACK
Some well marked bush tracks in the upper part of the Boundary Stream Reserve, but a bush tramping track only down to Shine Falls. Good farmland and bush track to Shine Falls from Heays Access Road. This description is from the upper Boundary Stream Reserve one way down to Shine Falls.

WALK TIME AND DISTANCE
One-way track through Boundary Stream forest to Shine Falls and on to road-end 4–5 hours (6 km). Shine Falls from Heays Road 1–2 hours (4 km) return.

ACCESS AND FACILITIES
From Napier drive 50 km north to Lake Tutira and take the Matahorua Road some 5 km to the Pohokura Road junction. For main access to Boundary Stream Reserve continue on Pohokura Road as it climbs past limestone outcrops with impressive views of Hawke's Bay. After 8 km you reach a carpark and information board.

ACCESS TO SHINE FALLS
From the Pohokura and Matahorua Road junction, take the Matahorua Road 5 km to Heays Access Road and another 5 km to the carpark and shelter by the sandstone bluffs.

It takes a while to get here but it's worth it. Boundary Stream has been turned into a predator-controlled 'mainland island' and a haven for bush birds including North Island kiwi. Rare birds such as kokako and saddleback have been introduced, and the forest is lush and rich.

If you can arrange transport, the best walk is right through the whole Boundary Stream Reserve to Shine Falls.

From the carpark on Pohokura Road the track meets an intersection, so turn onto the Tumanako Track. Excellent information panels and some nice views as the track skirts an escarpment and drops down to rejoin the main Kamahi Loop track. There is a continuous background noise of bush birds.

Predator control in the reserve is a huge community effort, and the results have been startling, with flocks of 50 tui and 30 kereru reported, and increasing numbers of New Zealand falcon and robin.

Follow the left-hand track choice as the track edges along the escarpment and reaches the cliff margins and the more open manuka. There are some good views before you descend a narrow spur to meet the other loop of the Kamahi Loop Track.

(For those not continuing to Shine Falls, the Kamahi Loop Track continues up beside a pretty sandstone stream, and at the top picks up an old packtrack or dray road before it sidles back to the main trail.)

The main track to Shine Falls becomes rougher, and descends a damp gully through sandstone bluffs to an attractive stream crossing. A good lunch spot here. The track annoyingly climbs up 100 metres from Boundary Stream itself, drops back to the stream, then climbs for a second time up to a terrace through tawa and rewarewa.

Finally it sidles down to Heays Bluff, with a sharp zigzag descent to Boundary Stream, and a right turn at the junction leads you to the base of the 58-metre Shine Falls.

This is one of the loveliest waterfalls you will ever see, named not from the sheen of water as it slides down the sandstone cliff, but after the Shine family, who pioneered a farm in this district and donated some of their land to the scenic reserve. On hot days, the large pool below the falls is popular and safe for swimming.

A well made track now wanders down valley across a footbridge, and the last part of the track crosses farmland underneath large sandstone cliffs that turn a gorgeous yellow in the evening light.

OTHER WALKS
Kamahi Loop Track 2–3 hours return; Bellbird Reserve nature walk 15 minutes return; Spooners Hill 2 hours return; Lake Opouahi 20 minutes return (now a predator-controlled kiwi 'crèche').

Shine Falls.

76. MOUNT KAWEKA
An alpine climb to the highest point of the Kaweka Range

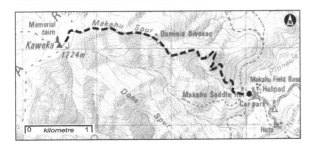

TRACK
Bush track initially, then a steady climb through tussock and scree to the alpine ridge. Suits well equipped and experienced walkers.

WALK TIME AND DISTANCE
4–5 hours (5 km) return. Total climb of 700 metres.

ONE-HOUR WALK
Ngahere Loop track, Dons Spur track.

ACCESS AND FACILITIES
It is 70 km from Napier to Makahu Saddle. Take the Rissington–Puketitiri Road, then Whittle Road and Kaweka Road to Makahu Saddle carpark and toilets.

Do not be put off by the 'mountain'. The long, lonely gravel road climbs to over 1000 metres, but you are still in the beech forest at Makahu Saddle. And then there is a surprise, for this sheltered area has a good choice of long and short tracks, including this one to the summit and soaring views of the Kaweka Range.
   A benched track travels quickly past scattered mountain beech and Makahu Saddle Hut (4 bunks), and climbs up through scrubland and pine trees onto Makahu Spur. The main track passes the Trials Spur Track (an alternative descent) then gets its teeth into the hill climb.
   Shrublands give way to tussock and steep shingle faces, and the poled track climbs steeply past the other end of the Trials Track to reach the battered Dominie bivouac. There are splendid views from here, and the track onward is not quite as steep. If the winds are picking up here (and Kaweka is famous for its winds) then the biv is a good turnaround point.
   The main track is well cairned for another 400 metres of climbing up to the easy rolling tops of the Kaweka Range. Turn south past the memorial cairn and onto the broad high point of Kaweka J and its storm-worn beacon.
   In spring there might be shy gentians and daisies in the foreground, and in the background, views as far as the three Tongariro giants.

OTHER WALKS
Littles Clearing (20 minutes return) and Trials Spur (2 hours return).

77. NAPIER CITY WALK — AHURIRI ESTUARY
Irresistibly easy estuary stroll

TRACK
Flat gravel paths and boardwalks.

WALK TIME AND DISTANCE
1 hour (4 km) return.

ACCESS AND FACILITIES
From Napier city it is 1 km to either the Humber Street carpark or alongside Meeanee Quay.

A short and sweet estuary walk, watching the wading birds, and the tides sifting in and out. The estuary is visually best in the early morning and at sunset, when the light turns the waters gold.

Over 55 bird species have been recorded at Ahuriri, so take some binoculars if you are keen on this sort of thing. Otherwise enjoy the peacefulness and excellent interpretation signboards.

From the Humber Street carpark the track crosses a footbridge and skirts a line of factories past plantings of ngaio and eucalypts. After 15 minutes the track reaches the embankment bridge, which is closed to cars and forms a perfect viewing platform.

Just here there is an unmarked side-trail that crosses a water control gate and follows a stopbank alongside the upper Ahuriri lagoon. This is a good place to look out for roosting spoonbills and the shyer waders. Migrant birds from as far away as Siberia, Alaska and Australia stop over at the Ahuriri estuary, including godwits, turnstones and knots.

The main track crosses the road bridge and winds over boardwalks through attractive saltmarsh ponds and glasswort back around to Meeanee Quay and the busy Pandora bridge.

Boardwalk over the Ahuriri estuary.

78. NAPIER CITY WALK — OTATARA PA
Authentic pa and palisades

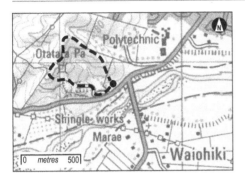

TRACK
Farm tracks and grass paths, with some up and down.

WALK TIME AND DISTANCE
1 hour (3 km) return.

ACCESS AND FACILITIES
From Napier and Taradale take Gloucester Street to the Springfield Road carpark. Toilets and information boards.

A splendid double pa site spread over 33 hectares, comprising both Otatara Pa and Hikurangi Pa. Defensive earthworks, site terracing and food pits are all evident, but what is particularly striking is the reconstruction of palisades and poupou (memorial poles). These give a haunting authenticity to the site, and reveal the personality and power of this pa.

It is not difficult walking. From the carpark an old vehicle track leads up under and around the extensive palisades, and you get a sharp idea of how invading tribes would have encountered the defensive fortifications. It also makes you realise how necessary those defences were.

Higher up, the track weaves past kumara pits and terracing to the top of the reserve, where the outlook is marvellous. The pa were situated here for the good defensive boundaries and for access to the rich natural lagoons that surrounded Taradale 800 years ago. An easy grass spur leads back down into the valley and carpark.

79. TE MATA PEAK
Walk circuit in a limestone landscape

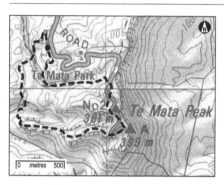

TRACK

Generally well signposted grass and forest trails, plenty of up and down. The information board at the Kiwani carpark has all the tracks marked on it. Study it carefully.

WALK TIME AND DISTANCE

2–3 hours (3 km) return. Watch out for track junctions and false trails.

ONE-HOUR WALK

Chambers Walk, returning via the Nature Trail.

ACCESS AND FACILITIES

From Havelock North take Simla Avenue to Te Mata Peak Road and the Kiwani carpark (the lower carpark).

Te Mata o Rongokako is 'the sleeping giant' or the face of Rongokako, and Te Mata Peak and Trust Park are extremely popular. You can drive to the top lookout, paraglide off the escarpment, mountain bike through the pine forests and walk along the limestone valleys. There is something for just about everyone, and this walk circuit takes in most of the best scenery, including the summit, the limestone faces and the redwood grove.

From the Kiwani carpark take the easy Chambers Walk as it sidles down to a track junction, then turn uphill past another junction onto the Nature Trail and into a dry limestone valley. The well graded track reaches another junction where you leave the Nature Trail and continue up to the middle carpark on Te Mata Walk. Fine views all round.

Cross the road here and follow the ridgeline Peak Trail as it sidles along the roadway and eventually zigzags up to the 399-metre summit — trig, carpark, seats and a glorious panorama.

Continue down the Peak Trail as it follows a long open grass spurline and winds down to the stately and silent redwood grove. There is a shelter here, and several track choices.

Continue along the Peak Trail briefly to the Nature Trail again, then, turning west, follow this track as it climbs steps up through the pine forest and swings around to a good lookout. The track then crosses the Chambers Walk (more redwoods here), and it is a steady but short climb up to the Kiwani carpark. A very good walk indeed.

80. CAPE KIDNAPPERS
Pointed peninsula and garrulous gannets

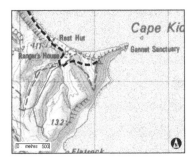

TRACK
Beach walking and a farm track up a hill at the end. A low tide in the middle of the day is essential, and if you start 3 hours after high tide you will not feel any pressure. The colony is closed from July to October to allow early nesting.

WALK TIME AND DISTANCE
6–8 hours (18 km) return. The distance along the shoreline can seem daunting, so come prepared with food and drink and take regular breaks.

3–4-HOUR RETURN WALK
Black Reef colony return.

ACCESS AND FACILITIES
From Highway 2 at Clive, drive on to the carpark and public toilets just before the Clifton motor camp, where if you are prepared to pay $1 you can use the motor camp carpark and save yourself 300 metres of walking (600 metres if you count the return).

You do not have to walk to Cape Kidnappers. There is tractor transport along the beach, or you can hire quad motorcycles. To book transport see the Napier Visitor Centre.

Cape Kidnappers would be impressive even without the gannets. This is a fine beach walk under white sandstone cliffs that seem to undulate like the surf coming onto the shore. Two-thirds of the way along is the Black Reef gannet colony, which in many ways is more interesting than the main colony. However, the climb up onto the final finger of the cape and looking down on the plateaus of gannets are sights to remember.

From Scotsman Point at the Clifton Beach Reserve Motor Camp you are immediately on the beach, which is a mixture of sandy bays and pebbles, with tidal platforms in places. As the tide goes out more sand is exposed, making it easier and faster walking.

The cliffs tower over you with remarkable striations, and streams break the white walls at several points. Black Reef Point can be a long time coming but it is worth it, with gannets nesting on small sea stacks, seemingly quite indifferent to humans standing and staring a few metres away.

Around the point, the beach route does not take long to pass the wide rock platforms and sandy coves to reach the shelter and toilets at the start of the farm track. This well marked trail climbs up onto Cape Kidnappers itself, passing the ranger's house and up the final grass slopes to the gannet colonies.

You are right beside the plateau colony and overlook the saddle colony, with a constant stream of gannets zipping overhead and making clumsy landings in an already crowded gannet city. Now it's time for lunch, and if you have started smartly enough, keen walkers will have a good hour before the tractor people arrive.

Top: The Black Reef gannet colony, on the way to Cape Kidnappers.
Above: The tussock faces of Te Mata Peak (see page 124).

81. SUNRISE TRACK
Through red beech forest to alpine buttercups

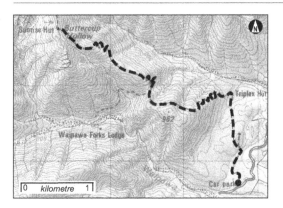

TRACK
A benched bush track that climbs steadily to an alpine hut.

WALK TIME AND DISTANCE
4–5 hours (8 km return). Total climb of 750 metres.

ONE-HOUR WALK
Triplex Hut return, Swamp Track circuit.

ACCESS AND FACILITIES
Turn off Highway 50 at Wakarara Road and travel 18 km to the junction with North Block Road, then 7 km to the Triplex carpark.

A highly accessible track to the tops, passing through a range of forest habitats. At the base there is kahikatea swamp forest, then red beech forest and mountain beech, finishing with alpine flora of daisies and buttercups. A sunny hut is sited beside a small tarn, with a panorama of Hawke's Bay and the Wairarapa.

From the carpark a vehicle track winds around the hillside past the Swamp Track junction to the start of the Sunrise Track. A few minutes later the vehicle track reaches Triplex Hut, which sleeps 12–16.

The Sunrise Track climbs slowly through red beech forest, with plenty of native birdsong. After passing the other end of Swamp Track the main trail climbs up to a small saddle, with mountain beech gradually displacing the red beech as the track puffs up the zigzag.

The track is so well graded that it is not as hard as you would expect, and Sunrise Hut pops suddenly into sight. For really good views scramble up to the rock lookout, where you get a prospect of mountains from Waipawa Saddle and on over the tortured scree ridges of the Ruahine mountains.

82. MASTERTON CITY WALK — HENLEY LAKE PONDS
Urban walk to a wetland wilderness

TRACK
Flat walking on gravel paths, stopbanks and mown grass strips.

WALK TIME AND DISTANCE
1–1.5 hours (4 km) return.

ACCESS AND FACILITIES
From Dixon Street in Masterton and the carpark at Queen Elizabeth II Park. There are toilets and a large children's play area.

A short, park-like walk alongside the Waipoua River to a series of wetland ponds beside the Ruamahanga River, linking to the Henley Lake Scenic Reserve. This is an unexpected wild area so close to town, with bird-hides and good scenery alongside the Ruamahanga. Great for families with small children.

From the carpark wander through the manicured gardens of Queen Elizabeth II Park and pick up the gravel path beside the west bank of the Waipoua River, which leads to Colombo Road. Turn left across the river and pick up the east bank track on the other side.

This continues along the stopbanks and paths, reaching the confluence of the Ruamahanga River and circling several wetland ponds that are linked by small waterways. Different tracks meander through this pretty area, with occasional footbridges and a bird-hide overlooking one pond. There is no shortage of ducks.

If you stick to the Ruamahanga River you arrive at the large Henley Lake, where there is a circuit walk around the lake. Then you can pick up tracks back to the Waipoua River on the northern side of the ponds, and retrace your steps to Colombo Road. This time stay on the east bank as far as the footbridge crossing back into QEII Park. A nice little urban trot.

Wildlife ponds, Henley Lake.

83. CASTLE POINT
An eventful sea coast

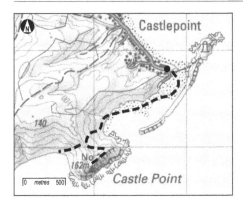

TRACK
Beach walking and grass trails up one very steep but short hill.

WALK TIME AND DISTANCE
Castle Point cliff 1–2 hours (2 km) return. Christmas Bay 2–3 hours (4 km) return.

ONE-HOUR WALK
Lighthouse lookout and reef return 30 minutes, cave return 20 minutes.

ACCESS AND FACILITIES
From Masterton take the signposted Castlepoint road about 50 km to the settlement, carpark and toilets.

You can see why Castle Point is popular — it is an eye-catching rock island with a strange claw-like reef, shielding the soft sweep of Deliverance Cove and its immaculate sands. Fishing boats are parked colourfully on the foreshore, and seabirds flock about, taking an interest in the catches of the many anglers who cast off from the reef.

Once you have explored the rock island, lighthouse and reef, another good walk is to Castle Point hill (162 metres). Follow the beach sands across to the far end of Deliverance Cove and locate the well worn trail up onto the saddle junction. People with vertigo might not want to carry on up to the high point.

The track sidles across the grassy face of the cliff, and although the track is not steep the faces are. It can get wet and slippery after rain. When the track reaches the edge of the ridge it doubles back and wanders up to the top where there are excellent views along the Wairarapa coast. Black-backed gulls have a nesting colony on the sheer cliffs of Castle Point.

Back at the saddle, there is a worn side-trail that drops down to the delightful Christmas Cove, a popular sandy bay, and opens up the possibilities of exploring further along the lonely coastline. The further you go the fewer people there are.

However, from the saddle there is a high-level track back to Castlepoint settlement. It circles around the top of the cliff edge, following the fenced farmland before descending easily through pine trees back to the carpark, and the summertime parade of people.

84. ATIWHAKATU RIVER
Graceful Tararua river track

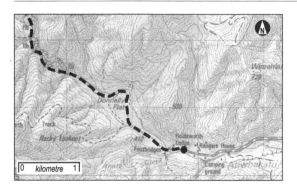

TRACK
A well graded bush track with many footbridges (including an all-aluminium one).

WALK TIME AND DISTANCE
4–5 hours (10 km) return to Atiwhakatu Hut.

ONE-HOUR WALK
To gorge return.

ACCESS AND FACILITIES
From Highway 2, turn left 4 km before Masterton into Norfolk Road, then take Mount Holdsworth Road (well signposted), and travel 15 km to the road-end and carpark. At the road-end there are picnic areas, toilets, a campground, a caretaker and Holdsworth Lodge, a roomy hut available for use by trampers, school parties and others (sleeps 30 people).

The Atiwhakatu is a gracious, gentle stream that runs through mature forest in the eastern part of the Tararua Forest Park. The benched track mirrors the easy swing of the stream, crossing 15 footbridges on its way to the Atiwhakatu Hut. Dry feet there and back.

From the carpark the track crosses the long footbridge over the Atiwhakatu Stream, passes the turn-off to Holdsworth Lookout and Gentle Annie, then continues through to the wide grassy clearing of Donnelly Flat.

After another kilometre the well graded track climbs easily above the short, crisp gorge, with some good river and forest views.

Holdsworth Creek is bridged and the East Holdsworth side-track is marked just on the other side.

It is an easy 3 km up a veritable tramper's highway to the new Atiwhakatu Hut. A good lunch spot, and a delightful return beside the sweet-running river.

85. TOTARA FLATS
Wide open grassland in the heart of the Tararua Ranges

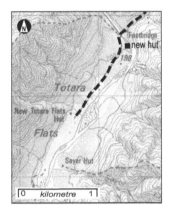

TRACK

A well graded bush track up the Gentle Annie, then a rougher track down the Totara Creek with some stream crossings to Totara Flats. Sandflies can get bad at Totara Flats.

WALK TIME AND DISTANCE

6–7 hours (18 km) return.

1–2 HOUR WALK

Rocky Lookout return.

ACCESS AND FACILITIES

From Highway 2 just before Masterton turn onto Norfolk Road then Mount Holdsworth Road and travel 15 km to the carpark. Ranger station, toilets, picnic area and 30-person Holdsworth Lodge.

'Gentle Annie' was the name of a popular sentimental goldminers' ballad of the 1860s, written by the American songwriter Stephen Foster. What it has to do with climbing hills is a mystery, but to get to Totara Flats walkers have to go up the Gentle Annie track.

The track then descends Totara Creek to the huge Totara Flats and one of a few large open clearings in the Tararua Forest Park. This is a full-day tramp, and even though it is not difficult it suits the fit and well prepared.

From the Holdsworth carpark cross the big footbridge, pass the two junctions to Donnelly Flat and start up the designer trail of Gentle Annie. The well graded track climbs 300 metres to Rocky Lookout, then a further 150 metres along the ridge to the track junction to Totara Flats on flat-topped Pig Flat.

A well worn, broad, rooty and muddy old cattle track gives away all your hard-earned climbing by dropping 300 metres to Totara Creek. This track crosses once (you might be able to keep dry feet) and wanders down the easy-going west bank of the creek that has several small side-creeks to hop across.

It's some 3 km to the enormously long footbridge over the Waiohine River, and you should spot the new Totara Flats hut. It sits on a sunny river terrace overlooking the confluence of Totara Creek and the Waiohine River.

Gas burners and a wood stove are found in the commodious hut — but Totara Flats itself is 10 minutes further through the bush. It's a sunny, golden flat, 2 km long and gradually being hemmed in by manuka. For those interested, there is a quirky historic hut on the other side of the river, originally built in the 1940s for a grazing lease on the flats held by a man called Sayer. A choice spot.

86. RIMUTAKA INCLINE
Puffing up an old railway line

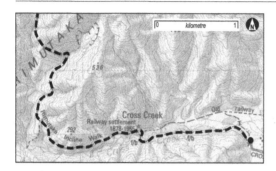

TRACK
A broad, well graded track that climbs steadily through tunnels to a saddle and descends on the other side. Take a torch. Walkers should be prepared for passing (and whooping) mountain bikers.

WALK TIME AND DISTANCE
5–7 hours (16 km) one way, so a whole day should be allowed. From either the Upper Hutt side or the Wairarapa side it is 3–4 hours return to the first tunnel. This description is from the Wairarapa side, as I feel there is more to see, and the walk can be shortened more easily.

ONE-HOUR WALK
Cross Creek return.

ACCESS AND FACILITIES
Just north of Upper Hutt on Highway 2 there is a signposted turn-off at Kaitoke, then it is 1 km to the carpark and signboards. For the Wairarapa entrance drive to Featherston and follow the Western Lake Road some 7 km to a signposted side-road where there is a carpark and signboard after 1 km.

The Rimutaka Incline was once the steepest railway in New Zealand, with a 1 in 15 grade, and specialist Fell engines that gripped onto a central toothed rail. The train assembly had four spaced locomotives weighing 200 tonnes, and the maximum speed was 10 kph up, 16 kph down. Often the train moved more slowly than most walkers or mountain bikers would achieve today.

The incline trains ran from 1878 to 1955, when the Rimutaka railway tunnel was completed. Tunnels, embankments and bridges have remained, and the gorse hillsides are turning into native bush.

From the Wairarapa carpark the track avoids farmland and sidles around into the Cross Creek valley before crossing the stream onto the site of Cross Creek township. There is a shelter here, and many historic photos and interesting anecdotes.

From Cross Creek you are walking on the railway line proper as it gradually snakes up the valley, climbing steadily before Prices Tunnel. The next tunnel is at Siberia, then the line reaches the very long summit tunnel that crosses the range and you pop out on the Upper Hutt side.

It is easy walking with good views as you wander past such places as Ladle Bend bridge, Pakuratahi bridge and the final tunnel at Pakuratahi. The line eases in grade somewhat and drops down past pine plantations to the Kaitoke carpark to complete this grand crossing.

87. BOGGY POND
Wetlands and waders

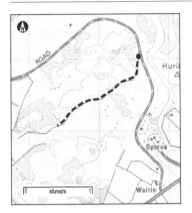

TRACK
An old flat stopbank alongside Boggy Pond. Grass paddocks to Lake Wairarapa.

WALK TIME AND DISTANCE
1 hour (3 km) return.

ACCESS AND FACILITIES
Take the Martinborough road, Highway 53, and turn down Kahutara Road for some distance to Parera Road. After about 2 km down this road you reach a DOC sign on a gate.

An amiable and unlikely walk along a stopbank that gives a fine vantage point over the wetlands that edge Lake Wairarapa. When this land is not inundated with water it is a peculiar savannah-like flatland of thick reedy grass and cabbage trees. The light is strong, the clouds washed in veiled colours with an almost Vermeer-like intensity.

There is no carpark as such, and the small sign does not promise much. The stopbank follows the road at first then turns away, with Matthews Lagoon on the left and Boggy Pond on the right.

The birdlife is diverse, from scavenging pukeko by the roadside to fantails among the scrub and cabbage trees, pied stilts on the swampy edges and a lone harrier hawk patiently working the skies. There is an old angler's hut on the water's edge about halfway along, and Boggy Pond is dotted with scaup.

After this the stopbank slips away from the waterline and reaches the return point by a fence and farmland. On the return, the unusual cabbage tree plains around Matthews Lagoon seem to have retained a visual landscape that is uncannily pre-European.

OTHER WALKS
Further along Parera Road there is another signposted walking track across the farmland to Lake Wairarapa itself. It is not well marked across the paddock and you have to thread your way past scrub pockets to the wide-brimmed lakeside. 1 hour return.

Cabbage tree savannah, Boggy Pond.

88. PUTANGIRUA PINNACLES
Hoodoos and sweeping views

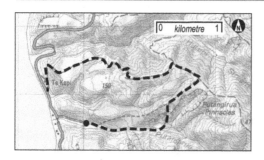

TRACK

Tracks and stream crossings, then a hill climb on bush trails and old vehicle tracks.

WALK TIME AND DISTANCE

3-4 hours (5 km) Pinnacles–Bush Walk–vehicle track–Te Kopi circuit. Total climb 300 metres.

ONE-HOUR WALK

Pinnacles return.

ACCESS AND FACILITIES

From Martinborough it is 35 km south past Pirinoa to carpark, toilets and camping area at the Pinnacles.

The Putangirua Pinnacles are a striking example of erosion, and the crumbling stones echo eerily in the dry silent gullies. The best walk is the full circuit, with views of the Pinnacles and Palliser Bay.

From the carpark and picnic area head upstream, passing the Bush Walk junction, and crossing the gravels where necessary to the Loop Track junction.

Wander into the heart of the amphitheatre of pinnacles, largely made of greywacke gravels exposed by rain and floodwaters. Harder layers of rock became 'caps', creating 'hoodoo' pillars. Some of the pillars are estimated to be 1000 years old.

Back at the junction take the steep Loop Track up a spur where you get excellent views of the formations. Follow up the pleasant ridge trail until it meets an old vehicle track on the ridgeline. This road wends its way back through beech forest, then over open farmland down to Te Kopi, with superb views of Palliser Bay and the Kaikoura mountains.

89. CAPE PALLISER TO NGAPOTIKI LODGE

A coastal journey

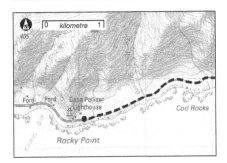

TRACK
Rough 4WD track all the way, with some climbing. This road is popular with four-wheel-drivers.

WALK TIME AND DISTANCE
3–4 hours (12 km) return.

1.5-HOUR WALK
Stonewall Stream return.

ACCESS AND FACILITIES
From Martinborough take the coastal road past Ngawi and around Cape Palliser, the seal colony and the striped lighthouse to the carpark and gate. Some of the last few kilometres can get rough, with at least one awkward ford.

The drive is along a magnificent coastal road that clings to the soft cliffy shoreline, and the steep dry hills of the Haurangi Range that plunge down to a shoreline where seals doze. Ngawi is a long row of beached fishing boats, and 'Kupe's Sail' is a naked rock slab. This coast has a raw edge to it, unfinished, untamed.

The walk itself to Ngapotiki Lodge is straightforward, at first weaving past some tremendous potholes, with good views along the coast, where sea spray can make the mountains look misty.

After about 4 km you reach Waitetuna/Stonewall Stream, with its distinctive drystone wall stretching from the sea to the hills. Stonewall Stream gushes out onto the shingle fan in a fine waterfall, worth a side-trip. Otherwise continue through scrubby flats across two more side-streams to where the road clambers up a vast scree slide.

This is the only real hill, and just down on the other side is Ngapotiki Lodge, rather pleasantly situated in a grove of trees.

The hut gets knocked about a bit, and this area is popular with surfers, anglers, four-wheel-drivers and drinkers, and those who combine all four activities. You can see the long reef at Te Rakau-whakamataku Point and a long way along the open, storm-singed Wairarapa coastline.

The old stone fence, looking towards Stonewall Stream.

90. QUEEN ELIZABETH II PARK CIRCUIT
Circuits in the sand dunes

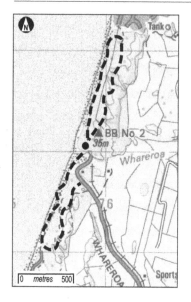

TRACK
Well marked grass and sandy tracks through rolling dunes.

WALK TIME AND DISTANCE
1–1.5 hours (6 km) return.

ACCESS AND FACILITIES
From Highway 1 at Paekakariki, turn down Beach Road then Wellington Road to the southern entrance of Queen Elizabeth II Park. A sealed loop access road leads to the start of the tracks, and there are several sheltered picnic areas with toilets.

Alternative access at Whareroa Road (MacKays Crossing) and carpark, where the trams are a big hit with kids. Great place for the family.

A different type of walk, through easy rolling dune country. There are plenty of short or long walk options, or beach walking, with no cars to worry about, and good views of the dark offshore mass of Kapiti Island. The full track is a figure of eight with the middle at the Whareroa Road carpark.

Take the inland track as it weaves through the dunes past an excellent seat and viewpoint. Further along there is another viewpoint before you reach the carpark off Whareroa Road.

For the northern dunes pick up the inland track as it crosses a bridge over Whareroa Stream, and there is a fine patch of coastal forest near the Raumati carpark.

The coastal pathway is usually gravelled, and easy to follow, with the option of beach walking all the way to the Paekakariki carpark.

OTHER WALKS
Wetland and kahikatea walk (30 minutes return), access from Whareroa Road.

Looking towards Kapiti Island from Queen Elizabeth II Park.
Facing page: Walkers on the rugged coast near Wairaka Point.

91. WAIRAKA POINT
Real raw coast

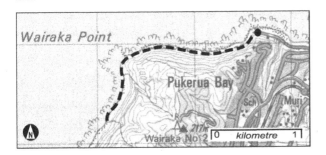

TRACK
Flat narrow coast paths and pebbly beach, ending in a quarry road. A start and end at Pukerua Bay is probably the most attractive walk option.

WALK TIME AND DISTANCE
1–2 hours (5 km) one way to quarry, or 1–2 hours (4 km) return from Pukerua Bay to Wairaka Point.

ONE-HOUR WALK
Sea arch return.

ACCESS AND FACILITIES
Turn off Highway 1 at Pukerua Bay onto Pukerua Beach Road then Ocean Parade and the appealing carpark and toilets at the far end.

A tough piece of coast, strewn with driftwood, and with kelp washing against the rocks at Wairaka Point. Little blue penguins nest along here and there are small karaka groves, perhaps planted by the Maori for food and medicinal use. Good views of Kapiti Island.

From the carpark pick your way along the narrow coast trail through the Wairaka Wildlife Reserve, created mainly to protect the rare Whitaker's skink. Around the first point there is an attractive sea arch. From here there is a generally reliable foot-trail at the back of the beach, with occasional pebble sections all the way to Wairaka Point. There is an attractive assemblage of small rock stacks that you have to clamber over, and a rusty ladder at one point.

There are good views along the beach from here, and just a little further is a stream and a grass clearing, marking the site of an old hermit's cottage. Many walkers might well return from here, following along the high-backed shingle beach to the quarry works, and the road on to Plimmerton.

92. COLONIAL KNOB
A blast out of the bush and onto the tops

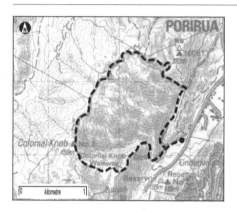

TRACK
Bush tracks and farm roads with a steady hill.

WALK TIME AND DISTANCE
2–3 hours (5 km) circuit. Colonial Knob is notorious for its wind, so pick your day and be prepared.

ONE-HOUR WALK
Reservoir loop track return.

ACCESS AND FACILITIES
From the motorway turn-off at Porirua, turn down Kenepuru Drive to Rahia Street, then Broken Hill Road to the carpark (just before the landfill entrance). There is other access off Rahia Street by Elsdon Youth Camp.

Threading your way through the industrial estates of Porirua, and nearly into the Porirua tip, is not an encouraging way to start a get-away-from-it-all walk — but persist. Only a short climb and you are way above the suburbs and enjoying the best views of Mana Island and Porirua estuary that you can find.

From the measly carpark at Broken Hill Road, take the main track up to the reservoir junction. Continue through the forest and up past the loop track, which returns back through the Spicer Botanical Park to the carpark. The main bush track climbs up a ridge through some pine trees and reaches open pastureland.

Marker poles march ahead — this is a hard slog up through the grasslands, with the noisy grind of the landfill and factories behind you. The track eases somewhat and you sidle around the main Colonial Knob (458 metres), with a black and white beacon on top, and go up to the Gulag assemblage of transmitter towers and buildings. But what a view — you look down onto Mana Island, and the far estuary glitters.

As you descend, the marker poles follow the 4WD tracks and pass the junction to the Elsdon Youth Camp exit. Then it is a steep descent down a bush gully with quite a few nikau palms sticking out, and you need to be sharp to pick up the return track to the reservoir.

It is a worn path that zigzags down to a fence and stile, then enters a secret bushy glen, which it follows all the way to the serene reservoir, and on to the not-so-serene carpark.

93. KOROKORO STREAM & BELMONT TRIG
Full circuit with secret gorge, bush hills and idyllic dam

TRACK
Good gravel paths and some steeper bush tracks and farmland to the trig. A total climb of 450 metres. Watch out for mountain bikes.

WALK TIME AND DISTANCE
5–6 hours (10 km) for full circuit. Farm track sections closed for lambing from August to November.

TWO-HOUR WALK
Korokoro Dam return.

ACCESS AND FACILITIES
Turn off the main Highway 2 (Hutt Road) by the Petone overbridge onto Cornish Street, where there is a carpark and signboards. Alternative access from Oakleigh Street carpark.

There is a bit of everything on this fine circuit, first up a lazy gorge, then past a perfect bush dam and on to the top trig of Belmont. The route can be shortened easily, although it might be smarter to lengthen the day.

The track leaves the ugly industrial conglomeration of buildings in Cornish Street and wanders up the tranquil Korokoro Stream, first through karaka and tree fuchsia forest, then opening out into a flax and tussock gorge.

As you pass the remains of the Mill Dam and cross several footbridges it is hard to credit you are so close to a busy city.

After 3 km you reach the pine trees and track junction at Korokoro Forks. Take the right-hand option and follow up through pine trees and regenerating natives to the Korokoro Dam, which is like an old-fashioned beauty spot.

For Belmont Trig continue up the main track past two junctions and over Korokoro Stream, and climb up through beautiful native forest of rewarewa and tawa. At the bush edge follow the orange marker poles across the farmland and up the Stratton Street track to the trig itself, where the fine views include the Kaikouras and Kapiti Island.

To complete the circuit, take the steep track down through wind-shorn peppertree (horopito) and then out into open country again on the Belmont Ridge. It is a mix of grassy knolls, gorse and mahoe forest, and open country down to Baked Bean Bend, where there is an unappealing grass camping area.

There are nine stream crossings down this pretty waterway to Korokoro Forks, but with some judicious hopping you should be able to avoid wet feet. There is still some way to go before you emerge from the slightly unreal haven of Korokoro Stream and into rushing reality.

94. MOUNT KAUKAU
Engaging bush tracks leading to a high peak

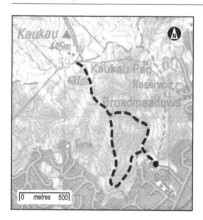

TRACK
Good bush tracks and some farmland on a steady hill climb.

WALK TIME AND DISTANCE
2–3 hours (3 km) Summit Track and Northern Walkway circuit.

ACCESS AND FACILITIES
Several access points, but the best are up Woodmancote Road, where there is plenty of carparking beside the swimming pool. A short path links to Clarke Street.

This attractive bush reserve nestles behind the suburb of Khandallah, with lookouts over the city, short bush tracks and a good circuit walk that includes the 455-metre-high peak of Mount Kaukau.

At Woodmancote Road there is a popular and sheltered area for families, with a children's play area, picnic grounds, toilets, summer swimming pool and excellent café (yes, that is a plug).

From the carpark follow the wide Summit Track as it occasionally crosses the gurgling Tyers Stream over several footbridges, past all the track junctions, until it turns uphill. The steps then get a bit remorseless as you climb through a healthy forest of kawakawa, rangiora and rewarewa, with a good and noisy sprinkling of fantails and tui.

On the spur the track meets the Northern Walkway Track, where it sidles quite quickly onto the pastureland. The bristling transmitter tower now looks very close, but the actual summit is marked with a beacon some 5 minutes beyond.

There is a lookout and peak-finding table, and you can see as far as the Inland Kaikoura Range.

A good variation on the descent is to follow the Northern Walkway Track downhill past the Summit Track, and at the next track junction (where there is a lookout, seat and picnic table) turn left along the benched track as it sidles through dense forest back to the Woodmancote Road play area. A fine circuit.

Left: Wellington's 'Eiffel Tower', atop Mount Kaukau.
Facing page: Silent gun emplacements, Makara.

95. MAKARA HEADLAND
Kaimoana and Raukawa Moana

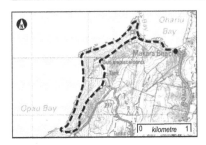

TRACK

A mixture of farm trails and stony beach walking. Total climb of 200 metres.

WALK TIME AND DISTANCE

3–4 hours (10 km) circuit. A low tide is useful but not essential. The headland part of the walk is closed for lambing from August to October.

ONE-HOUR WALK

Warehou Bay and Point return.

ACCESS AND FACILITIES

From Wellington city drive to Karori and take the winding Makara Road, some 16 km in all. Toilets at carpark.

Raukawa Moana is Cook Strait, and for the Maori at the pa overlooking Makara, Te Upoko o Te Ika, these waters were a good source of seafood, or kaimoana. Modern fisherfolk still come here, and kids like to fossick in the rock pools.

Paua shells look vivid on the grey boulders, and white-faced herons pick over the samplings with determined delicacy. This walk will give your lungs a good workout, and the sea views are stunning — Cook Strait, Marlborough Sounds, Mana Island, Kapiti Island.

Follow the vehicle track around Makara Beach to Fishermans Bay (Warehou), then a poled route heads up onto the faint terraces of the pa. The views are good already, and by the time you have managed the steep grass spur up to the old military fortifications you will have reached the highest point on the track circuit — 201 metres.

The gaunt gun emplacements were built hastily in 1942 because of the Japanese scare, but by 1944 were abandoned. There was a full barracks and quarters for the men. The South Island looks remarkably close here — as does the windfarm.

The marker poles continue to the top of an old sealed road, which makes for an easy descent to Opau Bay. Under the cliffs there is a worn trail that avoids the worst of the boulders, and once around Warehou Point you get back onto a good track again, picking its way through all the colourful detritus that Cook Strait sends ashore.

96. SOMES ISLAND
The heart of the harbour

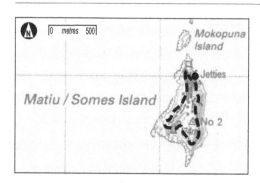

TRACK
Easy grass trails.

WALK TIME AND DISTANCE
1–2 hours explore, 2–3 km return.

ACCESS AND FACILITIES
Take a boat or ferry to the main wharf. There are toilets by the western jetty. The island is open from 8.30 a.m. to 5 p.m. daily.

In the middle of Wellington Harbour is the safe haven of Matiu/Somes Island. This rocky outcrop has for centuries been a place of refuge — and imprisonment — but today the island is a refuge for New Zealand's unique native plants and animals.

Since the early 1980s a revegetation scheme has replanted the 24.8-hectare island in native plants. There are penguins and many nesting seabirds here already, and tuatara have also been introduced — this is one of the few places on earth where they live.

Local Maori used to shelter here from invading tribes. In the early years of European settlement the island was used as a quarantine and clearing station for weary settlers. During both world wars the island was used to intern aliens and New Zealanders of Italian and German extraction; and it was an animal quarantine centre until 1995.

From the main wharf the track climbs up onto the plateau, and there is a circular track around the island, overlooking the many little cliffs and rocky bays. Some short tracks visit features like the gun emplacements. Wildlife is thick upon the land and in December the black-backed gull chicks think they own the place.

The light can change from minute to minute, swishing about the island like a sea itself, and Wellington city seems both close and far away; it is still within cellphone range, but leave the phone behind, go on, just once. It will be good for your soul.

97. WELLINGTON CITY WALK — INNER CITY
Motorway madness

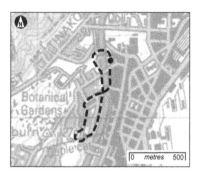

TRACK
Footpaths, bush paths, steps and quite a bit of up and down. There are many alternative paths.

WALK TIME AND DISTANCE
1–1.5 hours (2 km) circuit.

ACCESS AND FACILITIES
Bolton Street, best carparking on a weekend.

This walk fossicks around the heart of downtown Wellington, enjoying the intricacies of back alleys, bush paths and the tight muddle of streets behind The Terrace, Bolton Street and Kelburn Park. The complexity of city paths in this area is surprising, as is their seclusion from the constant humming motorway. It is a mad place for a walk, but that is its charm.

From the Bolton Street cemetery chapel/museum, take the path past the dell-like 'amphitheatre' onto the footbridge that crosses the motorway. There is a mess of paths on this side of the cemetery, but take the Hart Path on the left, then Powles Path as it plunges into a dark gully where the graves are permanently lost in the deliberate wilderness of tall macrocarpas and sprouting bush.

Powles Path leads to Easdale Street, then crosses Bolton Street to the sealed path that slips under Aurora Terrace. The healthy plantings of bush along this path include kowhai, karo, manuka, pittosporums, koromiko and many others. There are brick lunch shelters here, which never seem to get used.

Continue to the junction (the other track goes to Clifton Station on the cable car route and steps under the motorway) and then up some steps and across Everton Terrace to pick up a bush path that climbs into Kelburn Park.

At the first junction take the right-hand option, which brings you up to a sealed footpath by the university hostels. You pop out on Everton Terrace again, walk down this fractionally; then into the furtive Talavera Terrace.

At the end of the cul-de-sac take the steps down to San Sebastian Street then up onto Aurora Terrace, and follow it down over the motorway. Just here pick up the pleasant path that leads back to the start at Bolton Street, and that should be the end of your lunch hour.

98. WELLINGTON CITY WALK — ORIENTAL BAY TO MOUNT VICTORIA
Quick flick to Mount Vic

TRACK
Footpaths, steps, and bush trails. Inconsiderately steep! Signposting has much improved.

WALK TIME AND DISTANCE
1–2 hours (1.5 km) for full circuit.

ACCESS AND FACILITIES
Plenty of carparking at Oriental Bay. A public lookout and seats on top, and public toilets 50 metres away.

Most people who go to the summit of Mount Victoria drive there. But there is a lot of fun to be had exploring the tangle of steep Mediterranean-like lanes that lie between Oriental Bay and Mount Victoria. Every corner has a different surprise, with hair-raising tramways, quirky bush paths, expensive houses and the satisfaction of a panoramic view from the summit.

From Oriental Bay head/pant straight up the steep Hay Street, with the Mount Victoria tower framed by narrow houses, and a gingerbread house at the top.

Turn into Telford Terrace and follow the sealed footpath (signposted) to the junction, and take the uphill option (signposted 'Mount Victoria lookout', part of the southern walkway) along a path that climbs to Palliser Road. Note the home-built tramway.

Across the road keep on the southern walkway to a well marked track junction. The obvious main walkway track is wide and easy, sidling quite a distance to a lower grass clearing with a prominent white-barked gum tree. Follow up the open spur track as it climbs to a top grass clearing and follow the advice of the 'Mount Victoria lookout' signpost along to road and summit.

There are three summits: the first is the Byrd Memorial and noonday cannon; the second summit is the real summit and the trig beacon; and the third summit has a quaint 1950s shelter, which obviously has been designed to give no protection from the wind at all.

After your breathing is back to normal try this alternative route down through the posh suburb of Roseneath. Follow Mount Victoria Road to Alexandra Road, then turn onto Thane Road, into Palliser Road and along The Crescent. That distinctive tangy smell is money.

About halfway down The Crescent is a footpath leading down to Grass Street — an astounding 22 zigzags — and you are back on Oriental Parade, where you can now find a well deserved café.

Taranaki Falls, Tongariro.

Left: Karangahake Gorge, Coromandel.
Below: Hapuawhenua Viaduct, Tongariro.
Facing page top: Whitecliffs Walkway,
Taranaki.
Facing page middle: Syme Hut, Taranaki.
Facing page bottom: Coopers Knob, Port Hills,
Christchurch.
Following page: Sealy Tarns, Mount Cook.

Top left: Te Porere Redoubt, Tongariro.
Bottom left: Sawcut Gorge, Kaikoura.
Previous page:
1. Totara Flats Hut, Tararua.
2. Colonial Knob, Porirua.
3. Putangirua Pinnacles, Wairarapa.
4. Castle Hill, Canterbury.

Top: Kaikoura Peninsula.
Above: Hooker ice lake, Mount Cook.
Following page:
1. Hinewai Reserve, Banks Peninsula.
2. Blue Cliffs Beach, Fiordland.
3. Marian Cascades, Fiordland.

99. THE CATCHPOOL & ORONGORONGO VALLEY

Bush track to braided river valley and
idiosyncratic baches

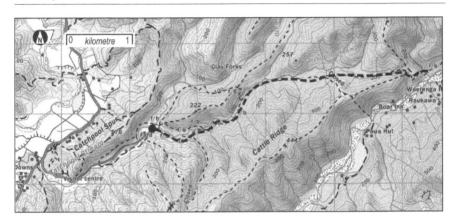

TRACK

A superbly graded forest track from the Catchpool Stream to the Orongorongo
River. If you want to explore the baches in the Orongorongo River you will need
a good map, and some tramping experience to cross the river.

WALK TIME AND DISTANCE

2–3 hours (7 km) return to Orongorongo River; exploring huts and baches
allow another 2 hours (4 km).

Note: The Orongorongo Track used to be known as the Five Mile Track, and still
is in some quarters. The Catchpool is also a common name for the area. This
name comes from an early settler, Edward Catchpool.

ACCESS AND FACILITIES

From Wainuiomata the Rimutaka Forest Park is 10 km south on the Coast Road.
Extensive carparking and picnic areas along the Catchpool Stream. Visitor
centre, toilets, huge camping area and information boards. The Catchpool
reserve gates are locked at dusk.

The Catchpool is a gorgeous valley, and on a hot summer's Sunday the place is
alive with day-trippers cooling off in the crystal sharp waters of the Catchpool
Stream, though the water temperature scarcely rises above chilly. At the end
of the track are the wide braided gravels of the Orongorongo River, with its
discreet and quirky collection of private baches tucked into every nook and
cranny. Well worth exploring.

The Orongorongo Track sidles gently upvalley from the carpark into native
bush, crossing occasional footbridges and passing various track junctions. It is
a broad and pleasant track, and climbs quietly to the saddle at the head of the
Catchpool Stream.

The bush is lovely, with every bit of ground space filled up with ferns. The track now descends past the McKerrow Track junction, and to the elegant arched bridge over the Turere Stream. Shortly there's a side-track out into the Orongorongo riverbed, and a well concealed toilet.

There are various options here. DOC signs indicate a good track up to the Big Bend Hut (40 bunks). This track continues upstream, and you pass and glimpse various private huts. If you cross the river you can reach the historic Baine-iti Hut, private but open to the public, and the oldest hut in the valley. 1 hour one way (3 km). Or you can cross the Orongorongo River directly from Turere Stream, and on the other side is a maze of tracks linking up with baches and huts all over the show. Some belong to DOC, some to tramping clubs, some are private.

There are nearly 50 huts tucked in the bush, harking back to a do-it-yourself era, when all a Kiwi family aspired to was a bach by the beach, or in the bush. Plenty of fresh air, slops out the door and possums in the dunny.

OTHER WALKS
Many short and long walking options here.

The Orongorongo bridge.

100. PENCARROW HEAD

Strolling alongside harbour waters to Cook Strait and the historic lighthouse

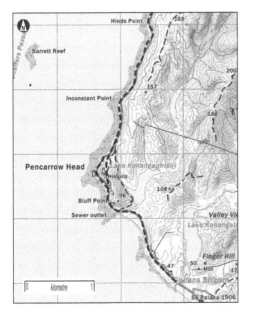

TRACK
Old road to lighthouse, tramping tracks to lakes. Good information boards at carpark.

WALK TIME AND DISTANCE
4–5 hours (12 km) return to lighthouse.

ACCESS AND FACILITIES
From Wellington or Lower Hutt take the Eastbourne Road right to the carpark and information signs at the end of the road by the locked gate.

During the summer a mountain-bike operator sets up shop, and since the 'track' is mostly a vehicle road, this is an option well worth considering.

Wellington's Latin motto is 'suprema a situ' or, in Kiwi idiom, 'a neat spot'. Nothing can match the capital on a fine day, and the harbour of 'Poneke' is one of the best and most sheltered in New Zealand, and at times one of the wildest.

The famous winds that come out of Cook Strait give rise to a good many of the jokes about 'windy Wellington' — and also some of its tragedies. From the Pencarrow walk you are only 500 metres away from Barrett Reef, which was the site of the sinking of the ferry *Wahine* on 10 April 1968. The Cook Strait ferries are a feature of this walk, as they (not surprisingly) tend to steer clear of Barrett Reef and come close to Pencarrow Head.

From the carpark at Burdans Gate and Point Arthur the vehicle track winds around numerous small stony bays. Each turn in the track reveals another angle on Wellington's hills. Rocky outcrops protrude from the pebbly beaches, and black-backed gulls patrol the shoreline. Little blue penguins come ashore at dusk.

Just before the working automated lighthouse on the shoreline, an obvious side-track climbs up to the historic lighthouse. This was built in 1858, the first lighthouse in New Zealand, and has the unusual distinction of being 'manned' at one time by New Zealand's only female lighthouse keeper, Mary Jane Bennett.

She lit the light for the first time on 1 January 1858 and worked at the light with her five young children till about 1865. She was assisted by a junior keeper from 1860. The light was finally closed in 1935.

On a fine evening the setting sun illuminates the cliffs and hills alongside Wellington Harbour, and provides some compensation for the long trudge back.

OTHER WALKS

Pencarrow Head area has a good track network along ridges and beside the twin lakes and wetlands of Kohangapiripiri and Kohangatera. Allow an extra 2–3 hours (3 km) to explore this interesting area.

Pencarrow coast.

101. RED ROCKS
Sea breezes, seals and the South Island

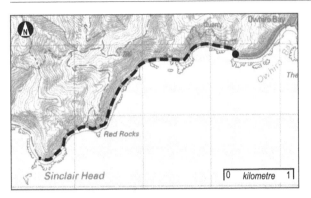

TRACK
Flat 4WD road. Plenty of mountain bikes.

WALK TIME AND DISTANCE
2–3 hours (8 km) return from Red Rocks and Sinclair Head. Good for mountain bikes.

ACCESS AND FACILITIES
Drive to Owhiro Bay and turn west to the large carpark and smart information shelter by the old quarry.

This is an invigorating pathway between the sea and the steep southern hills of Wellington, which has been popular for hundreds of years. Maori used this coast extensively for habitation and food-gathering, but today it is city slickers 'getting away from it all' who come to the Red Rocks coast. There are plenty of rock crannies and rock pools to loiter by as you fill your lungs with some of the sweetest air in Wellington — until you smell the seals.

Follow the 4WD track as it swings around a bay with baches huddled under the hills. There is a track junction here for walkers and mountain bikies up onto Hawkins Hill or to the old gun emplacements.

It is another kilometre along the coast to the strangely coloured red rocks, 'pariwhero', which are pillow lava, and around the corner there are more baches at Waipapa Stream, and then you reach Sinclair Head, which is a haul-out area for seals.

The road continues on to the Karori Stream baches, but somewhere about here either inertia, or a gale-force southerly, will spin you around for the way home. The interisland ferries slog on to the South Island, which now looks close enough to reach. So please read on.

*The 'red rocks', or pariwhero
(see previous page).*

SOUTH ISLAND

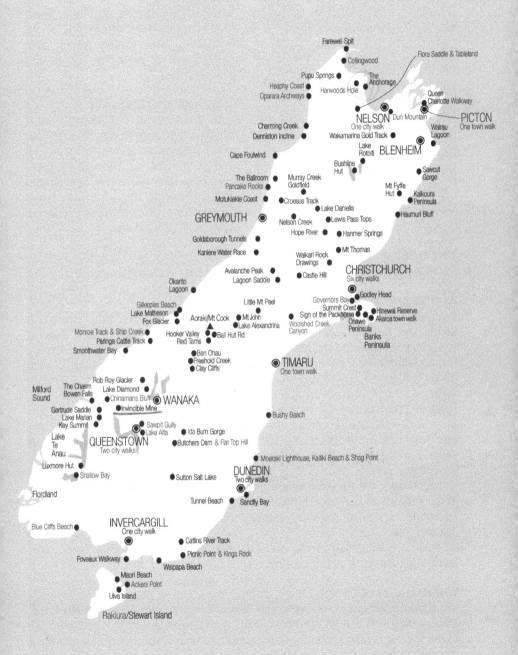

Farewell Spit

Collingwood

Flora Saddle & Tableland

Pupu Springs
Heaphy Coast
Oparara Archways
Harwoods Hole
The Anchorage

Queen
Charlotte Walkway

Charming Creek
Denniston Incline

NELSON
One city walk
Dun Mountain

PICTON
One town walk

Wakamarina Gold Track

Lake
Rototi

BLENHEIM

Wairau
Lagoon

Cape Foulwind

Bushline
Hut

Sawcut
Gorge

The Ballroom
Pancake Rocks

Murray Creek
Goldfield

Mt Fyffe
Hut

Kaikoura
Peninsula

Motukiekie Coast

Croesus Track

Lake Daniells

GREYMOUTH

Nelson Creek

Lewis Pass Tops

Haumuri Bluff

Goldsborough Tunnels

Hope River

Hanmer Springs

Kaniere Water Race

Mt Thomas

Waikari Rock
Drawings

Avalanche Peak

Castle Hill

CHRISTCHURCH
Six city walks

Lagoon Saddle

Okarito
Lagoon

Little Mt Peel

Godley Head

Governors Bay
Summit Crest

Gillespies Beach
Lake Matheson
Fox Glacier

Aoraki/Mt Cook

Mt John

Sign of the Packhorse

Hinewai Reserve
Akaroa town walk

Onawe
Peninsula

Lake Alexandrina

Woolshed Creek
Canyon

Banks
Peninsula

Monroe Track & Ship Creek
Paringa Cattle Track
Smoothwater Bay

Hooker Valley
Red Tams
Ball Hut Rd

Ben Ohau
Freehold Creek
Clay Cliffs

TIMARU
One town walk

Rob Roy Glacier

Milford
Sound
The Chasm
Bowen Falls
Lake Diamond

Chinamans Bluff
WANAKA

Gertrude Saddle
Lake Marian
Key Summit

Invincible Mine

Bushy Beach

Sawpit Gully
Lake Alta

Ida Burn Gorge

Lake
Te
Anau
QUEENSTOWN
Two city walks

Butchers Dam & Flat Top Hill

Luxmore Hut

Moeraki Lighthouse, Kaitiki Beach & Shag Point

Shallow Bay

Sutton Salt Lake

DUNEDIN
Two city walks

Fiordland

Tunnel Beach

Sandfly Bay

Blue Cliffs Beach

INVERCARGILL
One city walk

Catlins River Track

Foveaux Walkway

Picnic Point & Kings Rock

Waipapa Beach

Maori Beach
Ackers Point
Ulva Island

Rakiura/Stewart Island

102. FAREWELL SPIT & WHARARIKI BEACH
Sea, space and spit

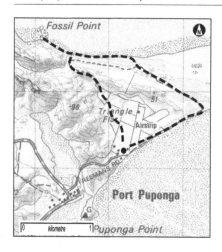

TRACK
Farmland and beach walking. Fossil Point circuit flat; Wharariki circuit and Hilltop Walk rolling. Mid- to low tide is good for both Fossil Point and Wharariki Beach.

WALK TIME AND DISTANCE
Fossil Point circuit 1–2 hours (4 km); Hilltop Walk 2–3 hours (6 km) one way; Wharariki Beach circuit 1–2 hours (3 km) return. Remember this is a working farm park, and care should be taken not to disturb stock. Some walks will be closed for lambing during September and October.

ONE-HOUR WALK
Fossil Point direct return; Wharariki Beach return.

ACCESS AND FACILITIES
From Collingwood in Golden Bay, take the Pakawau and Port Puponga road for 25 km. One kilometre past Port Puponga is a visitor centre, café, toilets, viewing telescope, information boards and carpark. The café is closed in winter. On the hilltop behind the visitor centre you can see Mount Egmont/Taranaki, 144 km away.

Farewell Spit has a mythic status, deservedly, for it stretches like a long curved kiwi beak from the top of the South Island. It is well worth the tremendous effort needed to get there. No less impressive is Wharariki Beach, with its armada of offshore islands and magic interplay of rocks and dunes. A truly memorable place.

For starters, the Farewell Spit and Fossil Point circuit is a good one. It begins at the carpark and follows the inland curve of the spit until it picks up a vehicle track and crosses through dry manuka forest to the windswept sands by the Tasman Sea.

There are windswept rocks and tidal platforms at Fossil Point, and a well marked return track to the carpark.

WHARARIKI BEACH
Wharariki Beach access is 6 km from the visitor centre down the Nguroa Road. Depending on the tides, the best walk is the full circuit, which leaves the carpark along a farm track, past the Dune Lake and then Island Lake, to a track turn-off to the beach and a marvellous descent to this remote bay.

A good track crosses through manuka around Pilch Point onto the main Wharariki Beach, and at low tide there are numerous sea arches and caverns to explore as you wander towards the Archway Islands at the far end.

A track leads through the dunes (Hilltop Walk starts here) back to the carpark. But Wharariki is a hard place to leave, and there are always a few backward glances.

OTHER WALKS

The Hilltop Walk (if you can arrange transport) is an excellent one-way crossing, wandering up and down beside the big cliffs with a rare view of the whole extent of Farewell Spit. It is mostly open farmland with some coastal scrub.

Wharariki Beach — it does not get any better than this!

103. PUPU HYDRO WALK & PUPU SPRINGS
An elegant investigation of a water race

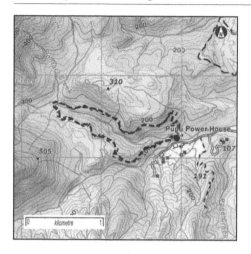

TRACK
Bush track up a hillside, then a flat walk along the water race with boardwalks. Children will enjoy this walk, but some of the drop-offs are steep.

WALK TIME AND DISTANCE
Allow 2–3 hours (5 km) return.

ACCESS AND FACILITIES
From Takaka drive 2 km to the Pupu Springs turn-off, and follow the winding road 6 km to the carpark at the end. Two fords.

This is an uncluttered walk along an old gold-diggers' water race, which was originally constructed in 1901, then in 1929 adapted to supply power to New Zealand's smallest power station. The toy-like power system still works, and the water flows brightly along rock channels and around bluffs — a chiselled masterpiece of the goldminers' skills.

At the powerhouse there is a viewing window through which you can see the power turbines. From the carpark the track crosses a bridge and climbs up a steep zigzag trail to the end of the water race. The penstock is a large pipe to carry the water down to the powerhouse.

The stopbank beside the water race is now the walking track, with boardwalks

and handrails where the canal gets narrow. Occasionally fluming (a sort of aqueduct) carries the water over a gully, and the water race curves cunningly through bush and bluffs for some 3 km before reaching the intake weir at Campbell Creek.

A pleasant place to boil the billy, and no doubt the early goldminers did just that.

OTHER WALKS
Waikoropupu Springs (known as 'Pupu Springs') are the largest freshwater natural springs in New Zealand, and have been dubbed 'a submerged Garden of Eden'. A well made 30-minute track travels around the springs, which are regarded as some of the purest water in the world.

A narrow boardwalk on the Pupu Hydro Walk.

104. COASTAL COLLINGWOOD
Golden beach and idiosyncratic coastal park

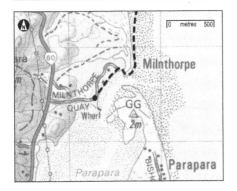

TRACK

Flat, easy beach walking, and bush paths through the Milnthorpe Reserve. Low tide not essential but handy. A local pamphlet on Milnthorpe Park shows the layout of the tracks, which is useful because they can be fiendishly difficult to fathom without a map.

WALK TIME AND DISTANCE

2–3 hours (8 km) return.

ONE-HOUR WALK

From the wharf take the estuary track, then onto the sand shore around to the beach, back through Milnthorpe Park on 'The Old Coach Road' track through to the Highway 60 carpark, then back down Milnthorpe Quay Road to the wharf. There are many other 1-hour options inside Milnthorpe Park.

ACCESS AND FACILITIES

From Highway 60 turn down Milnthorpe Quay Road to the old wharf beside the Parapara Inlet. Alternatively, take Nelson Street (off Milnthorpe Quay Road) then Kendall Street to the carpark beside the old stone bridge. At Collingwood there are cafés, shops, toilets and a children's play area.

Golden Bay — the name sounds good, and real estate agents are grateful it did not remain Murderers Bay, which is what Abel Tasman called it. But it does not take much to sell this place, famous for its benign climate and sweeping sands, and as a last refuge for hippies. This walk is an easy and graceful stroll along a small part of this golden bay.

From the old wharf a good benched track follows the edge of the estuary around to the old stone bridge, which provides an elegant high-tide footway to Milnthorpe Beach. Kids can spend hours playing in the little estuary and soft sands here. Follow the sand shore around to the main beach, which at low tide retreats far out into Golden Bay.

It is easy, flat walking along to Collingwood, an old goldmining town that in 1857 was touted as a future capital of New Zealand. The gold has gone but the cappuccinos remain; after a recharge, head back along the beach to Milnthorpe.

For an interesting variation on the way back, take the Redwood Trail into Milnthorpe Park, which plunges you into a rustling dry manuka forest. Tracks and junctions come thick and fast, but one very pleasant route is Redwood Trail, Rimu Flats, Ian's Incline, Elise's Way (nice by the stream here), then Blackwood Trail to Jimmy's Jungle, and Baas Deviation to Nelson Street and Milnthorpe wharf.

Remember, if you do get lost, the park is only 1 km wide between the highway and the sea, so you should make it out by nightfall.

Top: Parapara Inlet, on the Milnthorpe to Collingwood walk.
Above: Limestone rocks on Takaka Hill (see facing page).

105. HARWOODS HOLE
Huge sinkhole amongst weird limestone outcrops

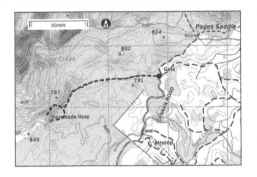

TRACK
Good bush track, some rock scrambling involved, particularly near the hole itself.

WALK TIME AND DISTANCE
1–2 hours (4 km) return.

ACCESS AND FACILITIES
Off Highway 60 near the high saddle of the Takaka Hill, turn down the unsealed Canaan Road over the 900-metre Canaan Saddle through exposed limestone rocks, some v10 kilometres to the signposted carpark. The road has been gradually improved over the years, though it might not seem so to the uninitiated. It feels very remote.

Camping area, toilets and information signs are at the carpark, and there are mountain-bike trails and several other walking track options.

This hole is 50 metres across, with encircling sheer walls of 80 metres, and a total vertical drop of 176 metres. Cavers abseil right down the throat of this gaping maw, and attempt to negotiate the complex cave system that leads out to the Starlight Cave and into Gorge Creek.

Streams from the Canaan plateau once tipped over a waterfall into Harwoods Hole, and ran underground through the Starlight system, but they now have found quicker ways to get through to Gorge Creek. Now only floodwater goes through the old cave system and so it is popular with cavers, though in recent years there have been several well publicised rescues from this underground complex.

From the carpark it is easy walking through beech forest at first, then you have to clamber around large boulders where the valley gets confined. At a track junction, the right-hand branch goes around to a lookout over Gorge Creek.

For Harwoods Hole itself, take the other track choice and be careful near the lip. It's a feature that's difficult to see into and you shouldn't try! Perhaps the chill of the cold air, and the powerful sense of something pulling you down to nothingness, is enough of an experience.

OTHER WALKS
From the Canaan carpark there are several good tracks: Wainui Saddle 2 hours return; Moa Park shelter 4 hours return, plus the mountain-bike trails which make excellent walking tracks as well.

Off Highway 80 on the hill road saddle, there is the well signposted Takaka Hill track: 2 hours (4 km) circuit in a strange limestone landscape.

106. THE ANCHORAGE
A coastal ramble to a beautiful bay

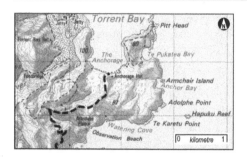

TRACK
A flat wide path, with some short climbs along the way. Many track intersections, so it pays to have a good map like the Abel Tasman National Park 273-07.

WALK TIME AND DISTANCE
3–4 hours (9 km) one way (assumes one leg of the journey by boat).

ONE-HOUR WALK
· Tinline Bay return.

ACCESS AND FACILITIES
From Motueka, drive north 5 km to the Kaiteriteri turn-off, then 8 km to Marahau carpark, toilets, information shelter and café.

A clever option is to take the launch back from Anchorage Bay to Marahau, or vice versa, depending on tides and boat times. There are several launch operators that run daily (in summer) along the coast, and these water-taxis add a unique dimension for walkers. This walk assumes you will take the boat, otherwise double the walking time.

Coastal walking does not get much better than this. A forested shore, a lapis lazuli sea, and tiny slivers of golden sand between. A dozen bays to explore, and many headlands to peer out from. If you do not mind sharing the track, and take plenty of sunblock and water, you will have a memorable excursion.

From the carpark and café, cross the Marahau boardwalk over the estuary, then follow the track as it hugs the coast for about 2 km to Tinline Bay, a sheltered open clearing with picnic tables and a toilet. A short way beyond is the junction with the inland track, and a good lookout off Guilbert Point.

After this the coastal track ambles along the sea edge 20–30 metres above the shore, past two pretty bays, Apple Tree and Stilwell. Side-tracks lead down to each bay, and there are pleasant picnic areas at both. It is not far from Stilwell Bay to Yellow Point and another tiny picnic area at Akersten Bay.

For the first and last time the track climbs quietly through the manuka forest up to a ridge saddle and a signposted junction. There is a muddle of track junctions here, but tracks to Anchorage Hut are all well signposted.

Turn right and follow along the ridge, after a while passing a side-track to Watering Cove, which was where Dumont d'Urville filled up his watering casks in 1827. The main track gives splendid views over The Anchorage and drops down to this brilliant sweep of sand, and the hut is just along the beach. Wait for the boat. Daydream.

107. NELSON CITY WALK — AIRPORT CIRCUMFERENCE
Estuary flights

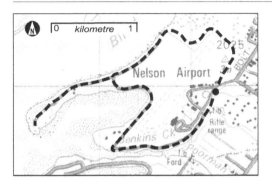

TRACK
Sealed road and grass paths.

WALK TIME AND DISTANCE
1–1.5 hours (4–5 km) return.

ACCESS AND FACILITIES
Drive to the carpark and koru sculpture just before the Nelson airport terminal.

This sounds bizarre — a walk round an airfield? You've gotta be joking? No really, Nelson's airport is by the sea, and this walk has no roads to cross and enjoys extensive views out over the Waimea estuary. In between planes it is quiet, and there are plenty of birds to be seen. If you like bird-watching, walking and aeroplanes — perfect!

From the sculpture follow the sealed access road between the perimeter fence and the lapping lagoon inlet. The road swings around a point then loops around another inlet to the shoreline.

Here there is an optional side-track along a vehicle track that leads right out onto a peninsula, with expansive views of the estuary and its islands.

Back on the main track the route follows the coastal edge and reaches the golf course, then follows the airport perimeter fence alongside worn grass trails. By keeping near to the fence you end up on Maclaren Street and then the main airport road, only 100 metres or so away from the carpark.

An alternative route at low tide, once you reach the golf course, is to follow the shoreline to Tahunanui Beach.

108. DUN MOUNTAIN CROSSING

A big alpine crossing over a saddle and down a historic railway line

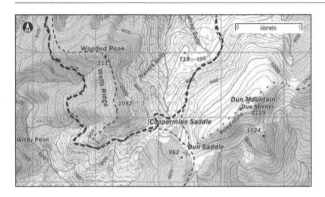

TRACK
Generally a well marked track, which is also a mountain-bike trail, as it climbs from the Maitai Dam to Coppermine Saddle. Then the track follows the broad, evenly graded historic railway back down to Brook Street motor camp. Total climb is 700 metres. Take the Nelson O27 map.

WALK TIME AND DISTANCE
Maitai Dam to Brook Valley Holiday Park 7–8 hours (15 km) one way; Brook Valley Holiday Park to Coppermine Saddle 6–7 hours (18 km) return.

ACCESS AND FACILITIES
From Nelson follow the winding Maitai Valley Road some 12 km to the Maitai Dam. Carpark and informations signs here. For the Brook Street motor camp, drive up Brook Street to just before the motor camp where there is a signpost for the Dun Mountain walkway. This is a closer start for people going to Third House and beyond.

This is a tremendous day tramp, climbing from the lonely Maitai Dam, crossing the strange geological formations at Coppermine Saddle, and descending down the long railway line to Nelson. This is now a mountain-bike trail, but it's also very good for trampers. It's still an alpine crossing, so take it seriously with good gear, and give yourself an early start.

From the Maitai Dam carpark, cross the footbridge and follow the signposts upvalley along a well graded road and packtrack. As the forest closes in you reach a stream fork, and a crossing, which might get bridged at some stage.

At first the climbing is gentle, then it starts to zigzag steeply up the scrubby hillside, with great views when you can get your breath back. After an almost 300-metre climb from the stream, the track levels out and starts to sidle underneath Dun Mountain.

It's much easier travel now, through a smidgin of beech forest, and the final zag up to the Coppermine Saddle. The rocks are weirdly coloured, and you can see why the miners were attracted to this area. Great spot for lunch.

Follow the graded track off Coppermine Saddle (past the original mine shaft) with fine views of the Richmond Range before you turn into bush. You are now on the old railway, and it's a long perambulating lollop past several track junctions down to the old Third House shelter.

Grab some sun in the sunny clearing before plunging into the forest again, as the track winds endlessly around Cummins Spur and reaches a track junction. This offers a more direct route down to the Brook Valley camp and Brook Street, and is worth taking.

Top: Coppermine Saddle.
Above: Rain clouds over the Dun Mountain track.

109. FLORA SADDLE AND TABLELAND

Historic packtrack leading to spectacular rock bivvies and karst tablelands.

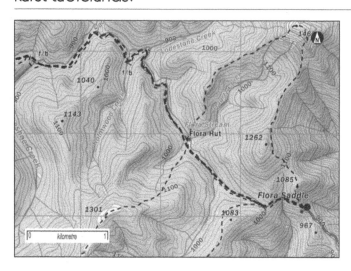

TRACK
A beautifully graded packtrack through forest, so it's pretty and quick travel. The Flora area is now being maintained as a predator-free 'mainland island', so you will see many bait stations for rats and stoats.

WALK TIME AND DISTANCE
Grid Iron Gulch is 3 hours return (12 km); Salisbury Hut 8–9 hours (20 km) return. This is alpine country and snow can occur throughout the year.

ONE-HOUR WALK
Flora Hut return.

ACCESS AND FACILITIES
From Highway 61 between Motueka and Kohatu drive to Ngatimoti (19 km from Motueka) and follow signs to Graham Valley and Mount Arthur. The last section of road is very steep, and can become greasy after rain. The carpark is at an altitude of 900 m, with information boards, intentions logbook and toilet. Superb views looking back to Nelson.

History is entwined through this peaceful forest, for it is the old goldminers' trail from Nelson to Takaka. The early explorers faced a bewildering landscape on the bush plateau riven with deep streams and karst limestone fissures. They made temporary homes under the limestone overhangs, caught weka, cooked them over beechwood fires, and finally scratched their names into the rock and passed on.

Your car has done most of the hard work for you, and it's an easy walk up the broad track to Flora Saddle. Here one side-track goes up to Mount Arthur Hut, and another side-track goes to Mount Lodestone, both excellent day tramps.

The main trail follows a gentle grade down to the historic Flora Hut with its distinctive twin huts sharing a common porch.

The packtrack now follows the soothing Flora Stream, across various footbridges, to the spectacular rock overhangs at Grid Iron Gulch.

The main rock has been enlarged somewhat and a dripline added, and domestic features have been built in, such as a fireplace and bunks. In case you missed it, just before the main rocks a trail zigzags steeply up the slope to another natural overhang, with a fireplace and a snug hut with its own glass murals. Quite a work of art.

From Grid Iron Gulch it's only another 15 minutes to a track junction, and then the track turns up Balloon Creek and passes the cute Growler Rock Shelter. Not much further another side-trail leads to an excellent rock shelter on the edge of open tableland, with many old names carved on the rock walls. Built-in bunks.

It is about 30 minutes on to the 30-bunk Salisbury Hut, which sits on the open tussock tablelands and has a superb view of the Arthur Range and the fierce-looking Twins.

The walk back isn't too strenuous, as it is mostly a flat walk to Flora Saddle. Time to appreciate the sinkholes, limestone outcrops, and that strange, rustling silence so characteristic of dry karst areas.

OTHER WALKS
Lodestone circuit 2–3 hours (6 km); Arthur Hut circuit 2–3 hours (6 km).

110. PICTON TOWN WALK — THE SNOUT
A delightful ridge walk to a splendid lookout

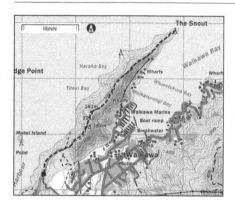

TRACK
Well graded bush tracks, which can get slippery after rain.

WALK TIME AND DISTANCE
3 hours (6 km) for full walk to headland; 2 hours (4 km) for Queen Charlotte Lookout return. Toilet at the lookout.

ACCESS AND FACILITIES
From Picton drive towards Waikawa, and turn off down Sussex Road into Victoria Domain. Map board here. A one-way sealed road climbs onto ridge past lookouts and after 1 km reaches the signposted The Snout carpark. This road carries on back to Picton. Note there are several other tracks and mountain-bike trails on this ridge.

As you look up Queen Charlotte Sound from Picton wharf, The Snout is the ridge on your right. It points a long finger into the sound, and has several good walking tracks, with particularly impressive views of this labyrinth of waterways.

At the carpark, walk past the locked gate along the wide unsealed road till it reaches a saddle and the bush track starts a gentle zigzag up the hill. The shrub forest is a mix of akeake, kawakawa, five-finger and mahoe, whose leaves turn skeleton-like on the ground.

The track eases into an old bridleway and sneaks around the high point, with

views of the bright waterways and dark silhouetted headlands. After a slight descent you pop out onto a fine lookout.

For many people this is a good return point and you can easily while away an hour watching the buzzing boats and changing water patterns on the sea

The actual headland is another 30 minutes further one way, and when you reach the rocky shore you can practically touch the huge white ferries as they glide by like stately dames, making a grand entrance to the ballroom arena of Picton.

View from the Snout Track towards Picton.

111. QUEEN CHARLOTTE WALKWAY (PORTAGE TO TE MAHIA)
Sea views on both sides of an open ridge walk

TRACK
From Torea Saddle a well-marked hill track through scrub and coastal forest. This is also a mountain-bike track.

WALK TIME AND DISTANCE
3 hours (6 km) one way.

ONE-HOUR WALK
Onahau lookout, 417 metres.

ACCESS AND FACILITIES
Off Queen Charlotte Drive at Linkwater, the Kenepuru Road winds along the shoreline, and just before Portage, take the Torea road to the saddle. Obviously having transport arranged is useful, or a car swap, or else a mountain-bike hidden at one of the road-ends. The carparking is miserly at Torea Saddle, and nonexistent at Te Mahia Saddle, though 300 metres down the road there is a large carpark for Mistletoe Bay. At Mistletoe Bay there is a camping area and three DOC lodges that can be hired.

The Queen Charlotte Walkway is rapidly becoming one of New Zealand's most popular tracks. It offers almost 55 km of ridge and coastal walking overlooking the glittering turquoise waters and endless peninsulas of the Marlborough Sounds. This walk is a snippet of the overall track, with swinging views on both sides of the ridge, a bit of gorse, a bit of forest, and on a hot day more than a bit of sweat. Take plenty of water.

From the stone war memorial the track from Torea Saddle (Portage) is steep, following a bulldozed line that has been softened by manuka forest as it zigzags up the ridge, with extensive views once you get higher.

After this the track settles down into a rolling pattern along the ridge tops. You are about 400 metres above sea level here. It can often be hot and dry, but as you near the peak of Te Mahia the track slips through pockets of bush.

Before you drop down to Te Mahia Saddle there is an excellent viewpoint with a picnic table from Mount Onahau overlooking the complicated waterways of the sounds. Allow 30 minutes return.

Then there is a fast bush descent down to the junction with the James Vogel track. This is a charming bush walk that goes down to Mistletoe Bay, where there is camping and picnicking at one of the prettiest and most sheltered harbours in the sounds. Otherwise follow the main track directly down to Te Mahia Saddle.

Views from Queen Charlotte Walkway (Portage to Te Mahia).

112. WAKAMARINA GOLD TRACK

Romantic miners' packtrack into a deep bush valley with historic huts

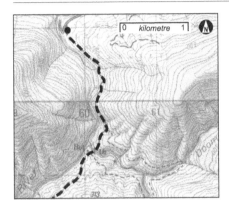

0   kilometre   1

TRACK
Vehicle road at first, then benched miners' packtrack. Some short hill climbs, but mostly easy walking.

WALK TIME AND DISTANCE
3–4 hours (12 km) Devils Creek Hut return.

ONE-HOUR WALK
Doom Creek return.

ACCESS AND FACILITIES
The Wakamarina valley is 10 km west of Havelock off Highway 6, and it is 15 km to the road-end, past the Dead Horse Creek ford, and finishing at the Butchers Flat carpark and the attractive and sheltered picnic area.

The ripe language of the goldminers is evident right from the picnic area. Dead Horse Creek, Doom Creek, Devils Creek — those guys did not mince words. A glance at the map shows Muttontown Stream, Mountain Camp Creek and All Nations Creek, a reference to all the hopeful nationalities that crowded into the Wakamarina in the brief goldrush glory days of 1861. What they left behind were some colourful names and an excellent packtrack that climbs all the way to the top of the Richmond Range.

From the picnic area the route follows a good vehicle track through pine trees some 2 km to the footbridge at Doom Creek. There's a circuit track up Doom Creek for people who want a shorter walk option.

A pleasant miners' packtrack now meanders upvalley, crossing from scrubby slopes into dappled beech forest, and after 4 km reaching Devils Creek Hut, which sits high above the river gorge on an attractive terrace. Behind the hut is the original Devils Creek hut, built of slab timber and still standing — just.

From Devils Creek Hut you have a couple of interesting options. You can explore the deep river gorge, which is off a side-track from the footbridge, or there is also an interesting side-track that negotiates up Devils Creek itself to the ruins of some historic stone huts. Allow 30 minutes return for the latter.

113. WAIRAU LAGOON
Slow times and gentle tides

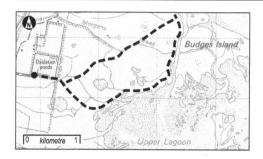

TRACK
Mostly firm-packed earth and sand, and nicely flat.

WALK TIME AND DISTANCE
2–3 hours (7 km) circuit. A low tide is useful but not essential. No water, except of the salty kind.

ONE-HOUR WALK
Budges Island return.

ACCESS AND FACILITIES
From Blenheim drive 2 km south on Highway 1 to Harding Road, then 1 km to the carpark and information sign (beside the oxidation ponds).

This is a luminous lagoon and estuary, permeated with understated textures. The glasswort is as intricate as Persian carpet, blending into dozens of subtle colours along the sinuous tidal waterways. Over 70 bird species have been recorded at Wairau, including nesting royal spoonbills. So much of the pleasure in this walk is in the morning or late evening light.

Shortly after leaving the carpark the track divides, and the right fork crosses side channels and wanders along the fringe of the estuary to opposite Budges Island.

The charm of the Wairau is its elegant flatness, and the absence of any structures that block the view. So it is a surprise after an hour when you reach the beached wreck of the *Waverley*, 30 metres long and built in 1883. It was scuttled and later pushed by a flood up this side channel, where it provides a sculptural site for roosting shags.

A short side-trail leads to a view of Wairau Bar, and there are information boards that tell the story of the Maori moa-hunter culture that lived in camps around the lagoon.

European settlement began on Wairau Bar in 1847, when an inn was built to cater for the coastal trading ships that had access up the Opawa River to 'Beavertown', the terrible name then given to Blenheim. Apparently the early settlement used to flood regularly.

The return trail cuts across the flat marsh meadows, and in late evening the colours in the sedge turn into a rich rug of reds and yellows.

114. SAWCUT GORGE
A peculiar alleyway of stone

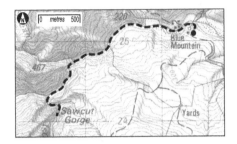

TRACK
Quite a tough walk, with 15 or 16 river crossings one way and river boulders. Suits the well equipped – i.e. not jandals. A normal to low river flow is important.

WALK TIME AND DISTANCE
3–4 hours (4 km) return; for Isolation Creek hut allow 5–7 hours (8 km) return. But remember the river crossings will slow you down.

ONE-HOUR WALK
Up to start of Waima River gorge.

ACCESS AND FACILITIES
From Highway 1 turn off to the Waima/Ure River, then it is 12 km of winding road to the Blue Mountain station. You have to park just before the homestead's front door (which seems odd and intrusive, but the occupiers do not seem to mind). Please inform the landowners of your presence by signing the logbook.

Sawcut Gorge is a strange feature, 50 metres long, 50 metres high and barely 3 metres across in some places. It looks as if a giant's circular saw simply ran through the limestone. The route up the Waima is short, yet it has lots of river crossings, great on a hot day, but some people find them awkward. It would be dangerous to attempt to go to the Sawcut after rain, for this area floods rapidly in a brutal brown gush.

From the carpark follow the vehicle track down to the Waima River to a good and wide ford. DOC has now marked the route with large orange triangle markers and the route keeps to the shingly river, crossing several times past Blue Mountain Stream.

Gradually the river is squeezed between steep walls, and soon the huge limestone face of the Waima gorge looms over the river, and a well marked track twists in and out of big boulders and bluffs past Headache Stream. The top river crossing can be awkward, but after that a good track continues on the south bank past some splendid totara trees to Isolation Creek.

Around a few bends in Isolation Creek and the Sawcut appears, a thin slit in the band of rock, the opposite walls almost close enough to be touched by outstretched arms. The creek bed is shingle and it is easy to walk up the length of the gorge.

At the other end of the Sawcut, Isolation Creek continues to wind narrowly and impressively (with some waterfalls) between high cliffs for just over 1 km to the top forks and a wide shingle flat, and there is a 6-bunk hut. Add another 2 hours return for this extra section, which is worth doing if you have the time.

115. KAIKOURA PENINSULA
Wildlife walk around a fine peninsula

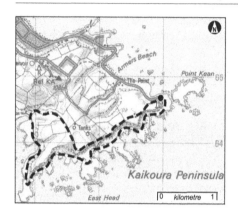

TRACK
Beach walking and some tidal platforms, with farmland tracks on the return. Generally good underfoot, but a low tide is essential to enjoy this walk.

WALK TIME AND DISTANCE
3–4 hours (5 km) return Shoreline and Clifftop walk circuit. If using the Whalers Bay track 3 hours. The Shoreline Walk is a low-tide route only.

ONE-HOUR WALK
Coastal route to Whalers Bay and return.

ACCESS AND FACILITIES
From Kaikoura township drive past the information centre to Point Kean carpark at the end of the coastal road, where there are information boards, a shelter and barbecue sites. There are toilets 1 km before the carpark. Access can also be gained on the other side of the peninsula, down South Bay Parade to the carpark, recreation area, toilets and impressive information shelter.

A feature of this walk is that the wildlife is visible, and unavoidable, and at low tide you have to take care not to step on a sleeping seal — they do not like it. There are over 12,000 red-billed gulls (tarapunga) nesting around the peninsula and they can get pesky in spring, with raids on intruders. Shags congregate on offshore rocks, and there are extensive roosting colonies of white-fronted terns.

When you include the remarkable tidal platforms and the dazzling white cliffs, it is little wonder the Kaikoura Peninsula walk is a must-do for many travellers.

At Point Kean seals may be sleeping only 30 metres away from the carpark, and at low tide you can wander around the base of the cliffs, exploring small bays and peninsulas on the way to Whalers Bay.

There is a shortcut track up onto the clifftop track, but at low tide you can keep following the dramatic shoreline almost to the finger-like Atia Point.

The track crosses the narrow peninsula and follows more extensive tidal platforms (with 'tramlines' running across them) back to South Bay. Here a track climbs up onto the clifftop and lookout and follows the crumbling cliff edges back to the carpark at Point Kean. Welcome views, and a walk that never gets boring.

116. MOUNT FYFFE HUT
A 'little' hill looking onto big mountains

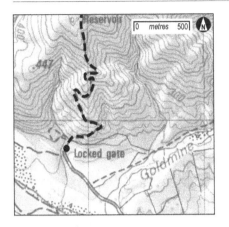

TRACK
A good vehicle track made in the 1970s to the hut, and a tussock ridge to the summit. Take plenty of water.

WALK TIME AND DISTANCE
4–5 hours (9 km) to hut return; 6–7 hours (13 km) to Mount Fyffe return. Total climb to hut 1000 metres.

ONE-HOUR WALK
Up to first 'saddle' return.

ACCESS AND FACILITIES
From Kaikoura township take Ludstone Road 8 km to the junction with Postmans Road, then follow Postmans Road 6 km to the bush carpark, picnic area and toilets.

This is a big sweat of 1000 metres to a hut perched on the summit ridge of Mount Fyffe. The slog is hard but the reward is majestic views. Up here the Kaikoura Peninsula looks squashed and small, but the Kaikoura mountains are massive, especially when covered with snow. With an early start and a packed lunch this walk is not as daunting as it seems, and the well graded road provides an even walking surface.

The walk description is easy. Walk up the road, and keep going until you give up, or get up.

It is about an 800-metre climb to Sandy Saddle following the zigzagging road. There is some scrub and forest lower down, but once you gain altitude you are in tussock and scree slopes. Many seats on the way up, as well as a good lookout and altitude signs.

From Sandy Saddle it is a steady 300-metre climb to the hut, and it does not get any flatter until just before the hut itself, which is a little oasis after the slog uphill. It has 8 bunks and a woodstove, and there is an old tarn beside it that is usually dried up, but has attractive native herbs fringing it. The view is spellbinding.

For summiters, the vehicle track continues up the barren slopes and rises another 500 metres onto the large beacon on top of Mount Fyffe itself. The views are not measurably better than from the hut, but you are standing at 1602 metres, a long way above the world.

Hot day, snowy mountains, on the way to Mount Fyffe Hut.

117. HAUMURI BLUFF
Secret coast and sea arch

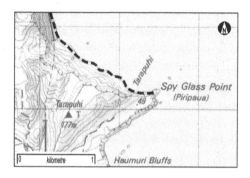

TRACK
A flat vehicle road, then slower beach and boulder scrambling. A low tide is essential.

WALK TIME AND DISTANCE
5–6 hours (11 km) return.

ONE-HOUR WALK
Mikonui Stream return.

ACCESS AND FACILITIES
From Highway 1 at Oaro, turn off on the south bank of the Oaro River and park in the large area just before the small settlement. There's no carparking further on.

The sea arch at Haumuri Point is a brilliant white outcrop of fretted limestone. It is not a difficult walk to get there, but you need a low tide at Haumuri bluff, and good balance, as there is plenty of rockhopping involved. Haumuri probably means 'wind at your back', a reference dating from when Maori used to regularly canoe around this promontory.

From the carpark walk through the snug Oaro settlement to the locked gate. Then cross the railway line and follow the access road beside it. Some derelict rolling stock helps form a melodramatic sea wall here.

Further on there is a disused railway tunnel on the right-hand side, mostly blocked up, and in the small bays there are stands of karaka trees that were probably planted by Maori as a food source.

Many of the shallow bays have attractive areas for pausing or picnicking, and interesting tidal platforms to explore.

At the Haumuri railway tunnel (about 4 km from Oaro) a steep track goes down to the beach, and from here on it is rockhopping along to the bluff.

On top of Haumuri bluff.

Seals often come ashore here for a midday doze because they mostly feed at night, and even elephant seals have been seen.

The archway is called Te Pupaki, the crab hole, and it is a wild place, with extensive offshore reef platforms. You can climb above the archway onto the bluff itself, and enjoy a panoramic view of this most excellent coast.

118. LAKE ROTOITI
The rebirth of the dawn chorus

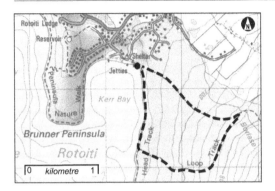

TRACK
Well graded bush tracks with information panels on the way.

WALK TIME AND DISTANCE
Honeydew Walk circuit 1 hour (3 km); Loop Track 1 hour 30 minutes (5 km); St Arnaud Range and Pinnacle Lookout (hill climb) 3–4 hours return.

ACCESS AND FACILITIES
From Highway 63 at St Arnaud (which has petrol, store and café), drive to Kerrs Bay picnic and camping area, with shelter and toilets.

DOC has made a commitment in selected places in New Zealand to recreate the dawn chorus, and at St Arnaud they are getting close. Intense predator control on this 'mainland island' has created a wall of sound from bellbirds, robins and kaka. This natural music of the forest has not been heard for a long time on the mainland.

Lake Rotoiti itself is a charming bush-edged lake, with great views towards the big Nelson Lakes mountains. The only downside of this magical spot . . . well, sit down for a while, and they will find you!

You have several walk choices. The negligible Bellbird Walk is just 10 minutes round — fall over a few times and you have done it.

The Honeydew Walk is longer, and named after the sweet, almost sickly scent of the honeydew excreted by a scale insect. The bellbirds love this stuff, and they are loud and melodious in appreciation. This walk has excellent interpretation signs all round to explain what DOC is trying to do, and the beech forest floor is smothered with a carpet of lush moss.

Then there is the longer Loop Track — about 1 hour 30 minutes — and for a big hill climb try the track up onto the St Arnaud Range and Pinnacle Lookout, 3–4 hours return.

Whichever track you choose will go through the heart of the predator-controlled beech forest. Do not touch the traps or bait stations — unless you are a rat.

119. BUSHLINE HUT
A healthy hill circuit to an alpine hut

TRACK
Bush tracks and tussock trail on this steep hill walk. Well marked tracks with snowpoles on the tops, but most of the route is exposed, so you need good weather. Take water.

WALK TIME AND DISTANCE
4–5 hours (5 km) return, total climb 500 metres.

ONE-HOUR WALK
Up the Pinchgut Trail for 30 minutes or so. Excellent views.

ACCESS AND FACILITIES
From Highway 63, 2 km west of St Arnaud, take the West Bay road for 5 km to the Mount Robert carpark, at the end of a steep zigzag.

This is a walk to remember, and although the steep scree faces of Mount Robert might put you off, the total climb is only 500 metres and the rewards are well worth it — definitely the best views over Lake Rotoiti, as well as a fine outlook along the Angelus Ridge. Bushline Hut, as its name suggests, sits on sunny slopes beside the bush edge in a particularly privileged position.

The beginning of the tramp is horribly steep. The Pinchgut Trail switches back and forth for 500 metres up through a burnt-off scrub face and some remaining beech forest to reach a small box shelter sitting right on the bush edge. The views are superb, and you have now done most of the climbing. Best of all you are above those pesky sandflies.

It is only a short distance from the shelter to the flat summit and the Relax Shelter Hut (seats only) then on to the signposted track junction to Bushline Hut. A downhill stretch now, past tall snowpoles on a wide, easy ridge, swinging past the private Kea Hut down to the 12-bunk Bushline Hut. Hard to find a better view to have lunch over.

Paddys Track continues down from the hut, snaking lazily through open tussock faces for 300 metres before easing into manuka forest and slipping into Robert Stream.

The zigzag track overlooking Lake Rotoiti, on the Bushline Hut walk.

There are fine lake views, then the track sidles under Mount Robert, slowly making its way to the access road, 100 metres from the carpark.

120. MURRAY CREEK GOLDFIELD
The gold gone and the tracks silent

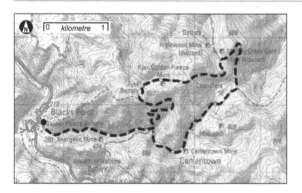

TRACK
Well graded miners' tracks on the Murray Creek and Royal Track circuit. Some hill climbing.

WALK TIME AND DISTANCE
4–5 hours (9 km) Murray Creek main track and return on Royal Track.

ONE-HOUR WALK
Energetic Mine junction return.

ACCESS AND FACILITIES
From Highway 7 at Blacks Point, 1 km from Reefton. There is a museum by the carpark.

Red beech leaves fall and scatter gold colour on tracks that are 100 years old, worn smooth by the plodding footsteps of the goldminers. The mining relics are crumbling away and might not impress, but the deep forest and tea-coloured streams take you into a long-lost world. It is hard to believe that these silent forests were once an important and noisy industrial landscape.

From the carpark the main Murray Track follows a broad packtrack through luxuriant moss and beech forest for 2 km, passing the junction to the Energetic Mine and the bridges at Cement Town. Not much here now, though gold was mined in the Murray Creek from 1870 until the 1930s.

Not long after this, the main track goes into a broad area of manuka forest at Chandlers open-cast coal mine, then reaches the Waitahu Track junction at a saddle.

Keep to the main track as it climbs steadily to the Inglewood junction, then it is only a short side-track past the Painkiller Track junction to the iron remnants of the Inglewood Mine.

Now take the Royal Track, which climbs up to another saddle and the remains of the horse whims. These are circular raised embankments where the poor horses walked round and round pulling coal carts.

Quite soon afterwards there is the Ajax Mine, a chilling 485 metres deep; then the Ajax Battery, which is the most attractive of the gold ruins. The old track has been closed and the new track follows the ridgeline to the spur, where it zigzags down very steeply some 400 metres right back to the carpark.

The remnants of a goldfield, Murray Creek.

121. LAKE DANIELLS
An easy bush stroll to a lake

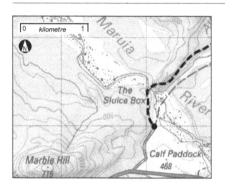

TRACK
Mostly flat bush track with a slow and subtle climb.

WALK TIME AND DISTANCE
3–4 hours (12 km) return.

ONE-HOUR WALK
Pell Stream seat.

ACCESS AND FACILITIES
From Highway 7 the Lake Daniells turn-off is 5 km east of Springs Junction at the Marble Hill picnic area. Camping area and toilets.

This is a well made path through dense beech forest to the lapping shores of the lake — a track anyone can tackle, with plentiful native birdsong and a crisp-cut gorge through the Sluice Box.

From the carpark, the track turns a corner and reaches the footbridge over the well named Sluice Box, where the Maruia River cuts through hard granite with a rush and flurry. Then the track sidles through groves of red beech, occasionally crossing matagouri river flats before reaching the Pell Stream confluence, where there is a seat.

The track starts to climb gently, and slips from the Alfred River valley into the attractive Frazer Stream, which drains Lake Daniells itself. The red beech changes to silver beech and the stream twists through moss banks, almost silent.

The lake is a surprise — a large, sequestered body of water, tucked under bush hills with a short jetty pointing out into it. Often you can hear kaka, with their creaky-door call, flapping wildly from one side of the lake to the other. A hut provides a good lunch shelter and the return walk is gentle.

Lichen, Lake Daniells.

122. LEWIS PASS TOPS
An accessible track to tarn-studded tops

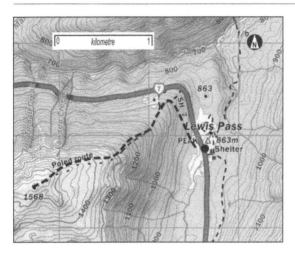

TRACK
A beech forest tramping trail up a short, sharp hill, about 600 metres all told. On the tops there is a worn trail and pole markers to the first high point, but beyond that you need a map, Lewis M31, and a good day.

WALK TIME AND DISTANCE
3–4 hours (4 km) return.

ACCESS AND FACILITIES
Off Highway 7, just before Lewis Pass itself, opposite the main carpark for the St James Walkway. This new access track avoids the hassles of the original carparking area

Short on distance but high on height, this is a fast track to the alpine tops of the Lewis Pass. The views are splendid, and in season there are carpets of alpine flowers such as celmisias and gentians.

The track now sidles a short distance through forest to where it meets the original track. This track does not muck about, climbing quickly through open, rocky country to a seat and junction with the lookout track. Then it is a steady 300-metre climb through old gnarled silver beech then mountain beech to the clean-cut bush edge.

Only now does the track take a breath, and a worn trail climbs up through the open tussocklands, with a steady 200 metres to the first obvious unnamed peak, which I have named 'Panorama Peak'.

The views are good, and the double-peaked Mount Gloriana up Cannibal Gorge looks as a mountain should look. Beyond that is Faerie Queene, and all around are the rolling, graceful tops of the Lewis Pass.

Further on there is a sprinkling of tarns, and anywhere along this ridge you can have lunch straddling the main divide itself — one foot on the West Coast, the other in Canterbury.

A snowpole marker, looking towards Cannibal Gorge on the Lewis Pass tops.

Cloud clearing from the wide valley of the Hope River (see page 180).

123. HOPE RIVER
Classic Southern Alps valley walk

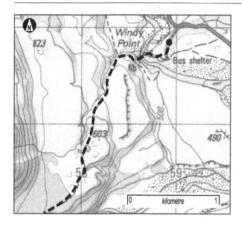

TRACK
A rolling track with one hill climb over tussock slopes, then through beech forest. Well marked.

WALK TIME AND DISTANCE
4–5 hours (14 km) return to Halfway Hut (or Hope Shelter).

ACCESS AND FACILITIES
From Lewis Pass, Highway 7, turn off to the Hope River/Windy Point carpark and shelter. There is an information board here, and a logbook further along the track.

The Southern Alps are the grandest feature in the South Island, stretching from Nelson Lakes to Fiordland, and this walk up the Hope River is typical of the scale of the scenery. The valley is wide, with beech forest cloaking the sides of mountains well over 1500 metres high, particularly majestic with snow on them. On the way there's a wee gorge, and a soft carpet of moss under the bush canopy — plenty of space and plenty of solitude.

From the shelter follow a short vehicle track past the huts at Windy Point, then down and over a long footbridge suspended across the impressive gorge of the Boyle River. After that the track climbs steadily, some 150 metres up over farmland terraces to the bush edge. Good views downvalley.

You are now meandering along in fine, dense beech forest for most of the way to Hope Shelter, staying about 100 metres above the river on a flat bush terrace. Every now and then you get superb views from grassy clearings of the Hope River and the mountains beyond.

The 6-bunk hut stands at the far side of a major clearing in the matagouri. It is a logical place for lunch — sunny and sheltered — and about 30 metres away there is a dribbling thermal spring, which is disappointing if you are in search of a hot bath. That will have to wait until you get home.

124. HANMER SPRINGS
Woodland walks, a fine 41-metre waterfall and thermal springs

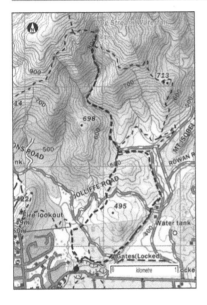

TRACK
Well formed trails in gentle rolling country. Note that forestry operations can close tracks at any time of the year.

WALK TIME AND DISTANCE
Woodland and Dog Stream waterfall 4–5 hours (8 km) return. Well marked, but many track intersections. If you just want to do the shorter option to Dog Stream waterfall, then drive from Hanmer up the Jollies Pass Road, McIntyre Road and Mullans Road to the carpark. From here the Dog Stream waterfall is about 2 hours return. A Hanmer Forest Recreation pamphlet is available from the information centre.

ONE-HOUR WALK
Woodland Walk circuit.

ACCESS AND FACILITIES
Hanmer Springs is off Highway 7, 130 km from Christchurch. The Hurunui Information Centre is right beside the Hanmer Springs thermal pools, with detailed information boards and pamphlets. There is an extensive network of mountain-bike trails in the Hanmer Forest, some utilising existing walking tracks.

'Forest' in Hanmer means either native beech or pine plantations; the two types mix together with sometimes incongruous and sometimes lovely results. This walk starts with the flat circuit by Woodland Ponds, but the track gets steeper near the waterfall, with a return down the Dog Stream track. There are many permutations and you should be able to design a walk circuit to suit your time and yourself.

From Jollies Pass Road beside Dog Stream there is a good track up steps and past a small, pretty waterfall to the two ponds and flax wetland. This is a tranquil enclave.

Head north along the Woodland Walk, pass the Majuba Walk junction and follow the Timberlands Trail. This starts in redwood forest and links with the Joliffe Saddle Track. The track wanders over a low manuka saddle and down to the Dog Stream track near Mullans Road.

If you want to go on to the Dog Stream waterfall, head west to the end of Mullans Road and follow the well graded track upriver through beech forest.

After two footbridges and a ford, the track gets steeper with several staircases before you reach the elegant waterfall.

Return to Mullans Road, and pick up the good track as it wanders through beech forest alongside Dog Stream. This can be followed all the way back to Woodland Walk. There are numerous track junctions (and track options) but stick close to the stream and you will be okay.

Woodland Walk.

125. MOUNT THOMAS
Beech forest and alpine views

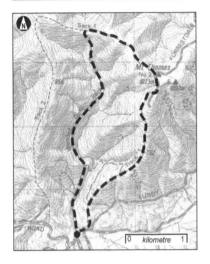

TRACK
Good bush tracks in a steady climb to the ridge, where there is a flattish trail through the tussocks to the summit. Keep alert for track junctions. Total climb of 700 metres.

WALK TIME AND DISTANCE
5–7 hours (7–8 km) return to Mount Thomas summit.

ONE-HOUR WALK
Wooded Gully and Loop 2 circuit.

ACCESS AND FACILITIES
For Mount Thomas drive north from Rangiora across the Ashley River, then take the road to Lowburn and Glentui until you reach Smiths Road (just before the Garry River). It is well signposted. At the road-end is a well sheltered and exceedingly pleasant picnic and camping area, with extensive grass terraces on several levels. Toilets, picnic tables and information board.

Mount Thomas is excellent day-trip country, and the peak has a fine view over the plains. There are various ways up the mountain but the Wooded Gully is the most attractive. It is well graded, with plenty of drinking water from the side-streams, but it is a surprisingly long and convoluted track as it sidles up the valley, with some ups and downs as it crosses side-creeks.

If you can drag yourself away from the charming picnic area, follow the Wooded Gully track over the footbridge, and pass both intersections with the Loop 1 track. Slightly further is the junction with the Loop 2 circuit, which is a good option for 1-hour walkers. The Loop 2 track drops down to the stream at a nice bush picnic site.

The main track starts to climb slowly, passes the junction with Red Pine Track, then drops down to the stream. It climbs a bit, crosses another side-stream and settles into a steady long zigzag up the bush face to the ridgeline.

From this saddle you can amble along through mountain beech onto the tussock grasslands and alpine herbfields to the Mount Thomas beacon. The view is excellent: the Port Hills, the Kaikouras and the Puketeraki Range. Track 1 is the fast, slalom way down.

OTHER WALKS
Options to the summit of Mount Thomas include Track 1 or Track 2 up different spurs, and there are several shorter track options including the Red Pine Track.

126. WAIKARI ROCK DRAWINGS
Dry land and fine drawings

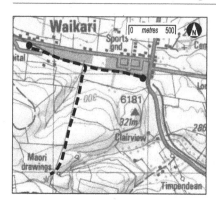

TRACK
Old flat railway line, then worn grass foot and sheep trails over rolling farmland.

WALK TIME AND DISTANCE
2 hours (3 km) return.

ACCESS AND FACILITIES
From Highway 2 at Waikari township, either beside the Waikari tearooms/café or down the Hawarden road 1 km to the signpost.

This is a striking display of Maori rock drawings, perhaps the best surviving in Canterbury, if not in New Zealand. This hot, dry limestone country was once forested, and provided seasonal shelter to Maori groups who hunted for birds like kaka, weka and quail, and the kiore (Pacific rat).

Whichever end you start the walk from, it follows the old railway line 200 metres to a signposted stile. The track then follows the grasslands beside the fenceline, climbing some 150 metres, with a good hilltop viewpoint over the limestone outcrops.

Continue down the fenceline into the limestone valley, part of the Timpendean farm, which is private property. A sign turns you right and it is a few minutes to the obvious rock overhang and the Maori drawings. Wire netting keeps out sticky fingers.

Some of the drawings have been touched up with house paint, and there is a confusing array of overlaying shapes, figures and drawings that are believed to be around 600 years old. What are the drawings for? Doodles? Religious icons? A guidebook for hunters? Graffiti? Marking property or territorial rights? Art? The comic strips of their time?

Whatever the artists' intentions, the drawings are enthralling.

127. CASTLE HILL
Sculpted stones in the high country

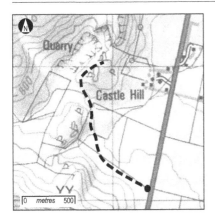

TRACK

Worn grass paths. Take care as you explore, for sudden drops can appear from nowhere. The area is also popular with rock climbers.

WALK TIME AND DISTANCE

1–2 hours wandering (2–3 km). Carry your own water.

ACCESS AND FACILITIES

Castle Hill is easily visible from Highway 73 between Christchurch and Arthur's Pass, and the start of the track is from the large carpark just before Castle Hill Station.

The setting of Castle Hill is superb. It is surrounded by an arc of high-country mountains, tipped with old snow, where cirrus cloud swishes across the brilliant blue sky and invariably heralds the famous hot Canterbury nor'wester.

Several generations of travellers have been attracted to the limestone formations of Castle Hill. Maori found seasonal shelter here, and left charred moa bones and rock drawings. Quite a bit of quarrying went on too (fortunately not marring the main outcrop) and a little of the limestone found its way into the old Christchurch Cathedral.

From the carpark follow the worn trail past the matagouri scrub to the base of the cliffs. The size of the stones is deceptive from the road and it is only when you walk among them that their true scale emerges.

Nearly all the rock shapes have an uncanny resemblance to something else: sheep, camels, mushrooms, Easter Island statues, whatever the imagination suggests. Among the main rock labyrinth is an ephemeral tarn, an archway, several holes and curious canyons — eerie, silent and evocative.

By skirting the lime quarry and the fenced reserve you can climb up 150 metres onto Castle Hill itself. A prominent clump of pinnacles stand on top, the tallest of which are 10–12 metres high.

OTHER WALKS

Cave Stream, a short underground tunnel of 360 metres, is signposted 15 minutes further along the highway from Castle Hill. You need torches, and one person who has been through the cave before. It's cold and you could get wet up to the waist. There's a scramble up a wire ladder at the end.

128. LAGOON SADDLE
Gold tussock and gracious wetland

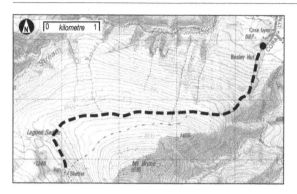

TRACK
A well marked and steady hill climb through beech forest and onto a tussock bench. Total climb of 500 metres.

WALK TIME AND DISTANCE
4–5 hours (10 km) return.

ONE-HOUR WALK
To bushline return.

ACCESS AND FACILITIES
Off Highway 73, between Christchurch and Arthur's Pass; turn at the Cora Lynn Wilderness Lodge sign and follow the road to a carpark.

There is a well known oil painting by Bill Sutton called *Dry September*, a bare, hot picture of a dry river and a peeling bridge in a nor'wester. After 40 years nothing has changed. The bridge is still there, and the hot, dry land is stark and familiar; yet this walk reveals some of the subtlety and beauty in these mountains. It climbs up through beech forest and across a tussock downland to a perfect wetland, a picture in itself.

A few minutes from the carpark is a classic old 6-bunker Forest Service hut, and from the hut a good track climbs up through beech forest and straggly pine trees about 300 metres to the open tussock slopes below Mount Bruce.

The poled route now sidles along a tussock bench, then steers past Lagoon Saddle and eases down through the bush to the A-frame lunch shelter. This track continues as part of the Cass–Lagoon Saddle track.

It does not take long to get to Lagoon Saddle itself, a perfect parkland intermixture of tarns, cushion plants, mosses, beech groves and alpine grasses. This is a very fragile area, so please walk lightly.

If you have the energy it is worth a detour up onto Mount Bruce itself, at 1630 metres (R.W. Bruce was one of the early owners of Cora Lynn). And what a view — from the gorge of the Bruce Stream, to the graceful greys of the Waimakariri River and on to the mountains of Arthur's Pass.

129. AVALANCHE PEAK
A rocky, rewarding peak

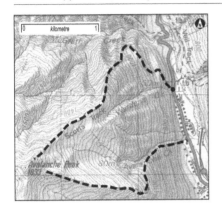

TRACK
A well marked but roughish tramping track through beech forest, then a poled route over the tops. It is recommended that you check the weather forecast at the Arthur's Pass Visitor Centre, and log in your intentions. There is a long history of accidents in this area, particularly with inexperienced walkers.

WALK TIME AND DISTANCE
5–6 hours (6 km) return to summit. Total climb of 1100 metres.

TWO- TO THREE-HOUR WALK
Bush edge return.

ACCESS AND FACILITIES
Arthur's Pass is on Highway 73, 155 km from Christchurch. There are three cafés, a store, petrol, toilets and a public shelter, and the National Park Visitor Centre. The easier track to Avalanche Peak starts 500 metres north of the visitor centre, opposite the Punchbowl Falls track.

It is a tough day tramp to the summit of this 1833-metre peak, but many people get immense satisfaction from just reaching the bushline or the top basin. There are alpine flowers in late spring, and sensational views. You do need clear weather, as cloud will ruin the views and there is some route-finding higher up.

There are two track options, but most people start up the gentler track north of the village and come down the steep track that exits by the visitor centre.

It is a steady climb leading up a rough and ready track through beech forest and mountain scrub, almost 500 metres to the alpine tussock, with good views along the way.

The track does get a little easier, but still follows the strong spur some 400 metres to the summit, although it is well poled and cairned on the way up. Mount Rolleston looks awesome, and you can also peer into the narrow Crow Valley.

The alternative spur down is basically due east of the summit, and again cairned and poled. It is relatively easy travel down to the bush edge, then the track does a steep descent beside a dizzying sequence of waterfalls before reaching the visitor centre and carpark.

OTHER WALKS
There are good walks in the Bealey Valley, to Punchbowl Falls, the Dobson Nature Walk, Otira Valley and Temple Basin Skifield Walk.

130. WOOLSHED CREEK CANYON

Coalminers' tramway leading through high-country tussock to a canyon

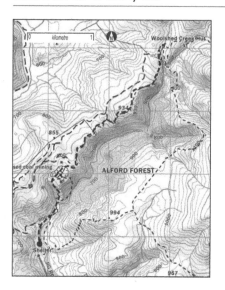

TRACK

Mix of well marked tracks, including a tramway, tussock trails and beech forest paths.

WALK TIME AND DISTANCE

4–5 hours (7 km) return.

ACCESS AND FACILITIES

From the Mount Somers township take the Ashburton Gorge Road (to Erewhon) and after about 10 km turn right down a signposted and gravel side-road 3.5 km to the Coalminers Flat picnic area. This is a large, grassy and sheltered picnic area and campsite, with information boards and toilets.

Mount Somers is a Canterbury walkers' mecca, with tracks and trails all over the mountain. This 'stroll' takes in the fascinating history of the coalmine, and explores the rock outcrops, watercaves, waterfalls and canyon at the headwaters of Woolshed Creek. Oh yes, and the views of the Southern Alps aren't half bad either.

From Coalminers Flat the track picks up the old jig road to the foot of the jig railway incline. Full 4-tonne hoppers of coal would plummet down from the mine and by means of a self-acting ropeway pull up the empty hoppers. Invariably a few hoppers ran off the rails, and there is a good example of a mangled hopper at the foot of this incline.

The Miners Track zigzags up the jig incline for a severe sweat to the bare bleached site of the 1928 Blackburn Coalmine. A reconstructed mine entrance has been built, where you can learn about 'gutsers' and 'banjos' and marvel at the sheer hard slog of the miners during the Depression.

From the mine site follow a well poled track which sidles in tussock gullies along the edge of Woolshed Creek canyon, climbing to Trig R, a splendid viewpoint. You can see the 3000-metre Mount Arrowsmith massif and the distant headwaters of the Rangitata River, the mythical land of 'Erewhon' that Samuel Butler made famous.

The poled route nimbly descends past a rocky lookout and drops right down to the gouged and twisted canyon, and to the large trampers' hut at the head of Woolshed Creek. To explore this area, a poled track goes from the hut and zigzags neatly around bluffs to the base of the roaring canyon itself. A very worthwhile 10-minute side-trip.

OTHER WALKS

If history is your thing, don't forget to have a look at the two historic sites signposted on the road to Woolshed Creek. Both are fascinating and the information boards are excellent.

Pinnacles, Mount Somers.

131. LITTLE MOUNT PEEL
Bush and alpine spur up to a Canterbury summit

TRACK
A well marked and steady climb through bush, with boardwalks across the tussock. Little Mount Peel is exposed and gets plenty of snow in winter. A day tramp rather than a walk.

WALK TIME AND DISTANCE
6–7 hours (6 km) return to Little Mount Peel. Total climb of 950 metres.

TWO-HOUR WALK
Tarn return.

ACCESS AND FACILITIES
Turn off Highway 72 and travel 12 km past the Peel Forest Visitor Centre to Blandswood Road, and follow this some 1 km as it turns sharply before a ford. The carparking area is signposted on the left. Peel Forest store and tearooms has all supplies.

There is not much left of any native forest in South Canterbury, and most of it is in Peel Forest. Some massive totara live on the fertile flat below Little Mount Peel, and this walk climbs up through the bush to a high alpine peak, with an eye-opening view of the patchwork plains.

From the Blandswood carpark walk up the road some 500 metres till the track starts. Take the Deer Spur track, which passes the junction with the Fern Walk and climbs steadily up through a mixed forest of tree fuchsia, broadleaf, lemonwood (tarata) and mahoe, with a glossy carpet of ferns.

There are occasional views of the plains as the track passes the junction with Allan's Track, and some southern rata (look out for the crimson flowers at Christmas time). The track then enters the upper alpine shrub belt, which consists of turpentine, flax and dracophyllums.

The tarn, which is at an altitude of 900 metres, might be something of a disappointment if it has not rained for a while, leaving little more than a sodden bogland. However, there are some splendid specimens of spaniard with razor-sharp leaves and flowering stalks that often reach over a metre in height.

The track winds up the spur onto the tussock, with extensive boardwalks higher up. The last 150 metres is a steeper, muddier climb to the small, sharp top of Little Mount Peel at 1311 metres. There is a beacon on top and a wee shelter 20 metres below (enclosed, with seats and water).

OTHER WALKS

There are various other walks in Peel Forest including Acland Falls (1 hour return); Dennistoun Bush Walk (1.5 hours circuit); Fern Walk (1.5 hours one way); and Kahikatea Walk (1 hour circuit).

A tarn on the way up Little Mount Peel.

Boardwalk over the wetland of Travis Swamp (see page 192).

132. CHRISTCHURCH CITY WALK — TRAVIS SWAMP
Superb suburban perimeter walk around a wetland

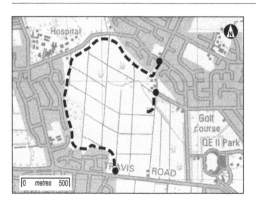

TRACK
Good gravelled tracks or boardwalks.

WALK TIME AND DISTANCE
1 hour (4 km) circuit.

ACCESS AND FACILITIES
From Anzac Drive ring road, take Frosts Road to opposite Beach Road, and drive to large carparking area. Signboards and information shelter a minute away.

My, how things change! At one time everyone wanted to drain Travis Swamp and no one wanted to live next to it. Now the Christchurch City Council has been busy sculpting ponds and waterways, and people are scrambling to pay expensive prices for a house with a view of this local treasure, where over 60 different bird species have been recorded, including more pukeko than you could throw a stick at. The wetland not only survived the earthquakes of 2011, it became even wetter!

From the carpark walk to the information shelter, which seems to float in its own pond. It has interpretation panels as well as a short walk to a bird lookout platform. Take the main perimeter track as it heads south, crosses a bridge and reaches a junction by Angela Stream.

This section is busy with waterfowl, and large, posh homes from Travis County come close to the track but do not overwhelm it. It is a peaceful walk along to Clarevale Reserve, then the track follows a boardwalk to a birdwatching platform.

Great lookout, then boardwalks continue through to open grass swales with good views. Now the Anne Flanagan Track passes a seat lookout (and carpark off Mairehau Road) before swinging round the northeast corner of Travis wetland to a path that leads back to Beach Road carpark.

133. HALSWELL QUARRY
Historic quarry track and sculptural surprises

TRACK
Gravel paths and mown grass strips, some short hill climbing.

WALK TIME AND DISTANCE
1 hour circuit (Rim Track); 1 hour return (Farm Track): both 2 km return. Note: The 2011 earthquakes temporarily closed the Rim Track but it is currently open.

ACCESS AND FACILITIES
Drive to Halswell and the Akaroa–Sparks Road junction then take Kennedys Bush Road to the signposted turn-off; 10 km from Christchurch city. Extensive picnic areas, walking tracks, sculptures, toilets and information centre.

This fine park has been formed out of an old council-run quarry and is a unique combination of botanical gardens and historic quarry buildings; a quiet, involving landscape, with plenty of discoveries and surprises on the way. Sculptures from other cultures are scattered among the garden trails, with ponds, seats and lookouts.

The main Rim Track starts from the carpark, goes up past the interesting assemblage of old quarry buildings and gradually follows the outer rim of the quarry. There are lookout points and interesting interpretation panels on the way. At the top, the faces of the rock quarry have striking rock patterns, and there are expansive views over the park, the plains and the southern mountains beyond.

The down-track passes a 10-minute side-trail up to Kennedys Bush Road, then goes through the shady Findlays picnic area and back to the carpark.

Other tracks include the Farm Walk (1 hour), a circuit around the other side of Halswell Quarry up to a high point with fine views. There are also many shorter rambles (10 minutes) among the Sister City gardens that are being developed: Seattle, Adelaide, Christchurch (England), Songpa-Gu (Korea), Sansu (China) and Kurashiki (Japan).

Some of the historic buildings at Halswell Quarry.

134. COOPERS KNOB & SIGN OF THE BELLBIRD
A classic skyline walk

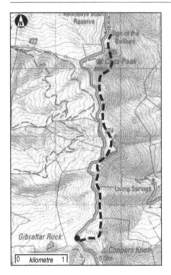

TRACK
A mix of bush tracks and tussock trails over rolling country. Occasionally rough underfoot, and a rock scramble to the top of Coopers Knob.

WALK TIME AND DISTANCE
2–3 hours (5 km) one way (Coopers Knob to Cass Peak/Sign of the Bellbird).

ONE-HOUR WALK
Coopers Knob return.

ACCESS AND FACILITIES
This track is part of the Crater Rim Walkway and it follows along the Summit Road. It can be accessed at several different points, but this description starts from the small carpark (and steps) beside Gibraltar Rock, just past Rhodes Spring. It assumes that you have arranged transport to pick you up at Cass Peak/Sign of the Bellbird. Toilets and picnic area at the historic stone resthouse, the Sign of the Bellbird.

This track follows the twist and twine of a volcanic ridge, slipping past rock tors and overlooking bluffs down to the lovely blue-green cleft of Lyttelton Harbour. There are extraordinary views from Mount Cook to the Kaikoura mountains, and despite the rugged terrain there is not a lot of climbing. On a fine day you would not wish to be anywhere else.

Take the steps opposite the carpark, and climb easily through gorse and tussock to the main Crater Rim Walkway. At this junction you can do a brief side-trip to Coopers Knob, by following the main track to an unmarked side-trail, then staying on the ridge before scrambling up the rocks of Coopers Knob. Hint: there's an easy way to the top on the back/south side.

This is the highest point on the Port Hills (572 metres) and the views are stunning. Lake Ellesmere and Kaitorete Spit are in the foreground, then the whole panorama of the Southern Alps, including Mount Cook (just to the left of Mount Somers), Mount Arrowsmith and Mount D'Archiac.

Back at the track junction, follow the broad track along the ridgeline almost down to the road. Skirt through a small bush reserve and around a prominent rock outcrop to another bush remnant, then the track climbs out along a rugged line of bluffs, with sweeping views on the way.

Cass Peak is 546 metres high, with the obvious meteorological golfball on top. The main track drops past a hang-gliders' launching pad then sidles on the dramatic east face of Cass Peak (or if closed take the easier west-side track), past a stone seat and around to the historic Sign of the Bellbird. This shelter provides seats and a splendid view.

135. SIGN OF THE KIWI
Unrivalled views and original tearooms

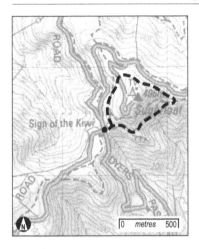

TRACK
Well marked bush tracks and tussock trails, with an easy hill climb of Sugarloaf.

WALK TIME AND DISTANCE
1–2 hours (3 km) circuit.

ACCESS AND FACILITIES
From Christchurch drive up Dyers Pass Road to Dyers Pass and the carpark beside the Sign of the Kiwi. An excellent lookout, but be warned: the crossroads can get busy with traffic on weekends.

The Sign of the Kiwi has information brochures, and offers teas, milkshakes and ice creams. Closed after the 2011 earthquakes, but should open again as it seems to be structurally sound.

This is a short, civilised, circular walk on the Port Hills, which explores bush reserves on the Lyttelton Harbour side and outstanding views on the Sugarloaf side; and you can end with a snack in the 1917 stone resthouse.

The start of this walk is over the crossroads, opposite the Sign of the Kiwi, where there is a stile and a sign saying 'Mitchells Track'. This bush track sidles slowly through a substantial hillside of native bush with dominant mahoe, lancewood, broadleaf and lemonwood, and some tuneful bellbirds and grey warblers.

There is an excellent lookout over the deep blue gash of Lyttelton Harbour. It takes about 30 minutes to amble up through the bush reserve and past the Smyth seat to the junction with Cedrics Track.

This track climbs gently uphill across tussock and around to the large Sugarloaf carpark, and it is worth the 20 minutes or so extra to walk up the sealed road to the Sugarloaf summit and television tower. At 496 metres you get superb views, and you can look along the length of the volcanic escarpment of the Port Hills.

Back down at the Sugarloaf carpark pick up the other half of Cedrics Track, which lollops down to the Sign of the Kiwi.

OTHER WALKS
Coronation Hill Walk (1 hour return) and the H.G. Ell Track to Victoria Park (1 hour one way).

Mount Sugarloaf, on the Sign of the Kiwi walk.

136. MOUNT VERNON
From suburb to summits

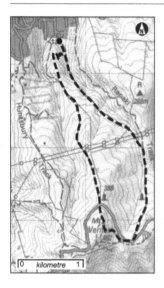

TRACK
Dry tussock trails and farm vehicle tracks up a long hill. The 4WD tracks also get used by mountain bikers.

WALK TIME AND DISTANCE
4–5 hours (7 km) Mount Vernon summit return.

ONE-HOUR WALK
Plane table return.

ACCESS AND FACILITIES
Off Centaurus Road and Hillsborough Terrace to a large carpark and signboard. The 2011 earthquakes closed this carpark but it should be open by 2013; otherwise use the alternative access up Hillsborough Road to the plane table.

This is a superb day-walk circuit, easy to access from the city, and exploring many facets of the Port Hills. There are tussock downlands, rock outcrops, a direction-finding table and seat lookouts, a historic Maori trail and two memorial poles to lost children.

Start from the carpark, and at an immediate track junction follow the zigzag up the hill to the spur, then follow the spur track to a lookout table. Good views from here already.

Continue up the spur track (also known as the farm track) to where it joins the farm vehicle road, and settle into a slow, steady slog all the way up to Summit Road. On the way you can glimpse the isolated pocket of native forest called Dry Bush.

At the Summit Road there is the Lamar Track for wheelchair access, a short, tidy circuit with plane tables and seats. There is also a memorial pole to John Lilley, aged 8, one of two children who died in a snowstorm in 1883. The other pole, to 10-year-old William Mason, is just off the side of the Rapaki Track. The poles were placed on the sites where the bodies were found.

The farm road continues up to the summit of Mount Vernon itself, with great views everywhere. From here pick up the Crater Rim Walkway and follow it down to Rapaki carpark. This rock was an icon to Maori as well as to today's rock-climbers, and marked the way of the Rapaki Track from Otautahi (Christchurch) to the Rapaki settlement in Whakaraupo (Lyttelton) harbour.

The Rapaki Track is a 4WD road and a broad, easy walk past the second memorial pole to where the valley track starts. The valley track is not well signposted, but obvious, as it starts from a low dip on Rapaki Track. If you miss it, carry on down Rapaki Track and take the signposted Rogers Track to the carpark.

The valley track leads gently past a dry streambed and an eccentric meditation kiosk (well, how else would you describe it?) back down to the Hillsborough Terrace carpark.

Top: Walkers on the valley track, Mount Vernon.
Above: Mount Vernon walkway kiosk.

137. BRIDLE PATH & CASTLE ROCK
Historic footpath and striking rock outcrop

TRACK
Gravel road up a steep hill, then a worn path through tussock up to Castle Rock. The Bridle Path track should reopen by 2013, though the circuit track around Castle Rock may never reopen.

WALK TIME AND DISTANCE
2–3 hours (3 km) return.

ONE-HOUR WALK
Seymour seat return.

ACCESS AND FACILITIES
From Christchurch city it is about 7 km to the gondola, and just beside it is the Bridle Path carpark. Picnic tables and water fountain.

The Bridle Path was surveyed and constructed in a feverish hurry over the Christmas period of 1850–51, and finished in the second week of January 1851. Originally the main road from Lyttelton to Christchurch was to go via Evans Pass, but progress was excruciatingly slow.

After a year the 'Sumner Road' was still uncompleted, and with the settlers due to arrive in December there was an urgent need for some sort of pathway to the plains. It was a tight finish. The Bridle Path was surveyed in November 1850 and the *Charlotte Jane*, the first of the four immigrant ships, arrived on 16 December.

From the carpark the broad vehicle track (the Bridle Path is technically a road) climbs steadily past seats and up a broad zigzag.

At the Seymour stone seat, named after one of the first four ships, the Castle Rock side-track is signposted the Kahukura Track. This beaten trail winds up under Castle Rock, climbing steadily, with expansive views over the estuary and the Kaikoura mountains.

It reaches a top track junction, and by turning left you avoid the slips and rockfall from the 2011 earthquakes. Castle Rock has significantly changed shape, losing a large middle section, so it looks like a tooth has fallen out.

Once you reach Summit Road, follow it down to the top of the Bridle Path and its historic shelter to the pioneer women. The plunge back down to the carpark will be steep, but at least you will be unhindered by Victorian crinolines.

138. GODLEY HEAD
Cliff coastline, precarious baches, interesting
military history

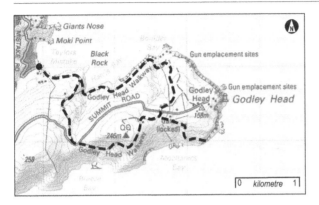

TRACK
Broad, well graded tracks on an open tussock peninsula. You will need a torch
for the optional tunnel track. It was planned that Godley Head tracks would
start to reopen by 2012 or 2013.

WALK TIME AND DISTANCE
4–5 hours (6 km) for circuit (including tunnel).

ONE-HOUR WALK
Boulder Bay return.

ACCESS AND FACILITIES
From Christchurch city drive 14 km to Taylors Mistake beach. Picnic area and
toilets at Taylors Mistake.

Penguins like this coast and so do people, and this is a popular walkway that has
a swag of good views and some curious facets of history, including a military
tunnel. Maori knew Godley Head as Awaroa or Otokitoki, while another early
name was Cachalot Head, probably named by the crew of a French whaler.

Taylors Mistake is a fine sandy beach with baches, clumped under the cliffs,
hanging as perilously as a shag's nest. From the beach the track follows a
coastline eaten out into bays and caves (some of which were inhabited once)
and cuts cleanly around headlands to where a few baches snuggle down at
Boulder Bay.

Nesting sites for spotted shags and the white-flippered little blue penguin are
found along this coast.

It is a steady climb from Boulder Bay up to the top of the peninsula, where
the track crosses Summit Road to the carpark and toilets.

There is a good side-trip to the tunnel, if the track has been reopened.
The tunnel track descends past the remains of old military buildings (also a

side-track to a coastal lookout), then zigzags sharply down to the 110-metre tunnel, which you can walk through to the two searchlight 'pillboxes'. Splendid headland views, and on a fine day a popular place for fishing.

At the ridge carpark, follow the main track as it rambles along the side of the tussock peninsula, past a lookout, and down to Breeze Col. It then descends dramatically to the bay. Several mountain-bike trails have been constructed on the peninsula, and these can be utilised by alert walkers. A great walking circuit.

139. GOVERNORS BAY COAST
Coastal wandering

TRACK
Old flat road for most of the way.

WALK TIME AND DISTANCE
2 hours (5 km) return (Allandale to Sandy Bay).

ACCESS AND FACILITIES
There are several entry points but carparking at many of them is awkward. There is little carparking at the Governors Bay jetty, only a few places at Sandy Bay, not much at Church Lane carpark, but plenty at the attractive Allandale picnic area, right by the shoreline.

This is an easy-going shoreline walk, rambling along the old coastal road with refreshing views out over Lyttelton Harbour and the humped rolling peaks of Banks Peninsula. The walking is surprisingly private once you leave Allandale carpark, and you get glimpses of houses up on the terraces, including a handsome old stone mansion.

Around the point, the road swings past some swirling rock patterns in the soft cliffs, and it is very peaceful beside the oystercatchers and shags picking over the mudflats. Governors Bay has a long finger of a jetty, and the road ends.

However, if you are feeling frisky, a good bush trail fossicks around the circumference of Governors Bay, past boatsheds and bushy backyards to the carpark at Sandy Bay.

There is a benched track past the old jetty, and a side-track heads down to a secluded bay with baches tucked under the cliffs. The tide platforms are extensive at low tide, and it is hard to drag yourself away.

Governors Bay coast track.

140. SIGN OF THE PACKHORSE
A hut in lonely limbo

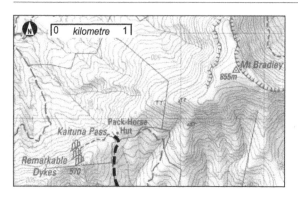

TRACK
The track is well signposted and poled, following vehicle tracks up a steady hill climb.

WALK TIME AND DISTANCE
3–4 hours (5 km) return.

ACCESS AND FACILITIES
Access to the Packhorse Hut is off the Christchurch–Akaroa road, Highway 75, into the Kaituna Valley, then about 7 km along the Kaituna Valley road, and turn off into Parkinson Road 500 metres to carpark.

The Sign of the Packhorse is perched in a fine romantic situation, alone on the tussock pass that looks from Lyttelton to Kaitorete Spit. It was built in the 1920s, when walking became popular on the peninsula.

The hut was once part of a network of hostels, and early photos show a homely place with curtains at the windows and flowers on the table. At the hostels it cost walkers a shilling for a bed, a shilling for a meal, and lunch (thick bread and butter with cheese) was sixpence.

The track is well signposted and poled, and from the carpark sidles past the farm, following vehicle tracks up a bush-filled valley then climbing onto a big spur. There are extensive patches of scrub forest in the Kaituna Valley and you can hear quite a few native birds, including kingfishers and bellbirds. Kanuka trees are dominant here, with lots of kowhai as well.

After a while the track stops climbing up the spur, and sidles on a farm track past Parkinsons Bush Reserve to the saddle and an old stone hut. The hut has bunks and mattresses, a wood stove and a rainwater tank. In summer the water supply cannot be relied upon — unlike the views.

OTHER WALKS
The Packhorse sits in the centre of a web of tracks. For the fit, a poled track leads behind Mount Bradley and on to Mount Herbert, the high point of the peninsula

It is shorter, and not difficult, to go directly on to Mount Bradley. Another poled route continues down from the Packhorse Hut, past the Remarkable Dykes (an outcrop of volcanic rock) and then on to Gebbies Pass, 2–3 hours one way.

Tussock saddle with Mount Bradley beyond, part of the Sign of the Packhorse walk.

141. SUMMIT CREST
A wild way on a high ridge

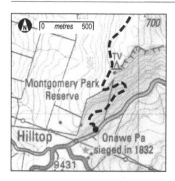

TRACK
Farm tracks and 4WD roads. The walking is generally easy and rolling, but there are quite a few climbs as the route follows a rather zany course along the main ridge. The route is poled, and follows legal paper roads for the most part, and it is sometimes called the 'double fence track'.

WALK TIME AND DISTANCE
4–5 hours (10 km) one way from the Port Levy/ Little River road saddle to Montgomery Park. You will have to prearrange transport, as the road-ends are a long way apart.

ONE-HOUR WALK
Waipuna Saddle return.

ACCESS AND FACILITIES
From Little River take the tortuous Western Valley Road up to the Port Levy saddle, a dramatic site.

These Banks Peninsula tops are wild, and the crouched shapes of the totara trees give a fair idea of what the weather can be like up here. The three hillside reserves of Mount Fitzgerald, Mount Sinclair and Whatarangi Totara Reserve have surprising subalpine plants — like mountain holly and spaniard. Pick a clear day and you will have a rewarding walk.

From the Port Levy saddle it is 1 km through stands of stunted totara to Point KK (738 metres), then a brief drop down to Waipuna Saddle and an easy swing around tussock slopes up to Mount Fitzgerald (826 metres). The route drops down to a saddle then up to Mount Sinclair (841 metres), about 3 km.

The tree 'graveyards', particularly on the eastern slopes of Mount Sinclair, are striking; both beautiful and ugly at the same time, with intricate patterns etched into the stumps.

Tree graveyards on Summit Crest.

There is a big descent from Mount Sinclair to the tiny Whatarangi Totara Reserve, then the track crosses open grasslands to an unnamed rocky peak (700 metres) overlooking Montgomery Park. The track is poled into, and through, Montgomery Park, and this dwarf of a reserve has some giant totara trees. Quite astonishing; you simply do not expect such a size of tree in such a tight space.

142. ONAWE PA

Historic Maori peninsula in gorgeous harbour

TRACK

Beach and grass trails up to a low summit. A low tide is essential.

WALK TIME AND DISTANCE

1 hour (3 km) return.

ACCESS AND FACILITIES

Drive to Duvauchelle on the Christchurch–Akaroa road, Highway 75, then turn onto an unsealed coastal road for 1 km to the small carpark.

From a distance the Onawe Peninsula looks like a greenstone pendant dangling in the smooth waters of Akaroa Harbour. It is now a peaceful place, and the quiet lapping tides make it an island at high tide.

But this was no defence for Ngai Tahu Maori who occupied this pa site when Te Rauparaha's warriors approached in 1831–32. The slaughter was immense, and was followed by a cannibal feast on the beach. Today there is no trace of this conflict except, fancifully, in the red-stained and contorted rocks that are exposed at low tide.

From the carpark a short vehicle track drops down to the pebbly beach.

There are striking rock patterns in the tidal rocks. Onawe is connected to the mainland by just a thin, razor-like ridge, which broadens out into a wide and rising grass slope to the beaconed summit 100 metres above sea level.

A good trail climbs up to this summit, which is further than it looks, and the outlook is fine. Some false trails look as if they lead down from the summit to the shoreline at the head of the peninsula, but these are for goats, and keen goats at that.

Manuka forest and thick grass now largely obscure the details of the pa site, but nothing can obscure the magnificence of the harbour landscape.

Coming down from Onawe Pa.

143. AKAROA TOWN WALK
Backyard exploration of a historic town

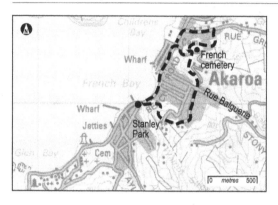

TRACK
Footpaths and grass trails. Some short hills. If you get lost it's not very far back to town.

WALK TIME AND DISTANCE
1–2 hours (2 km) circuit.

ACCESS AND FACILITIES
85 km from Christchurch on Highway 75. There are cafés, a good visitor centre, museum, toilets, beach, wharfs and shops in Akaroa. Plenty to do.

Akaroa is a charming town, started by French settlers in this most English of provinces. Historic cottages, overflowing with roses and wisteria, can be found up and down the narrow bylanes of the town. Views are unexpected and everywhere on this backyard trail, and to round off the walk there are numerous cafés supplying a quality of café au lait the early settlers could only dream of.

On Rue Lavaud, the signposted walks to Stanley Park start near the fire station and bakery corner, and the track ambles up from the sea, with a good view back over the harbour. The track crosses Penlington Place and carries on to Watson Street.

Follow this down to Rue Balguerie, then walk up Settlers Hill Road. It is a steep climb, but immediately on the left is a bush track that sidles easily around to the green, secluded site of the old French cemetery, dating from 1842.

You could continue down the road to Pompallier Street and Rue Lavaud, or take the pretty bush track down from the cemetery and turn right at the first junction. This leads on a rambling sidle to Libeau Lane, which can be followed down to Rue Grehan and Rue Lavaud. Follow this back to the whiff of croissants.

OTHER WALKS
Garden of Tane (20–30 minutes); Purple Peak (4–5 hours); Britomart Memorial
(10 minutes); and Woodills Loop Track (1–2 hours).

A quiet morning in Akaroa.

144. HINEWAI RESERVE
A forest being reborn

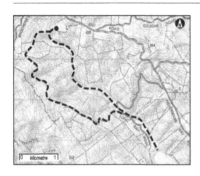

TRACK
Good bush trails, and the track signposting is superb. There are information boards and pamphlets available at most carparks, and first-time visitors to Hinewai should study the maps carefully. A fire in 2011 damaged some parts of the reserve.

WALK TIME AND DISTANCE
5–6 hours (9 km) for the full Hinewai circuit. Fire is the major threat to this reserve, so no fires, billy boiling or smoking at any time. No dogs allowed.

ONE-HOUR WALK
West Track, Big Kanuka Track, South Track and climb up East Track to the visitor centre.

ACCESS AND FACILITIES
From Akaroa take Long Bay Road up to the Summit Road junction (known locally as the Cabstand), then turn down Long Bay Road to the main entrance and carpark. For Otanerito Bay, continue down Long Bay Road all the way to the lower carpark near the Otanerito homestead. 90 km from Christchurch.

There is a visitor centre with interesting displays on Hinewai Reserve and what is being achieved here. Please take boots off before entering. Toilets.

Hinewai Reserve is one of the most extensive walking areas on Banks Peninsula. Almost 12 km of well marked tracks run through this unique 1000-hectare bush reserve, which is privately owned and managed by the Maurice White Native Forest Trust, but open to the public. Regenerating forest runs virtually from sea level to the summit, and gives an insight into how an ecologically managed area can be successfully restored.

From the visitor centre take West Track along to the Big Kanuka Track and South Track. The attractive Hinewai Falls is worth a look. At Boundary Falls continue down the easy Valley Track past a cascade and a big kahikatea to the Otanerito road.

For the beach cross the road and follow the trail beside the stream and farmland to Otanerito Bay. The bay is sandy and sheltered, with big sea cliffs guarding the entrance, and a sprinkling of private baches around it.

Return to the road again and the carpark. From here it is a solid climb up through the tall kanuka forest of The Stones Track to the junction with Lisburn Track. This track follows up the pleasant Waterfall Gully and sidles round to Lothlorien lookout.

Lisburn Track merges with Broom and Manatu tracks, with good views over upper Hinewai. At the junction with South Track, follow Beech Terrace Track to Tawai Track and West Track, which sidles easily back to the visitor centre.

145. MOUNT JOHN
Perspiration for a perfect panorama

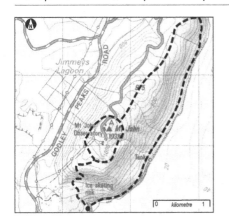

TRACK
Pine forest trail up a steady hill, then dry tussock slopes.

WALK TIME AND DISTANCE
2 hours direct return from summit; 3–4 hours (8 km) for full circuit.

ACCESS AND FACILITIES
From Lake Tekapo township take the road to the lakeside motor camp and continue to the carpark just before the hot pools and ice-skating rink.

Mount John sticks up like the proverbial sore thumb above the Mackenzie plain, in its isolation acting as a marker post for Lake Tekapo. There is a perfect panorama from the summit, from Mount Cook to Lake Alexandrina and Lake Tekapo, then back over the arid Mackenzie Country to Burkes Pass and Mackenzie Pass. And there's a café on top!

It is not that far to climb, about 250 metres, for Lake Tekapo is already at 800 metres and Mount John summit is 1031 metres. So you could fit in a quick jaunt to the summit on the way to Queenstown.

From the carpark the track climbs steadily through the larch forest and reaches a junction with a loop track that circles the summit. Already the views are good.

Head on up to the summit café for your well deserved treat. Mount John is surprisingly flat on top and Himalayan chukar (partridge, introduced as a game bird) are sometimes spotted on the top slopes.

One longer walk option is to continue on the summit loop then take the track north down the long easy spur some 2 km to where it drops sharply down to Lake Tekapo. Staying 50 metres above the lake, the track sidles around the base of Mount John, back to the skating rink and carpark.

The top stile on the Mount John track, with Lake Alexandrina behind.

146. LAKE ALEXANDRINA
Solitude at a high-country lake

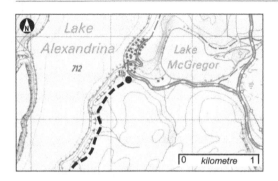

TRACK
An easy anglers' casual track across dry tussock country. Some mud.

WALK TIME AND DISTANCE
1–2 hours (4 km) one way; 2–3 hours (8 km) return.

ACCESS AND FACILITIES
From Highway 8 (6 km south of Lake Tekapo) take the Godley Peaks road 3 km to a turn-off to the south end of Lake Alexandrina, or 8 km to the middle of the lake and Lake McGregor. There are baches at both road-ends, and toilets, camping and information boards at Lake McGregor.

There is something subtle and silky about Lake Alexandrina, which sits in an old glacial gouge alongside its much bigger and more blustery sister. Powerboats are not allowed, and the crested grebes patrol the willowy edges in calm, persistent ripples. This is a land that takes many seasons to appreciate, and the colours are harsh: blue-grey waters, yellow shores, black mountains.

From the Lake McGregor baches and road-end a trail wanders south alongside the lake. However, the best plan is to climb straight up from the carpark about 50 metres to a flat-top hill. A stile crosses the fenceline, whose main purpose seems to be to stop four-wheel-drivers trashing the tussock.

Along here the unmarked trail wanders down to the lakeside again, and the footpath settles into some definition as it rounds the point and goes down to the baches at the south end of the lake. This is another feast of bach architecture.

Unless you have had the foresight to organise transport you will have to wander back the same way — no doubt wishing you'd brought your fishing rod.

The serene Lake Alexandrina.

17/2/2020

147. HOOKER VALLEY
A perfect and popular mountain walk

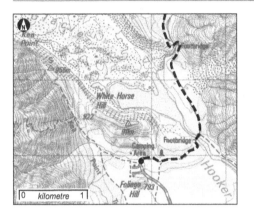

Stunning
weather !

TRACK
A well marked track, easy and mostly flat at first. Later it becomes rougher, with some clambering. Two dramatic footbridges and the sidle by the Hooker River gorge can unnerve some walkers.

WALK TIME AND DISTANCE
3–4 hours (8 km) return to ice lake.

ONE-HOUR WALK
Return walk to second swingbridge.

ACCESS AND FACILITIES
From Highway 80 turn off just before Mount Cook village and go to the large carpark and camping area under White Horse Hill. Picnic tables, public shelter and toilets.

The Hooker Valley is the perfect frame for Mount Cook. The dark and dirty V-shaped valley, with its rumbling moraine walls, is precisely mocked by the pristine and soaring A-shape of Mount Cook.

This short walk is packed with interest and drama, and walkers have been making this mountain pilgrimage for over 100 years. So you will not be lonely on the track, unless you go off-season or early in the morning — hotel breakfasts rarely start before 7 a.m.

The track starts from the White Horse camping area and passes the original site of the Hermitage and an alpine memorial, and groves of matagouri and some colossal spaniards (*Aciphylla*), with very sharp leaves and huge flowering stalks.

The track zigzags down to the first swingbridge across the milky-blue Hooker River. Good views continue upvalley, past the Mueller Glacier terminal lake, and the track cuts along a gorge with a spectacular swingbridge. You can often find native edelweiss in the cliffs here.

After the bridge you turn a slight corner in the valley and get some photogenic views of Mount Cook, and in summer there can be a profusion of Mount Cook lilies (or properly buttercups).

Stocking Stream shelter was named for walkers in the nineteenth century who would take off their shoes and stockings here. There are toilets and a plane table, which is stuck rather oddly on top of a rock.

After a flat section with some boardwalks, the track crests a slight rise and you reach the ice lake, the terminal lake of the Hooker Glacier. There might be small icebergs drifting in the lake.

The Hooker was named after William Hooker, an eminent English botanist; and Mount Cook was named after the explorer Captain James Cook, but to Maori the peak is Aorangi (or Aoraki to South Island Maori), sometimes translated as 'cloud piercer' — and you have to admit it's a better name.

The second footbridge over the Hooker River, heading up the Hooker Valley.

148. RED TARNS
Secluded alpine wetland

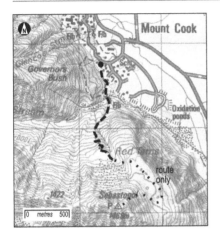

TRACK

A hill walk, sometimes steep, but well marked. Gravel path at first, but it gets rougher in places. Beyond the tarns the track becomes a worn route over boulders up to the Sebastopol ridgeline.

WALK TIME AND DISTANCE

2–3 hours (2 km) return to tarns. For Sebastopol ridgeline add 1 hour. Total climb of 250 metres.

ACCESS AND FACILITIES

Start from the public shelter on the Mount Cook village loop road, not far from the shop and beside Governors Bush. Toilets and information panels here.

The Red Tarns are a quiet escape from the tourist hubbub of Mount Cook village — a crystal sprinkling of ponds, like two clear eyes in the stony face of Sebastopol. In summer the waft of flax, turpentine scrub and totara berries can be quite heady, and soothing — a meditative refuge.

At the public shelter, signs direct you along a gravelled path beside a bubbling creek, then out of the village to a long footbridge over Black Birch Stream.

The track then starts to climb steeply through the alpine scrub, crossing occasional gullies on its way to the lip of the basin. It is a 500-metre climb to the tarns, where there is a seat and a plane table.

The tarns get their name from the red pondweed that grows in them. On a still, sharp day you get a perfect reflection of Mount Cook.

A rough track with cairns continues on to the Sebastopol ridgeline, with excellent views. Allow another 1 hour return from the tarns.

149. BALL HUT ROAD
Road to nowhere

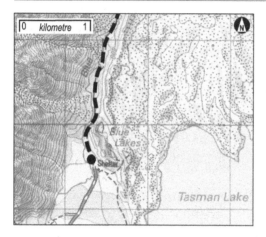

TRACK
Flat, easy walking initially on a gravel road, then a 4WD track, then a trampers' track on a moraine terrace.

WALK TIME AND DISTANCE
5–6 hours (16 km) return to Ball Hut.

ONE-HOUR WALK
Celmisia Flat return.

ACCESS AND FACILITIES
From Highway 80 just past Mount Cook airport, turn onto the Tasman Valley road and drive to the Blue Lakes carpark, shelter and toilets. A chain blocks any further access up the road.

An unusual walk in many ways, and not everyone's cup of tea. It is a long bash up a 4WD road, with steep, rotten hillsides of the Mount Cook range on one side and the huge, grinding rock factory of the Tasman Glacier on the other. It can be hot work too, with little shade, which makes you wish for a mountain bike.

But you are following in the footsteps of history. In February 1882 the Reverend W.S. Green and his Swiss guides Emil Boss and Ulrich Kaufmann slowly trekked along this moraine wall, camping by the streams and searching for a route to the unclimbed peak of Mount Cook. They almost made it, too, but for 'a mere matter of detail', a lack of daylight and 10 metres short of the summit.

Later the Ball Hut road was built and in the early 1890s a climbers' hut (one of several) was established at the far end, with parties in the early part of the twentieth century having to walk up onto the glacier. But this region is a textbook study of rock processes and rapid erosion. The Tasman Glacier retreated and shrank under its mantle of rock, and the moraine's walls crumbled and took away the hut and parts of the road.

The road now peters out into nowhere, some 6 km from Blue Lakes at Husky Flat. There is a worn foot-trail that threads along the terrace and reaches an unexpected oasis of grass and alpine shrubs beside the small Ball Hut shelter.

About 500 metres further on the moraine wall itself ends at the top of a nasty eroded access valley nicknamed 'Garbage Gully' by generations of climbers. But the view is anything but rubbish.

Blue Lakes, beside the Ball Hut road.

150. BEN OHAU
Little hills have big views

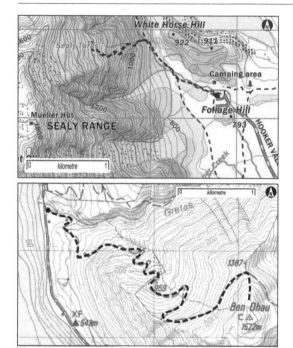

TRACK
An old farm 4WD track zigzags most of the way up a very big climb, with the last 150 metres to the summit across screes and tussock. Carry lots of water and have lunch on top.

WALK TIME AND DISTANCE
4–5 hours (6 km return); total climb 1000 metres.

ONE-HOUR WALK
Good views of Lake Ohau, but the Mackenzie Basin is still hidden.

ACCESS AND FACILITIES
You will need a good road map. From Highway 8 north of Twizel look for 'Glen Lyon Station' signs, and follow the Pukaki and Ohau Canal roads (all sealed). Eventually you get to Lake Ohau and the seal ends, and the narrow road twists along past huge drystone road walls. There's a DOC sign by the derelict barn.

In Scotland 'ben' means mountain — although you might not consider Ben Ohau to be much of a mountain. It sits beside giants on the edge of the Mackenzie Basin, a mere mole on the body of the Southern Alps.

Nevertheless at 1550 metres it is not a hill to be sneezed at, especially when you start to walk up the 1000 metres or so to the top. Suits the dedicated hill-walker.

Follow the farm road past an old rabbiters' hut, and the rustling beech forest by Gretas Stream. This is the last of the shade; the road then zigzags powerfully up the mountainside spur and up to a small basin. A brief reprieve from climbing then the vehicle track gets steep again as it slices across the face of Ben Ohau to a high saddle.

The unmarked route leaves the road and cuts up the scree and tussock slopes to the high-point rocks covered with a curiously hairy lichen. Expect a breeze — 'O hau' means 'place of wind'. But the reward is a view of four lakes — Ohau, Pukaki, and the artificially made Benmore and Lake Ruataniwha.

An old rabbiters' hut at the start of the Ben Ohau farm track.

151. FREEHOLD CREEK
From easy to alpine

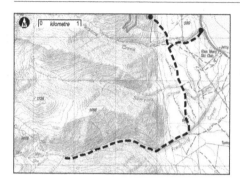

TRACK
A good signposted path through rolling tussock and scrub, followed by a steady hill climb in beech forest on an old logging line.

WALK TIME AND DISTANCE
5–6 hours (18 km) return from bushline (from Ohau skifield road), 4–5 hours (12 km) return from Parsons Creek carpark.

ONE-HOUR WALK
1 hour return will get you to Sawyers Creek from Parsons Creek carpark. Or 1 hour one way from the Ohau skifield road to exit at Parsons Creek, a nice cross-country trip.

ACCESS AND FACILITIES
From Highway 8 take the Lake Ohau road to either the Parsons Creek carpark or 2 km further to the turn-off to Ohau Lodge and skifield road. Follow this road 1 km to a ford and the start of the track. Signposted.

There is a bit of everything on this walk, which suits both the unfit and the keen. You start on soft sunny slopes and somehow end up in big, bluffy country, the real heart of the Southern Alps.

From the carpark at Parsons Creek, follow the well marked track up through beech forest (past the seat and lookout) and through tussock and matagouri terraces to a well signposted junction with the main track from the Ohau skifield road. The track ambles across open landscapes, with Lake Ohau dominating the view, and the Ben Ohau Range across the way.

The track crosses the footbridge over Sawyers Creek and follows tussock terraces to the beech forest at Freehold Creek. You slip into a green, bouldery valley, and after a little climbing reach a footbridge over the creek. This is another good return point, say 2 hours total from the road-end.

Now the track gets a little more serious as it climbs up through the forest past a large camping area and on to the sudden fringe of the bushline. If you are game enough, a cairned trail leads quite clearly into the alpine basins to the top forks, with waterfalls gushing down the side-creeks, and well fed alpine plants in every cranny.

If you are still keen (and within your time budget) it is not that far up to a large, broad saddle, but there is no track up to here. You have strayed into wilderness.

152. CLAY CLIFFS
Beautiful badlands

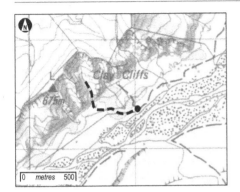

TRACK
Easy farm road, but scrambly amidst the pinnacles themselves. Watch for falling debris.

WALK TIME AND DISTANCE
1 hour (2 km) return.

ACCESS AND FACILITIES
Access is 3 km north of Omarama off Highway 8, turning left onto Quailburn Road, then Henburn Road, and driving a few kilometres to a farm gate and signpost. Currently there's a $5 per person charge. There's a box here or you pay at the Omarama information centre.

The gravel road continues 3 kilometres to another gate and onto a '4WD only' sign and carpark beside the clay cliffs.

These cliffs are not really 'clay', but the name does have excellent alliteration. Maori called them 'Paritea', which means 'white or coloured cliffs', and the early morning light brings out the subtle colours and textures of the sediments.

Erosion of the soft sediments and shingle by water has left deep ravines, with striking pinnacles wearing little caps of turf. The cliffs are 30–50 metres high in places, and just crumbling away. Some tracks have been made, but these all get undermined by the constant movement of the rocks.

On a hot, glaring day there is something spooky about the shady silences inside these chasms, with the tinkling sound of pebbles bouncing and falling off the sides, and the unexpected whoosh of pigeons (the boring kind) in the air.

You often come away with a distinct sense of relief, possibly because you are grateful nothing has fallen on top of you; or perhaps there is something unnerving about seeing geological processes in such an accelerated form.

The badlands of Clay Cliffs.

153. HEAPHY COAST
Nikau palms and luxuriant forest down to wild beaches

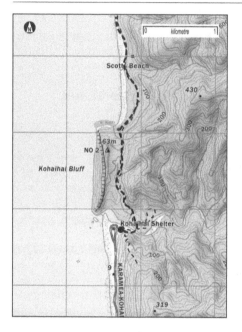

TRACK
Well graded packtrack.

WALK TIME AND DISTANCE
Scotts Beach circuit 2 hours return
(4 km).

ACCESS AND FACILITIES
From Karamea it is a 15-km drive
to the Kohaihai River and road-end.
Extensive picnic and camping area,
toilets, shelter, phone and lookout
track.

This is still an unspoilt coastline. A
dark mosaic of hills, covered with
sullen clouds, runs down to the
noisy surf, where abrupt headlands
interrupt sweeps of yellow sands.
The salt-laden forest has a profusion
of plants like karaka, kawakawa,
tree daisy, kamahi, kiekie and the
iconic nikau palm. Late evening light can illuminate this landscape as if pouring
through stained-glass windows.

Nikau palms are the southernmost member of the palm family, about 10
metres tall, with a tuft of leaves reminiscent of a feather-duster. The fruits are
enjoyed by native birds, particularly the native pigeon. Early travellers ate the
crisp kernel of the nikau, which was said to have a sort of 'nutty flavour'. Maori
wrapped food in nikau leaves before cooking it, and the large leaves were also
used for baskets, as carpets and thatching for huts.

From the lovely camping area, cross the huge swingbridge over the rich tea-
stained Kohaihai River. Then follow the Heaphy Track as it climbs easily to the
Kohaihai Saddle, and down to Scotts Beach.

This is a lovely run of sand leading for 2 km north up the coastline. Beyond
here is Big Rock Beach, Koura Beach and Crayfish Point. You can walk as far as
you like along this enticing shoreline, but at some stage you have to turn back
regretfully and face the slow hill to Kohaihai Saddle and the carpark.

OTHER WALKS
Lookout Track 1 hour return; Nikau Walk nature trail 40 minutes return.

154. OPARARA ARCHWAYS

Spectacular natural archways with a gelid river running through pristine rainforest

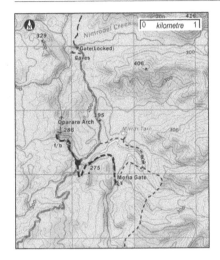

TRACK
Well marked bush tracks, sometimes muddy.

WALK TIMES AND DISTANCES
Oparara Arch 40 minutes (2 km) return; Moria Gate or Little Arch 1 hour (2 km) return.

ACCESS AND FACILITIES
From Karamea drive north for 10 km, then turn inland following the signposts for 15 km to the carparks and walking tracks. The road is winding and narrow but is in reasonable condition for cars.

The Oparara River has etched a sinuous and sensuous course through a limestone basin, creating three lovely and distinctive arches, two of which can be visited. Rainforest has disguised this geology and gives Oparara its mysterious and forgotten aura.

The arches are what people usually come for, and they are impressive. You can walk through the largest, Oparara, which is 43 metres high and 219 metres long. The inside is dry and roomy, with stalactites and stalagmites. The Moria Gate or Little Arch is smaller and prettier and you enter it via an unexpected cave. It is 19 metres high and 43 metres wide.

Once you've seen the arches, don't forget the podocarp/beech forest that sets the scene, with rimu, matai and kahikatea overtopping the red beech. There are also two short caves to explore, both 5 minutes' walk in. Crazy Paving has a distinctive mud floor, and Box Canyon is a high dry cavern. Take a torch.

Oparara is home to quite large bird populations, including great spotted kiwi, kaka, kea, tomtits, bellbirds, parakeets, native pigeons and tui. For the serious birdwatcher there is the chance to see rare whio (blue ducks) in the Oparara River.

On the ground look for the large-shelled *Powelliphanta* snail, a nocturnal carnivore that feeds on worms. The shells are colourful spirals of brown, gold and orange, and it is illegal to remove them, even when empty. Rats, weka and even kea and kaka prey on these fist-sized snails, the largest of which may be 10–20 years old.

OTHER WALKS
Mirror Tarn 30 minutes (1 km) return; Box Canyon and Crazy Paving Caves 20 minutes (1 km) return.

155. CHARMING CREEK
Old tramway through a granite gorge

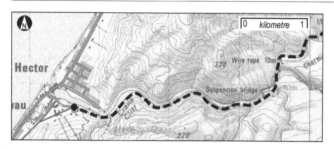

TRACK
Flat gravel track on an old tramway.

WALK TIME AND DISTANCE
1–2 hours (6 km) Ngakawau Gorge return.

ONE-HOUR WALK
Irishmans Tunnel return.

ACCESS AND FACILITIES
From Westport drive 35 km north to Ngakawau. The walkway is signposted just before the river; drive past the Stockton Coal cableway 200 metres to the carpark on the right. Don't drive down the walkway itself!

There was never a more apt name for a walk. Charming Creek has tunnels, walk verandahs, waterfalls and many other features all packed in on a dense trip into the cramped and gloomy spaces of a gorge closely overhung with sombre native forest.

Excellent information boards detail the coal-extracting operations in the area. From 'The Bins' terminus you quickly follow the slick dark waters of the Ngakawau River through the S-bend of Irishmans Tunnel (a mistake in alignment), and through another 'tunnel' which is in fact a natural rock arch. The granite gorge is at its narrowest here, as the tramway crosses the long suspension bridge with spectacular views of the Mangatini Falls.

There is another 50-metre-long tunnel, a boardwalked verandah, then the confluence of Charming Creek and Ngakawau River. The river always carries a thin line of foam and creates elaborate swirls and patterns as it joins the Charming.

Just around the next corner is Watsons Mill, where there is a toilet and shelter, and after the bridge a short casual trail goes down to the picnic rocks by the dark tea-stained river. A salubrious spot for lunch.

From here on, the walkway changes character as it leaves the gorge and enters a chewed-over forest of mine debris, relics of the old steam sawmill, a sulphur hole and the Papa Tunnel. If you continue right through, either arrange transport at the other end, or allow 2 hours return (6 km extra).

156. DENNISTON INCLINE
The remains of a mighty enterprise

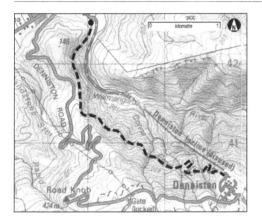

TRACK
A bush track up the original bridle path hill to Denniston township, with steps at the top.

WALK TIME AND DISTANCE
4–5 hours (8 km) return.

ONE-HOUR WALK
One Mile Log return.

ACCESS AND FACILITIES
From Westport travel 14 km on Highway 67 to Waimangaroa, then take Conns Creek Road to the carpark. If you continue along Conns Creek Road you reach the historic site at the actual base of Denniston Incline. This has been recently cleared so you can see the whole path of the incline.

For the top access, follow the signposted Denniston road as it climbs the 700-metre plateau, then down a side-road to the carpark and lookout over the top of the incline. One Mile Log carpark is on the Denniston road and offers a shorter walk to the top. Obviously if you can arrange transport to drop you off at the top of the incline, the walk is easier and the walk time is halved.

The Denniston Incline was built in 1878–79 and operated until 1967. When it was built it was proudly considered New Zealand's biggest and best engineering project. Water-operated brakes slowed the coal-laden wagons (in a descent that was 1 in 1.20 over the 548-metre drop) and helped pull up the empty wagons. Once 250 miners and their families lived and worked on this bleak plateau, and ultimately 12 million tons of coal were taken from Denniston.

At first the walk goes through regenerating forest and past the old brickworks site, climbing 2 km up to One Mile Log. After this the forest becomes more substantial, with tall rimu and red beech.

This bridle track was built in 1884 when the hazards of riding down on the incline wagons became all too obvious — namely, when someone died.

After two-thirds of the climb there is a short side-track to Middle Brake, where you can get an idea of the uncomfortable steepness of the incline. There is an old viaduct below Middle Brake but it is unsafe to go on; indeed, the incline is generally too steep and insecure to walk on.

On the main track, the last part zigzags up stone steps to the lonely and rusting machinery at the top of the incline. On misty days the place seems haunted, which perhaps it is — haunted by memories.

OTHER WALKS

Coalbrookdale Mine (1 hour). A 10 minute drive from the top of Denniston to the start of this walk.

Top: The top of the Denniston Incline.
Above: Tauranga Bay (see facing page).

157. CAPE FOULWIND
The smell of seals and the sea

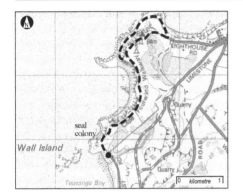

TRACK
Benched gravel track all the way. Well worth trying to arrange a car pick-up at the other end so you can walk right through.

WALK TIME AND DISTANCE
2–3 hours (3 km) one way.

30-MINUTE WALK
Seal colony return.

ACCESS AND FACILITIES
From Westport it is 12 km down the Cape Foulwind road past Carters Beach to the large carpark, information boards and toilets at Tauranga Bay.

The winds howl and crack their cheeks on this corner of the West Coast, and in 1770 James Cook called it 'Foulwind'. The name has stuck, and so have the seals, to one of the most publicly accessible seal colonies in New Zealand. Other attractions include the colony of friendly, thieving weka at the carpark, and the glorious golden sweep of Tauranga Bay.

From the carpark an excellent track climbs up onto the headland and leads down to the lookouts over the seal colony. At breeding time the colony is spectacular, with as many as 100–150 pups.

The New Zealand fur seal is found only in New Zealand waters and off the south coast of Australia, and the seals arrive at the Cape to give birth in November and December. By March the number of pups are at their peak, and a lively lot they are.

From the colony the track is well graded and follows the cliff-tops with a wonderful view. Past the astrolabe and the lookout, the track sidles around to the lighthouse and on to the northern carpark.

But just before here an unmarked trail leads down to the shore and follows the banking of the old railway line, which was used for moving quarried rock. On stormy days this is a wild piece of shore. Straggler seals often haul ashore here, no doubt trying to get some peace and quiet from the noisy quarrels at seal city.

158. THE BALLROOM & FOX RIVER
Deep river to a vast natural overhang

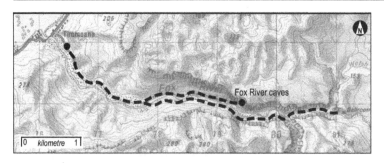

TRACK

A good benched track to Fox River ford, continuing on the south bank to the Dilemma Creek junction. Only one river crossing separates the two tracks, but from near the Dilemma Creek junction there are several deep river crossings on the way to the Ballroom.

This walk is suitable for experienced walkers and trampers. It should not be attempted in wet weather, as river levels can rise quickly and dangerously. Get good weather information from the visitor centre at Punakaiki. Maps: Paparoa National Park 273-12, Punakaiki K30.

WALK TIME AND DISTANCE

5–7 hours (11 km) return.

ONE-HOUR WALK

Fox River ford return.

ACCESS AND FACILITIES

From Highway 6 beside the Fox River take the short side-road to the carpark. There is a toilet at the Ballroom. At Punakaiki there is a good visitor centre, toilets, cafés and a craft shop.

This is a deep gorge that cuts into the heart of the karst syncline of Paparoa National Park. You can get a long way into this heartland with only one straightforward river crossing, but to reach The Ballroom you will get wet knees (at least). This is a wilderness walk, with tall forest, and limestone rocks that have been shaped into sculptures by the emerald river.

The marked track starts as a stopbank that becomes an old gold-diggers' packtrack, and crosses two low bush spurs via old miners' cuttings. It crosses a dry side-branch of the Fox River where the granite boulders glitter with quartz, and shortly afterwards reaches the first Fox River ford.

(The Fox River Tourist Cave track continues along a benched track, becoming gradually rockier, then steeply follows up a creek bed to the entrance of the cave, which can be explored for a short distance. Take a torch.)

For The Ballroom cross the river here and join the well benched south bank track that continues most of the way to the Dilemma Creek confluence.

The Fox Gorge is striking, and every twist in the river breaks open new angles of rock and light. At Dilemma Creek the rock walls have formed a sharp prow, splitting the two rivers. The track has now ended, and you have to start fording the Fox River. Some of the fords can be deep but the river is usually slow-moving.

It is about six to eight crossings upstream to the high natural rock shelter called The Ballroom. This is a massive overhang curved over a grassy flat, and you could fit a few houses under here comfortably. There is no record of any ancient balls ever being held here, but it is a lovely idea

Fox River.

159. PANCAKE ROCKS & TRUMAN/TE MIKO TRACK
Strange rock formations on a rugged coast

TRACK
Pancake Rocks: well made gravel paths; Truman Track: well made gravel paths and some beach walking.

WALK TIME AND DISTANCE
Pancake Rocks 30 minutes circuit; Truman Track 30 minutes return. Both 1–2 km return.

ACCESS AND FACILITIES
Drive to Punakaiki on Highway 6 (60 km from Westport, 45 km from Greymouth), to the information centre, café, tearooms, toilets, shop and large carpark. The Truman Track is 2 km north at the signposted carpark.

The Pancake Rocks are a peculiar rock formation, with limestone rocks layered in elegant towers. The BBC imposed digital flying *Ornithocheirus* on these rocks, for their *Walking with Dinosaurs* television series — and it did not look odd.

Surf surges into the caverns and, with the right sea running, can blast up through the blowholes underneath the rocks, creating a memorable short walk.

Opposite the visitor centre, the track starts through coastal bush then dense flax (harakeke) and cautiously circumnavigates a surging sea chamber. There are good information signs at the many lookouts. These rocks were formed by sedimentation of shell debris, accumulated and compressed over millions of years, and then uplifted.

Shrubs cling to the very edges of the blowholes, which have names like 'Sudden Sound', 'Chimney Pot' and 'Putai' (sea spray). On a clear day you can see Mount Cook in the far distance, though often the Paparoa coast seems to 'smoke' from the heavy spray of the pluming sea.

TE MIKO OR TRUMAN TRACK

Slightly north of the Pancake Rocks, this track plunges down through a coastal jungle of rimu, matai and entanglements of vines such as kiekie and supplejack. Walk through the final flax belt and you are on an exposed rock shelf above the sea.

The broad tidal platforms are stained with colours, and sea stacks take the brunt of the West Coast surf. Seals haul ashore up and down this coast, and little blue penguins nest here.

Steps go down to a gorgeous beach, where shallow sea caves have been carved out and glisten with subtle colours of lichen and moss. The sea fairly barrels into this tight little bay, but at low tide it is possible to scramble around the greasy rocks to the next bay. It is an ancient, relentless shore.

Sea caverns under the Pancake Rocks.

160. MOTUKIEKIE COAST
Low-tide exploring past sentinel sea stacks

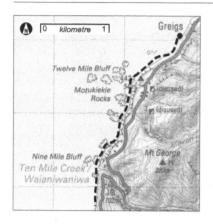

TRACK
Beach walking and low-tide scrambling. A low tide is essential, and the surf should not be too big either. If you follow the route right through, wet feet are a probability.

WALK TIME AND DISTANCE
1–2 hours (5 km) return. The golddiggers' terminology on this coast is confusing, since Nine Mile Bluff is at Ten Mile Creek. And the distance between Nine Mile Bluff and Twelve Mile Bluff is not 3 miles (or 5 km) but 2 km! The frequency of gold-diggers' 'shanties' in the 1860s, serving 'cold tea' along this coast, may have contributed to the confusion.

ONE-HOUR WALK
Twelve Mile Bluff return.

ACCESS AND FACILITIES
Off Highway 6, just past Greigs settlement at the rest area carpark. For Nine Mile Creek beach and carpark, there is an unmarked gravel side-road that leads past a bed-and-breakfast place to a rough carparking area by the beach.

This walk explores a cliff-hanging coast, with sea stacks at Motukiekie and a hole in the rock at Ten Mile Creek. Dodging the surf will keep you fit and is exactly what the early travellers had to do. Motu means 'island' in Maori, and kiekie is the rambling, salt-tolerant vine that makes the cliffs such a jungle.

From Greigs walk across the wide exposed sands onto the tidal platforms that swirl out to the sea like solidified ribbons of seaweed. Close to Twelve Mile Bluff large conglomerate boulders have tumbled onto the shore, some coloured terracotta and as fine as Roman mosaics.

Motukiekie is a sensational stand of sea stacks, topped by some tenacious plant life that manages to survive on the spume-soaked headland. It's an amazing place, and there is an emergency escape track up to the highway if you get stuck — it's hard to find but the locals use it.

Around the corner from Motukiekie there is a short sandy beach, and another headland to clamber over where the rocks have slumped, then a passage across tidal platforms to Ten Mile Creek and a surprise — a large hole in a rock. Local legend says the early goldminers scrambled through it to avoid the high tide.

To get to Nine Mile Creek beach and carpark you will get wet feet across Ten Mile Creek, then there is a short rocky clamber over big boulders and under a cliff. You have to hit a low tide right on the button to get through, but then it is an easy, broad beach. There is a safe, if rugged, escape up Ten Mile Creek to the highway.

161. CROESUS TRACK
Classic packtrack to the tops

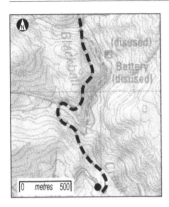

TRACK
A well graded goldminers' packtrack to the bush edge, with a short off-track wander up onto Croesus Knob itself. Total climb of 900 metres.

WALK TIME AND DISTANCE
7–9 hours (18 km) return from Croesus Knob (including a side-trip to the stamping battery).

ONE-HOUR WALK
First Hotel site return.

TWO-HOUR WALK
Second Hotel site return.

FOUR-HOUR WALK
Garden Gully stamping battery return.

SIX-HOUR WALK
Ces Clark Hut return.

ACCESS AND FACILITIES
From Blackball township drive 1 km on Roa Road and turn onto the Blackball road, which winds through forest for 4 km to the Smoke-Ho! carpark. The road is narrow and can get rough, though it is usually suitable for cars.

This walk is a wonderful leg-stretcher, following a historic, perambulating track that never loses interest. Indicated above are several shorter return walks for people who do not fancy the full workout, but do not be put off by the times. The easy gradient makes the hill seem far gentler than it really is, and on a fine day you really have to try for the top — the view of Mount Cook is awesome.

Take the track from the Smoke-Ho! carpark as it passes a logbook, and stay on the top track option to the First Hotel site, in a large, grassy clearing. There are good easy grades up to the Second Hotel site (past Perotti's Mill junction), and up past a couple of lazy zigzags to the Garden Gully junction.

This side-track crosses a saddle down to the old Garden Gully Hut then climbs up a side-creek to arguably the best preserved stamping battery on the Coast.

The main Croesus Track zigzags steadily upwards past the old Top Hut, reaching the bush edge at the Ces Clark Memorial Hut. Dedicated to a ranger who died on the track, this was the first mountain hut to be opened by a prime minister (David Lange, in August 1986 — and no, he did not walk).

Fine views already, but once out into the tussock basins the views get better and better, especially if you can manage the final fling up onto Croesus Knob itself. On top is the remains of the aerial cableway for the Croesus Mine — and his proverbial wealth is still not as good as the views.

162. NELSON CREEK
Tricks of track and tunnels

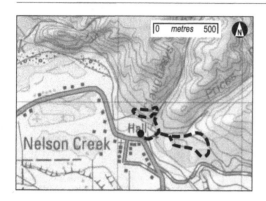

TRACK
Bush trails with streams running through the tunnels. Mostly flat.

WALK TIME AND DISTANCE
Nelson Creek 1 hour (3 km) full circuit (Tailrace Walk and Colls Dam Walk).

ACCESS AND FACILITIES
From Highway 7 just north of Ngahere turn onto the Nelson Creek Road for
6 km to Nelson Creek. Carpark and toilets.

A short walk through a fascinating landscape of tunnels, tailraces and tailings,
created by goldminers in desperate need of water. Ground sluicing was the
dominant technique used at Nelson Creek, but too much water was as much a
nuisance as too little.

The miners dug tunnels to gain a healthy pressure of water to attack the
goldbearing gravels and trap the heavier gold in riffle boxes, but they also cut
tailraces and sludge channels to drain water and the excess tailings away. You
can see the fruits of their hard work and admire their skill.

From the Nelson Creek carpark the track starts spectacularly — through a
tunnel! Then it is over a long suspension bridge and around to the Tailrace
Walk, past the turn-off to Colls Dam, Callaghans and the Tunnel Walk.

The Tailrace Walk is a 20-minute circuit around a number of cleverly incised
tailraces. Back at the junction with the Tunnel Walk have a look at the beginning
of the tunnel. This discharges a small stream into Nelson Creek, and you can
walk down it, though you will need a torch. There is a large swimming hole at
the Nelson Creek end.

Lastly, go back to the Colls Dam Walk and enjoy this peaceful circuit past
Colls Dam then continue round, crossing numerous other tailraces.

163. GOLDSBOROUGH TRACK & TUNNEL TERRACE TRACK
Mossy creeks and the art of tunnelling

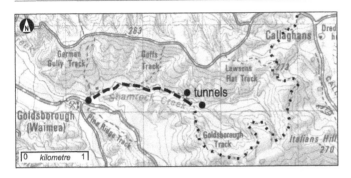

TRACK
An even-graded packtrack in bush, with river crossings and wet feet to reach the miners' tunnels.

WALK TIME AND DISTANCE
1–2 hours to tunnels (4 km) return; complete Goldsborough track 3–4 hours (7 km) one way.

ACCESS AND FACILITIES
Turn off Highway 6 at Awatuna onto the Stafford–Dillmanstown road and follow this some 10 km to a large carpark, picnic area and campground.

The great 1865 goldrush was the foremost historic event on the West Coast, and changed the landscape irrevocably. At Goldsborough the land has been completely trashed by generations of goldminers who shifted creeks, stacked pyramids of rocks, and inadvertently created an artistic labyrinth of tunnels. They did things with the pick and shovel we would not attempt with a bulldozer, and the Goldsborough Track is a marvellous testament to their endeavour.

The main track from the carpark initially follows Shamrock Creek quite closely in regrowth bush, then crosses the creek beside a bluestone cliff. Over a low spur there is a side-track back down to Shamrock Creek.

There are two tunnels, the first just 100 metres downstream, over smooth boulders in the mossy riverbed. It is a beautiful piece of work, built to eliminate a bend in the river so as to assist the miners in flushing out the tailing debris.

Upstream 5 minutes is an even better tunnel, some 30 metres long. Both tunnels are well fashioned examples of the gold-diggers' art, with crypt-like arched ceilings in the green, cloistered riverbed.

TUNNEL TERRACE TRACK
This track starts 5 km before the Goldsborough carpark, on the Stafford–Dillmanstown road. Clearly signposted. The kids will love it, even the small ones. It starts through a water-race tunnel, loops around old stone stacks of tailings past the entrances to other tunnels, and pops out on the road through the clever finale of a tunnel. 15 minutes of frolicking fun.

OTHER WALKS

The Goldsborough Track continues for another 2 hours to Callaghans Road and the Manzoni Claim, with its huge man-made tunnel.

An elegant, mossy tunnel on the Goldsborough Track.

164. LAKE KANIERE & THE KANIERE WATER RACE
Lovely lake and easy walk along a goldminers' water race

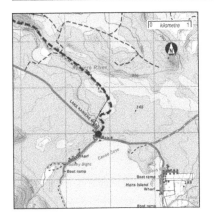

TRACK
Well graded and gravelled all the way.

WALK TIME AND DISTANCE
1–2 hours (4 km) return to Wards Road.

ACCESS AND FACILITIES
Drive to Lake Kaniere, where there is a carpark and picnic area by the control gates. Lovely picnic area at Sunny Bight and a spacious and attractive DOC camping area at Hans Bay.

Lake Kaniere is one of the scenic gems of Westland, serene, secluded, almost completely surrounded by bush, and it has several beautiful walks. At the north end of the lake at the Sunny Bight picnic area, there is the gorgeous Kahikatea Walk, about 10 minutes circuit. Drive past Hans Bay about 3 km to Dorothy Falls, a 2-minute stroll to a magnificent gusher. There's a 4–5 hour lakeside track that goes from Sunny Bight all the way to the south end of the lake at Lawyers Delight beach.

The Kaniere water race was built in 1875 to provide water to boost the flagging Kaniere goldfield. The water flowed but alas not the gold, so by 1916 the race was used for power supply instead, and it has stayed that way. The fully automated Kaniere power station is one of the smallest in the country and supplies between 100 and 125 houses in Hokitika.

The water-race walk is easy going, through bush forest and past tunnels, with the constant sweet accompaniment of the rippling race.

From the control gates by Lake Kaniere the first part of the walkway goes through cutover manuka forest with some emerging kamahi. Freshwater mussels can be seen in the race, and it is a cruisy 3 km to Wards Road. This is a good turnaround point. The old raceman's hut has been removed.

In the next section the race disappears briefly into three tunnels and you get good views of the river below, before reaching Tunnel Hill, where a 2-km tunnel takes the water race through to the power station. The track picks up an uninteresting bulldozer trail then drops down quickly to a gravel road, which is followed down to the Kennedys Creek carpark.

The track alongside the Kaniere water race.

165. OKARITO LAGOON
Packtrack to a wilderness lagoon

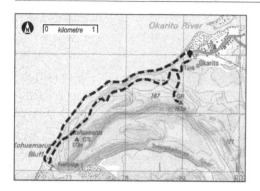

TRACK
Good bush packtrack one way, easy beach walking the other. A low tide is essential.

WALK TIME AND DISTANCE
3–4 hours (6 km) return.

ONE-HOUR WALK
Okarito trig return.

ACCESS AND FACILITIES
From Highway 6 at 'The Forks' it is 13 km to Okarito, where there is a campground, information post (in the wharf shed), signposted walks and a boat-launching ramp. Tide tables at the beach noticeboard.

This is a 150-year-old bush packtrack that once sturdily carried goldminers to the Three Mile Lagoon, but now carries walkers. The views of Mount Cook and Mount Tasman across the tea-stained waters are jaw-dropping, and on the beach return there may be sleeping seals on a shoreline that rarely gets disturbed. Okarito was a gold town that lasted from 1865 to about 1868 — three glorious, mad, drunken years, all gone now except for the packtrack.

From the new large carpark (before the beach carpark) the track swings across a boardwalk over a wetland, then sidles up to the original packtrack. From here it's an easier gradient to a track junction with the Okarito trig. If the day is fine this is a most worthwhile 40-minute return side-trip, on up to a lookout platform with views of Okarito in the foreground and the long horizon crammed with the snowy peaks of the Southern Alps.

The main packtrack rolls along to Three Mile Lagoon, sometimes coming close to the cliff edge, with a good crop of ferns and mosses beside the track. It drops sharply to a junction, the left-hand fork going to a long bridge over Three Mile Lagoon. The other fork goes on to the wide beach. The lagoon entrance is often blocked by a sandbar.

With a low tide the beach walk is easy, and quicker than the packtrack with not much rockhopping, and the constant surf rolling in. Occasionally a seal hauls ashore, but often it is just the gulls that take an interest in you on this restless, rollicking coast.

Mount Cook from Three Mile Lagoon.

166. LAKE MATHESON
Reflections around a pristine lake

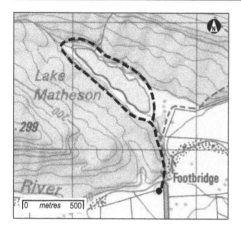

TRACK
A high-grade flat track and boardwalk around a lake. Most people go clockwise.

WALK TIME AND DISTANCE
1–2 hours (2 km) return.

ACCESS AND FACILITIES
From Fox Glacier village drive 4 km down the Cook Flat Road, and turn onto Lake Matheson Road 1 km to the carpark, where there are toilets, café and art gallery.

In the last century Lake Matheson would have been called a 'beauty spot', and that is still true, as 20 coach tours a day confirm. The backpacker buses try to get in early for the famous 'view of views' and the tranquil waters that giveth off the perfect picture.

God, however, does not always supply the perfect weather, and cloud has ruined many a fine reflection, but the lake is still pretty and pristine.

The track starts between the groovy café and the art gallery, crosses the Clearwater Stream bridge and goes to the first viewpoint, but you need to go to the head of the lake and climb up to the View of Views platform to get the 'classic' placemat and calendar view. On the way the rich rainforest is made up of tall kahikatea, rimu and matai, with a lush understorey of shrubs and ferns.

A few minutes on from the View of Views there is a side track to Reflection Island, a particularly appealing perch beside the lake. The famous reflections partly result from the brown coloration of the water, which is caused by organic matter leached from the humus on the forest floor. The calm surface of the lake accentuates any birdsong.

The main track then moves away from the lake and follows the forest around to farm paddocks with splendidly isolated kahikatea trees.

167. FOX GLACIER
Kea and ice

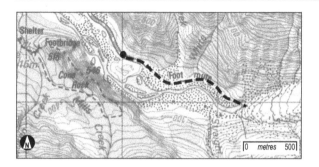

TRACK
A well marked track follows the riverbed to the foot of the glacier. This track constantly changes according to the whims of the river and the glacier.

WALK TIME AND DISTANCE
1 hour (2 km) return.

ACCESS AND FACILITIES
From Highway 6 by the Fox River, follow the signposted glacier road to the carpark. This road and the track are often subject to change and closure due to river floods.

Alternatively, there is a walking and mountain-biking track signposted from the village all the way to the glacier carpark.

The glaciers are retreating again. After some interesting advances in the late 1990s the Fox and Franz Josef glaciers are following the centuries-old pattern of shrinkage, but there is still a lot of glacier to go. The scale of the mountains, the sheer cliffs and the crumbling tongue of the glacier make for an awesome short walk. And the kea, alpine parrots, are never in retreat.

The drive in alone is worth it, crossing the Fox River floodplain and winding under the severe cliffs of Cone Rock. At the carpark there are usually kea, which cock their heads obligingly as the cameras click.

Currently, the track wanders across the riverbed, and edges along the scree slides. Streams are bridged.

You cannot touch the ice, for obvious reasons — a large lump might fall on you (it has squashed one or two incautious people) — and the glacier tongue is roped off. Still, you can feel the icy air rolling off the glacier, and photograph an object that, if you came back the following month, would have already moved on.

168. GILLESPIES BEACH
Coastal forest, lagoon and a historic tunnel

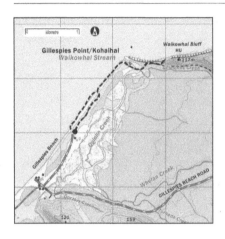

TRACK
Well marked tracks and a boardwalk across the lagoon.

WALK TIME AND DISTANCE
To the lagoon and back 1 hour; to the historic tunnel 2 hours return.

ACCESS AND FACILITIES
From Fox Glacier (Highway 6) it's 20 km to Gillespies Beach, and 11 km of this is unsealed. This is a narrow road with many blind corners. Carpark, camping area, toilets and signposted walks.

A wild coast with a battering surf and driftwood piled high on the beach — Gillespies has presence. On a fine day the mountains stand above the black swamp lagoon like a mirage and the spume from the surf creates its own mist. Sunsets are very fine.

Gillespies got its name from James Edwin Gillespie, who detected payable gold on the beach sands here in 1865. A small town sprang up but it did not last long. Gold dredges later turned over much of the beach frontage, but apart from a few remnants of metal there's hardly a thing left to mark the glory days — just the cemetery and the proliferation of gorse.

There are several walks at Gillespies. From the camp area and carpark the suction dredge ruins are down a short side-track. If you head north on the inland track you pass the remains of the bucket dredge, slowly slipping into the mire. This track continues to the beach.

Along the beach north is the lagoon, with its long trestle bridge and the dark tidal water offering some dramatic reflections. You can get some impressive views from here.

Across the bridge the packtrack goes through swamp and coastal forest and climbs to a junction, one branch going to the tunnel. The tunnel was cut in the 1890s to avoid the awkward Gillespie Point headland, and you can walk through to a viewing platform.

It is no longer permitted to go north along the beach to Galway Point as it disturbs the seal colony too much. Alternative access north is along the Galway Point track.

169. PARINGA CATTLE TRACK
Historic route over the mountains

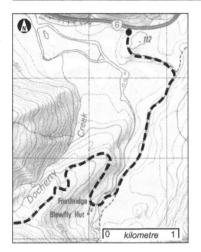

TRACK
Good benched track, but can get wet and muddy underfoot. Flat to Blowfly Hut, then a steady but graceful climb up to Maori Saddle. This is a big day-trip, so start early. Maps: Haast F37, Landsborough G37.

WALK TIME AND DISTANCE
7–8 hours (20–22 km) return to Maori Saddle Hut. Total climb of 500 metres.

TWO-HOUR WALK
Blowfly Hut 4 km return.

ACCESS AND FACILITIES
Off Highway 6, signposted 5 km short of Lake Moeraki.

A historic cattle road, climbing into the high mist and memories of another time. It was once a Maori trail, then a cattle road until the early 1960s, and you can still see an old (renovated) roadman's hut and the remains of the telegraph line. Now it is a splendid walking track, with your only companions the ghosts of roadmen past, and the squawking of kaka.

From the Lake Moeraki end the track is muddy at first then connects onto a good packtrack that sidles through bush over to the big suspension bridge over the Moeraki (or Blue) River. Blowfly Hut (see photo overleaf) sits in a clearing. I did not notice the blowflies but I can vouch for the sandflies.

From here the excellently graded track starts its slow perambulations up to Maori Saddle hut. The forest is rich in rimu and silver beech and the birdlife is equally profuse. Kereru, tomtits, fantails, bellbirds and kaka add sound to a rarely silent forest.

Old totara posts on the trackside indicate the telegraph line, and the flat stones in the creeks were laid to make the passage of the cattle easier.

After an hour you reach the narrow Whakapohai Saddle, but the track keeps climbing steadily, meandering past several side-creeks, then descends a little to the spacious hut at Maori Saddle.

The hut stands in a cleared beech glade and has 12 bunks and a wood stove. It is a cosy place for lunch, especially as rain is not unheard of in this locality, and you have a long, easy romp downhill to look forward to.

170. MONRO TRACK & SHIP CREEK

Majestic wilderness beaches with pretty lagoons and rare pingao grass.

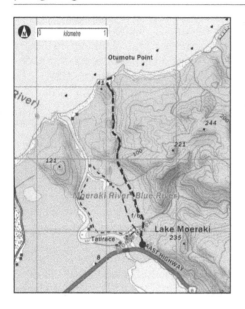

TRACK
Well made bush tracks, some beach walking.

WALK TIME AND DISTANCE
Monro Track 2–3 hours (5 km) return; Ship Creek 1 hour (1 km) return.

ACCESS AND FACILITIES
For the Monro Track follow Highway 6 to Lake Moeraki Wilderness Lodge and take the short signposted side-road to the carpark and information signs. No dogs.

For Ship Creek drive south from Lake Moeraki another 9 km. Ship Creek is about 10 km north of Haast. Carpark, shelter, toilets, information signs and lookout tower.

These are two fine beaches, only a few kilometres apart, and both can be enjoyed in an afternoon. Similar, but different, and the two of them illustrate much that is special and harsh about the South Westland coastal landscape.

MONRO TRACK

This enjoyable short walk is well graded, and plunges the visitor into a thick forest of mixed podocarps and coastal plants such as the kiekie vine. The beach is sandy, with the usual West Coast sea-rollers making it dangerous for swimming.

A colony of Fiordland crested penguins nest in the forest behind the northern part of Monro Beach; they are one of the world's rarest birds. The word 'penguin' comes from the Welsh 'pen gwyn' or 'white head'.

They nest several hundred feet up thick bush slopes and return to the same place year after year. They lay a clutch of two eggs in about August–September and the young birds are fledged by November–December and ready for an independent life. People are requested not to pass beyond the penguin sign if they see birds on the beach.

SHIP CREEK

At Ship Creek, a small tidal stream twists down through orange-red pingao-topped sand to the plunging sea. Driftwood stands crouched and polished. A lone headland shuts off access north at high tide, and south there is a long beach, so long you can hardly make out where it ends.

In fact it goes all the way to the Arawhata River, and once the settlers used it for taking their cattle up to the markets in Hokitika, via the beach and the Paringa cattle track.

The 'ship' has long been battered into nothingness. It was the stern part of the *Schomberg*, a wooden sailing ship that was wrecked off the coast of Australia in 1855; sections of the submerged ship drifted right across the Tasman.

In the evenings the sunsets give a brilliant shine to the dark tidal creek, and if it wasn't for the sandflies you'd stay for hours, absorbed in the scenery.

OTHER WALKS
Swamp Walk 1 hour, utter perfection.

Blowfly Hut on the Paringa Cattle Track (see page 241).

171. SMOOTHWATER BAY
Wet feet to a secluded bay

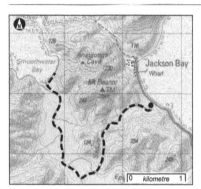

TRACK
A good, easy packtrack, then a river to follow. Wet feet are unavoidable — it is part of the joy.

WALK TIME AND DISTANCE
3–4 hours (6 km) return.

ACCESS AND FACILITIES
From Highway 6 follow the sealed road some 45 km to Jackson Bay. The Smoothwater carpark is 100 metres before the information shelter and toilets.

At the bottom of the West Coast is Jackson Bay, where today there are a few houses, a wharf and some fishing boats. Many tourists don't make it this far, but they probably should. An old packtrack goes over to Smoothwater Bay, a remote and lovely end-of-the-world sort of place.

Both Jackson and Smoothwater bays were sites for ill-fated government settlement schemes — Irish, English and German at Jackson Bay, mainly Scandinavian at the Waiatoto River, Italian at Okuru River, and Polish at Smoothwater Bay. What a beautiful land to fail in — and fail they did. Isolated and poorly equipped in a wretched climate, the colonists slipped away to somewhere more favourable (and presumably drier).

The track starts from Jackson Bay, following the old packtrack that was probably built by the Polish settlers in 1875. A gentle climb and fall.

The Smoothwater River is a wide, shining path, rarely more than knee-deep, and you walk on soft, easy gravels. On a sunny day splashing down the river is delightful. It is about 1.5 km down to the coast, crossing the stream maybe eight or ten times.

There is a marked flood track on the true right of the Smoothwater River if you want to reduce the chance of wet feet, but the river route is quicker.

The beach is a curvaceous curl of sand and there is a grass terrace overlooking the bay, where both you and the sandflies will no doubt enjoy an excellent lunch.

SMOOTHWATER–STAFFORD COASTAL ROUTE AND INLAND ROUTE
At low tide (mid-tide won't do!) you can walk south to the Stafford River and hut, and be rewarded by sea stacks and strange rock 'flowers'. Some scrambling involved over headlands which have marked tracks.

If you are keen then you walk up the Stafford River to Stafford Hut and pick up the well marked track that leads over the Stafford Saddle to the Smoothwater again.

This is an excellent but big day tramp. You need to be experienced and have a map, but no rain, and a low tide at Smoothwater Bay is essential. Allow about 7–9 hours for full circuit.

172. BUSHY BEACH
Gorgeous orange beach and penguins on parade

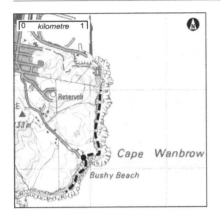

TRACK

Bush tracks, beach walking and low-tide platforms. Note that the clifftops are prone to erosion; maintenance has proved difficult and these tracks are sometimes closed.

WALK TIME AND DISTANCE

1–2 hours (4 km) return. A low tide is best for this walk.

ACCESS AND FACILITIES

From Oamaru take Tyne Street to the top of the hill, then drive via Bushy Beach Road to the carpark. Graves Walkway has been closed for some time due to cliff subsidence, but Bushy Beach at the south end of Graves Walkway is still a popular track.

At the harbour there is a grandstand for viewing the twilight penguin parade of little blues (korara) that scuttle across to the fenced-off burrows under the cliffs. Little blues weigh about 1 kg, with a height of 25 cm. There is a warden and a charge for viewing the parade.

This is a short, charming coastal track that features good views, a secluded beach and the home of one of the world's rarest penguins — the yellow-eyed penguin or hoiho. A striking bird, half a metre high, with yellow feathers around the eye and a yellow crown, this penguin weighs between 5 and 8 kg.

From the carpark the boardwalk trail meets a junction: one section goes around to the penguin viewing hide at Cape Wanbrow; another drops down to the beach.

From the hide a worn trail drops down the cape to the beach, and at low tide you can easily walk north along the attractive tidal platforms to the next headland. The track north of here is the old Graves Walkway.

Bushy Beach itself is a lovely run of orange sand (not kidding) with more tidal platforms to explore at the south end.

Both the little blue and the rare yellow-eyed penguin nest at Bushy Beach. The best time to watch for penguins is in the morning or late evening as they cross the sands. The birds will not come ashore if they see people on the beach. All penguins are vulnerable to disturbances throughout the breeding and moulting seasons, so follow the advice on the information boards, and watch from a distance at the specially made hide.

173. MOERAKI LIGHTHOUSE, KATIKI BEACH & SHAG POINT
Penguin peninsula and a beach of boulders

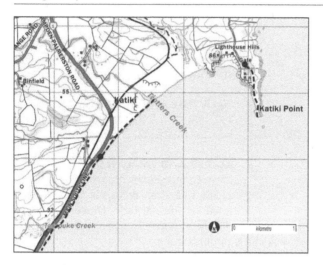

TRACK
Moeraki Lighthouse: grass paths and some scrambling; Katiki Beach flat, easy walking; Shag Point some rock scrambling. A good low tide is important.

WALK TIME AND DISTANCE
Moeraki Lighthouse: 1 hour (1 km) return; Katiki Beach 1–2 hours (3–4 km) return; Shag Point 2 hours (1 km) return.

ACCESS AND FACILITIES
For Moeraki lighthouse: from Moeraki village take the Lighthouse road 5 km to the carpark by the lighthouse itself. Moeraki has a motor camp, toilets and restaurant.

The coastline between Oamaru and Dunedin has many surprises, which the average punter who stays on the main highway will never enjoy. Apart from the famous Moeraki boulders, Highway 1 resolutely avoids the interesting places, so do yourself a favour and turn off to one of these places; Moeraki is a good choice. You'll find a pleasant fishing and holiday village, with a fish restaurant on the wharf.

MOERAKI LIGHTHOUSE
Follow the signpost over the hill to Moeraki Lighthouse, which is a great wee spot. The track descends past a viewing hide to an impressive coastline of rock platforms, sea cliffs and a surging sea. Notice the orange sand coves.
 The little peninsula will certainly see the cobwebs blown off, because it is rare not to get at least a breeze along this rugged coast.

KATIKI BEACH

Katiki Beach is a wild shore with its own mini-parade of Moeraki boulders. On the beach itself there's no sight or sound of the highway, and it is easy walking on the gorgeous wide sands. There are several rest areas alongside Highway 1. The two either side of Back Creek are good starting points.

There are many small, isolated boulders, but near the low cliffs you get an interfusion of tidal platforms and boulder shapes, with mini-domes encrusted with sea moss.

Concretions are formed by the precipitation of calcium carbonate around a small nucleus, like a piece of wood or shell, and can take millions of years to form. Because they are harder than other rocks, the surrounding mudstone gets washed away and the boulders become exposed, as on these lovely beaches in Otago.

SHAG POINT

Shag Point is a low headland south of Kaitiki Beach. It was once the site of one of Otago's largest coalmines, with half a million tons of coal extracted from undersea coal shafts from the 1860s to the 1980s. They also found a fossil plesiosaur here, a large marine reptile, inside a cretaceous concretion dated to between 65 and 135 million years old.

Once you've driven past the cribs and start exploring Shag Point, the beauty of the place becomes apparent. Massive tidal platforms are exposed at low tide, and shags flap vigorously along the coastal edge. There are pretty sandy coves, and fur seals loll about in lots of unexpected places.

The are several Moeraki-like concretions, but these Katiki concretions tend to erode from the inside out, and there are many stages of this process arrayed attractively on the low-tide rocks.

174. DUNEDIN CITY WALK — ROSS CREEK RESERVOIR
Mossy glen and still reservoir

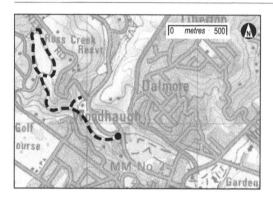

TRACK
Flat at first, then a short hill walk on a good gravelled track. Well signposted at junctions.

WALK TIME AND DISTANCE
1 hour (3 km) return.

ACCESS AND FACILITIES
From central Dunedin turn off George Street into Duke Street then Malvern Street, then Woodhaugh Street. Alternative access off Rockside Road.

An easy urban walk into a rich, fern-filled gully and up to the serene pond of the Ross Reservoir. This historic dam is one of only two working nineteenth-century dams in the country; the other is also in Otago, in the Eweburn. The Ross dam was built in 1867 of local stone and puddled clay, to supply the rapidly growing city of Dunedin, flushed with gold and hope. The artistic valve tower became a showpiece on picture postcards of the time.

The walk is a satisfying woodland promenade only 2 km from the city centre, and it would be true to say that it has remained popular for well over 100 years.

At Woodhaugh Street, where there is reasonable carparking, the track follows the Water of Leith (Leith Stream) past a boulder trap. Then it continues across a footbridge and on up past a quarry over another footbridge to the track junction with Rockside Road. There are some excellent information panels on the way.

The broad track now gets very shady and green as it climbs along the deep, mossy creek with brooding gorge cliffs above you. A last short steep climb up onto the dam and the seldom-rippled reservoir.

There is a circuit track around the lake, and the valve tower is worth a look. What is surprising is that after leaving the bustle of downtown Dunedin the view from the dam is almost completely rural.

OTHER WALKS

It would be relatively easy to connect the Ross Creek Reservoir tracks with the Dunedin Botanic Gardens, via Woodhaugh Gardens. Indeed, there are pleasant path connections and student backstreets that could be linked all the way alongside the Water of Leith to the University of Otago.

The valve tower, Ross Reservoir.

175. ORGAN PIPES & MOUNT CARGILL
Classic hill climb

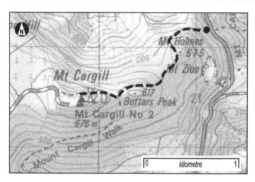

TRACK
A hill walk on a good gravel track, steep only at the beginning. Well signposted.

WALK TIME AND DISTANCE
2–3 hours (4 km) return.

ONE-HOUR WALK
Organ Pipes return.

ACCESS AND FACILITIES
From central Dunedin drive into the North East Valley up North Road, which blends into Norwood Street then Mount Cargill Road, almost to the ridgeline saddle. There is a pitiful carpark.

Mount Cargill has a central position in Dunedin's geography and psychology, helped no doubt by the massive 104-metre television transmitter tower. The mountain can be seen from many parts of the city and the peninsula, and the name — a reference to Captain William Cargill — taps deeply into the city's pioneering past. So it is a 'must do' walk, but it is also a very good walk with fabulous views and includes the Organ Pipes.

From the carpark there are steep steps, then the track settles down as it passes a rock cave before zigzagging up to the foot of the rock outcrop called the Organ Pipes. Curious yes, but overrated, and they seem rather small.

Large, segmented volcanic chunks are piled below the outcrop; indeed, some of these segments have been utilised thriftily to make the steps for the track.

The track is steady from here to a saddle and a side-track to Buttar's Peak (617 metres), with a good view on top. The native scrub is growing well up here and the views are getting less, with emergent totara and tall mountain cedars.

There is a flat section then a junction with the track to Bethunes Gully. The views in the tussockline are now very good, and the track sidles around the base of Mount Cargill and turns quickly to the summit.

This is not a beautiful place. There is an ugly assemblage of concrete boxes and unlovely metallic structures; but at the other end of the summit from the tower there is a rock outcrop that makes a fine rest area. On a fair day you need an hour to absorb the view, because practically everything can be seen.

176. SANDFLY BAY
The bay where sand flies and seals lie

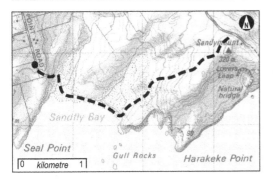

TRACK
Easy down to Sandfly Bay on farmland and sand dunes, but a steady hill climb
up to Sandymount carpark. No dogs allowed.

WALK TIME AND DISTANCE
1–2 hours (4 km) one way to Sandymount.

ONE-HOUR WALK
Sandfly Bay return.

ACCESS AND FACILITIES
About 18 km from Dunedin. Take Highcliff Road on the Otago Peninsula (which
leads to Larnach's Castle) and follow it to Pukehiki, and shortly afterwards take
Seal Point Road to a carpark at the road-end. Signposted.

There is alternative access via Highcliff Road, then Sandymount Road to
a high carpark. From here there is walking track access to Sandymount, The
Chasm and Sandfly Bay.

There is a strong sense of welcome as you cross the farmland towards Sandfly
Bay. The headlands' two strong arms seem to reach out to you, and the sand
and sea glitter. The gravel track drops quickly downhill to a lookout, then you
can let yourself go at the top of a huge sandhill, with a glorious romp down to
the beach plain.

There is much to see. The wind manufactures small ventifacts, rocks shaped
curiously by the abrasion of wind-blown sand, and everywhere the sand is
patterned in absorbing and delicate shapes. Sandfly Bay is named after the
wind, not the insects.

A small fur-seal colony exists on the far western end of the beach, and
there are yellow-eyed penguins. There is an observation hide behind the dunes,
though the birds are rarely seen except at dusk and dawn.

Just at this end of the beach a poled route climbs up through the sculpted
sand dunes to the scrubline. The obvious route follows a fenceline and a
250-metre climb up to the carpark at Sandymount. When you look behind, the
bay looks lovely.

177. TUNNEL BEACH
Sea cliffs, sea stacks and a whimsical tunnel

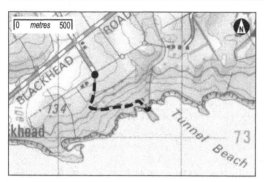

TRACK
A downhill walk on a gravelled and grass track, with afterwards an uphill slog to the carpark. A low tide is useful.

WALK TIME AND DISTANCE
1 hour (2 km) return.

ACCESS AND FACILITIES
From Dunedin follow Highway 1 to Green Island, then take the Brighton Road to just before Waldronville, and turn onto Blackhead Road about 3 km to Tunnel Beach Road, and carparking area. The track is closed for lambing from August to October.

If you are rich you can afford some eccentricity, and some privacy. Captain Cargill had a tunnel built through this sandstone headland in the 1870s to give his family exclusive access to their own private beach.

But now even we peasants can get there, and what a place it is — a powerful carved coastline of arches, sea stacks and sandstone cliffs, where the honey rock colours contrast with the wild blue sea.

From the carpark it is a steady downhill walk to the top of a broad sea arch, and views along the coast to other sea stacks. The tunnel has concrete steps and drops steeply to the surging bay. I do not fancy swimming here myself, and it is not recommended (Captain Cargill's daughter drowned here), but what a beautiful and battered shoreline. The only downside is the 150 metres of climbing needed to regain the carpark.

The cliffs at Tunnel Beach.

178. SUTTON SALT LAKE
Sliver of skinks and a sort of inland salty sea

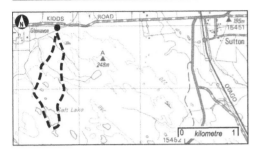

TRACK
Well marked tussock trail, mostly flat.

WALK TIME AND DISTANCE
1–2 hours (3 km) return.

ACCESS AND FACILITIES
From Highway 87, just south of Sutton, turn down Kidds Road and travel 2 km
to the signposted carpark.

You cannot equivocate with a place like Central; either it satisfies the soul or
it resembles a bleak wilderness. Here, even the sky has its own peculiarities,
with vast cauliflower cumulus clouds building over the Rock and Pillar Range.

And the salt lake is peculiar too, as far away from the sea as you can get,
yet rainwater runs over these arid rocks and brings out tiny traces of salt that
over years have accumulated and encouraged the odd situation of salt-tolerant
coastline plants fringing an inland lake.

The track is circular, threading through a tussock plain and schist rock
outcrops that every now and again hold a shiver of light where a skink had
been basking.

The occasional falcon
flicks high above, and if the
lake has water in it (sometimes it dries up) there will
always be a pair of paradise
ducks. The lake soothes
this desperately dry land,
and if it is hot, you will
probably want to quench
your thirst . . .

A lone walker at Sutton Salt Lake.

179. IDA BURN GORGE (OTAGO CENTRAL RAIL TRAIL)
An open-air history book

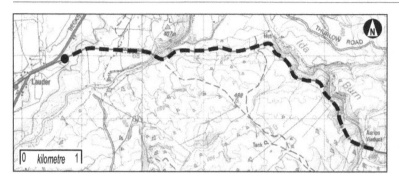

TRACK
Easy and flat, with a gentle climb on a gravelled track. Note: There is some confusion as to whether this gorge is the Pool Burn or the Ida Burn gorge. The topographic map clearly marks it 'Ida Burn' but the Otago Central Rail Trail brochure calls it 'Pool Burn'.

WALK TIME AND DISTANCE
3–4 hours (12 km) return.

ONE-HOUR WALK
40 minutes return to Manuherikia River bridge.

ACCESS AND FACILITIES
From Highway 85 at Lauder a signpost and a short road lead to a picnic area, passing a toilet on the way. Lauder's other main claim to fame is that it has the (officially) coldest recorded temperature in New Zealand — minus 25°C; but in compensation temperatures can also reach the high 30s during the summer — if that is compensation.

Old railway lines make excellent walking tracks, and the Otago Central Rail Trail is one of the best. Once the railway closed, the line was developed for mountain bikers. It is doubtful that you will want to walk the whole of it, but this is one of the best bits.

The trail wriggles alongside the pretty Pool Burn/Ida Burn gorge, negotiating two bridges and two tunnels on the way, and you pass through a landscape that is rarely seen.

The start of the rail trail is well signposted, just past the gun club, and it is about 1 km to the Manuherikia River bridge. This is a fine iron bridge, with an information panel detailing its history.

It is then a further 3 km to the Pool Burn gorge and the first tunnel. You could get away without a torch, but the tunnel has a kink in it so both ends are hidden, and you literally cannot see your hand in front of your face. You have to use it as a guide against the wall.

The second tunnel is 1 km further on, and straighter, and then it is a short distance to the Auripo viaduct, the highest on the entire rail trail — quietly spectacular.

A short distance further on the gorge ends, and there are views over the flat, soothing land. The lenticular rocks seem to mimic the saucer-like clouds, and this is a good meditative location in which to admire a land that has no equal in New Zealand.

A historic railway bridge on the Ida Burn gorge trail.

180. BUTCHERS DAM & FLAT TOP HILL
Wild lands and wild thymes

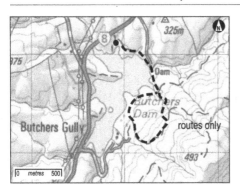

TRACK
Well graded, easy, 1 hour circuit; longer walk on farm tracks and through tussock to ridge.

WALK TIME AND DISTANCE
1 hour on short circuit; 2–3 hours (3 km) to ridgeline return.

ACCESS AND FACILITIES
Off Highway 8, 5 km south of Alexandra. Large carpark and information signs.

This track gives you quick, easy access to a typical Central Otago landscape. There is a superb 1-hour circuit track with excellent information panels on the geology, flora and fauna and gold history of this fascinating area. All around you there are expansive and stunning landscapes of rock and tussock.

From the carpark, cross the attractive dam with its permanent rainbow lurking below it. Beyond the stone hut, the main track quickly divides and a circuit can be followed through old gold workings.

Botanically, Flat Top Hill is interesting. There are 180 native vascular plants and several rarities, including a native forget-me-not.

What mostly thrives here, however, is the ghastly briar, the scented thyme, and the downright weird woolly mullein. If you are lucky, you might see and hear the endemic New Zealand falcon, and harrier hawks are often scouring the tussock for prey.

Beyond the main trail, there is a longer poled circuit which leads up into a strange landscape of rock tors that have an almost human-like quality; faces sometimes seem to peep out, or eyes seem to stare. These are the ghosts of shepherds and gold-diggers who moved through here — their hopes soon turned to stone in Otago's blighting weather.

Butchers Dam.

181. CATLINS RIVER TRACK
Silver river through an emerald forest

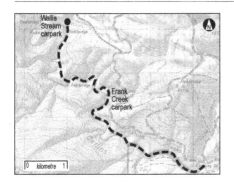

TRACK
Often flat travel on a forest trail beside the river, but some climbs over spurs and back up to the carparks.

WALK TIME AND DISTANCE
3–4 hours (9 km) one way from Wallis to the Tawanui camping area. 1–2 hours (4 km) one way from Wallis to Frank Stream carpark.

Full Catlins Wisp to Tawanui 5–6 hours. The signposted times seem pretty generous to me. If you take the Wallis to Frank Stream option you could walk back along the forestry road, which is quite easy and pleasant walking; about 3–4 hours for the round trip.

ACCESS AND FACILITIES
From Highway 92 turn onto Catlins Valley Road at Houipapa, about 8 km south of Owaka; well signposted. Follow the signposts some 6 km to the Tawanui camping area, where there are toilets and picnic tables. From here on the roads are forestry roads — gravelled and narrow but well maintained. It is about 7 km from Tawanui to the turn-off to the Wallis Stream carpark, and a steep 500-metre descent to the carpark itself. This last stretch can get muddy and a 4WD might be useful after rain.

The inland geography of the Catlins is a munched-up crazy paving of bush reserves, farmland, gum plantations and leftover logging areas. Some of the best forest left is alongside the Catlins River, which spins a silver thread through a mossy and green-bearded beech forest. The river is popular with anglers, and provides welcome seclusion from some of the Catlins' more squally weather.

At Wallis Stream the track passes the junction with the upstream track to the Wisp (great name!) and follows gently alongside the river. Here and there the river slicks over rock cascades, and the silver beech forest is healthy and mature.

After 1 km the track climbs steadily over a side-spur then drops down to a long footbridge over the river. Another 1 km or so brings you to another swingbridge and a track junction. It is a short climb up a gully to the main Catlins road.

Otherwise, continue downstream, with mostly easy travel apart from one short climb, some 5 km to the Tawanui camping area. A soothing walk.

182. PICNIC POINT & KINGS ROCK
Estuary and exploration

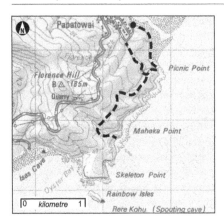

TRACK
Flat walking to Picnic Point on the beach or gravelled bush track, but there is a small hill to Kings Rock with some mud on the way. A low tide is almost essential to enjoy the estuary and rock platforms.

WALK TIME AND DISTANCE
2 hours (4 km) return to Kings Rock.

ONE-HOUR WALK
Picnic Point return.

ACCESS AND FACILITIES
From Highway 82 at Papatowai store (a remarkable place, selling everything including most foods, good wine, takeaways and petrol) drive through the crib-lined backstreets down to the foreshore and picnic area. There is a children's play area up the road a wee way.

The Catlins is a coastline that demands exploration, and rewards it. A quick drive through the area on Highway 92 (now fully sealed) will miss the magic of the place entirely. You will not see much coastline, or enjoy the wonderful Southland light that squabbles over and illuminates it. At Papatowai the Tahakopa River swings out into the bay and has manufactured a small, brilliant estuary at Picnic Point.

From the carpark wander out onto the low-tide sands of the estuary and head south. After less than 1 km is a seat commemorating local landscape painter Edna Robinson. There are some excellent tidal platforms here.

From the seat a very good bush track leads back to Papatowai. However, just past the seat is a track junction, and to go to Kings Rock the track starts to climb quite steadily through dense coastal forest.

You get occasional glimpses of the coast, then the track reaches a fence and farmland, and a poled route leads down a gully back to the shoreline. Kings Rock is obvious, and there are other rock platforms to explore. It does not look quite possible to return to Picnic Point via the rocks at low tide — but you could give it a go.

The beach at Picnic Point.

183. SLOPE POINT TO WAIPAPA BEACH
A severe and southern coastline

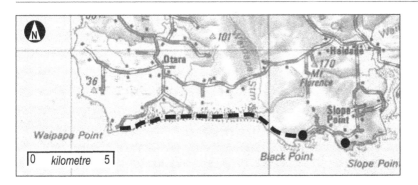

TRACK
Mostly flat on a 4WD sand road, beach travel and sand dunes. Take a topographical map: F47 Tokanui. It is useful to have a low tide, and there is some quicksand. It may not always be possible to cross the Lake Brunton outlet.

WALK TIME AND DISTANCE
2–3 hours (10 km) one way.

ONE-HOUR WALK
Waipapa Stream return.

ACCESS AND FACILITIES
From Invercargill turn off Highway 92 at Fortrose onto the coastal road to Waikawa Bay. It is about 10 km to the signposted turn-off to Waipapa Point and 20 km to the signposted turn-off to Slope Point. Follow the Slope Point road to the end, 2 km past Slope Point carpark and track, to a small turning area where the road ends by a 'Four Wheel Drive Vehicles Only' sign.

At Waipapa Point there is a carpark, toilets and information shelter.

A raw and restless coastline, with a long, wild beach and stark bits and pieces of human history — a cemetery built for a shipwreck, the bucket chain of an old gold dredge, a solitary lighthouse. This is not a comfortable walk, for Slope Point is the southernmost point of the South Island and gets blasted by winds that often have bits of Antarctica in them. But if you want something a little different, this will suit you.

At the 4WD sign follow the sandy road (a legal line) as it cuts through gorse some 2.5 km out to Waipapa Stream. If it is low tide you can probably sneak across the outlet without getting wet feet, but chances are you will have to take your shoes and socks off and wade across. Did I mention the quicksand?

It is strange stuff, not especially threatening, as it lies in a narrow margin of 1–2 metres alongside both sides of the stream. The sand looks solid but your feet puddle into it like porridge. Remember, there is no quicksand under the free-flowing stream water, so that is a safe haven.

Otherwise, for the cautious, walk upstream on the dune banks and cross higher up. One hundred metres past Waipapa Stream is the remains of a gold dredge, tucked behind the main sand dunes out on a flat and pondy area. All that is left is the bucket chain, which has obviously been restored to some extent. It is rather evocative, and worth hunting about for.

Waipapa Beach stretches a long way in front now, some 4 km to Lake Brunton, which may also have soft sand or quicksand by its outlet. When Lake Brunton is full and breaks out to the sea, the outlet becomes impassable.

About 1 km past the Lake Brunton outlet there is a slightly lower part of the sand dunes, and if you cross this area you should find the Tararua Acre.

This is a cemetery built to hold most of the 131 victims from the SS *Tararua*, which hit Otara Reef off Waipapa Point in 1881. It is a bleak, lonely scene matched by the loneliness of the little wooden Waipapa lighthouse, 2 km further along the beach, built in 1884 specifically because of the tragedy.

OTHER WALKS — SLOPE POINT

Off the Slope Point road there is a short signposted walk across farmland to the southernmost point of the South Island. There is a nice sign to take your photo by. 30 minutes return walk.

An old gold dredge, Waipapa Beach.

Kahikatea wetland, Thomsons Bush (see facing page).

184. INVERCARGILL CITY WALK — ESTUARY CIRCUIT
Wetlands and waders

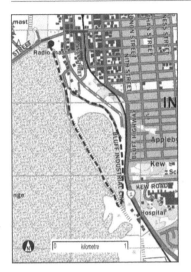

TRACK
Broad and firm gravel paths and boardwalk. Used by mountain bikes also. Eventually a combined walking and mountain-bike track will continue from here all the way to Bluff as part of Te Araroa trail.

WALK TIME AND DISTANCE
2-hour circuit.

ACCESS AND FACILITIES
From Invercargill drive down Tweed Street to the Stead Street bridge, and turn into the carpark and Scout Hall at the historic Stead Street Wharf beside the New River Invercargill Estuary. Excellent information boards.

This is a charming walk combining estuary views, wading birds, and insights into Invercargill's fascinating history. Spend a few minutes reading up about the replica steam train that originally ran on wooden rails, and the replica cutter that once served this busy wharf. There has been a massive revegetation of this once derelict area.

From the carpark the broad track wanders along the estuary edge 15 minutes or so to a track junction. Continue along the seaside embankment with occasional information panels that tell you this was once a popular bathing site.

Cross the footbridge over the tidal inlet and you reach another track junction — and useful shelter when the sou'wester blows. Turn onto the Roger Sutton Boardwalk that zigzags amiably across the inlet. Plenty of wading birds here, with large populations of black swans.

Where the boardwalk ends there is a link with a carpark and road, but the main track edges around the inlet with a good lookout seat at the end. The trail finishes by climbing up onto another carparking area (with seats) and the track meets the original trail and completes the loop.

OTHER WALKS
Thomsons Bush is a pleasant bush reserve beside the Waihopai River in Invercargill city, and has been much improved over the years. 1-hour stroll.

185. FOVEAUX WALKWAY
A blast at Bluff

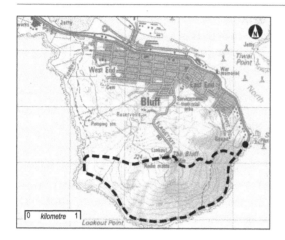

TRACK
Mostly good travel, on gravel tracks. Some mud.

WALK TIME AND DISTANCE
3–4 hours (5 km) return.

ONE-HOUR WALK
Glory Track in lovely rimu forest via the gunpit track return.

ACCESS AND FACILITIES
Drive from Invercargill to Bluff township, through to the Stirling Point carpark, world signposts, an impressive chain sculpture and the termination of Highway 1. There is a café and restaurant overlooking the carpark.

It is a rare day without wind on this track, something to do with the gale-force personality of Foveaux Strait. The trees get bent, and the sea thrashes along the coast. In compensation there are brilliant light bursts along the squally horizon, and a healthy forest with bellbirds and fantails enjoying the bracing climate.

From Stirling Point the track follows through coastal forest, past good information signs. Beyond the Glory Track junction, the track turns the corner to the Foveaux Memorial and the Millennium Track.

This track climbs steeply through bush up to Motupohue, or The Bluff, at 265 metres. Great views from the lookout. The dark shape of Rakiura/Stewart Island is omnipresent, and squalls blur the horizon.

For the downhill section, take the Topuni Track 20 minutes or so down to the Glory Track junction, then go past the old Second World War gun site back down to Stirling Point. A fine coastal circuit.

186. LAKE DIAMOND
Steep tracks to glittering views

TRACK
Well worn and marked tussock trails up a steep, short hill.

WALK TIME AND DISTANCE
2–3 hours (4 km) return.

40-MINUTE WALK
Lake Diamond lookout return.

ACCESS AND FACILITIES
From Wanaka, about 16 km on the Mount Aspiring road to a roadside carpark and signposts. This track is closed during the winter months, June, July and August. Toilet at Lake Diamond.

A rewarding shortish walk, from a secluded lake to hot tussock tops. It is almost a 400-metre climb to the high point, with a panorama of views over Lake Wanaka and arguably the best view of Mount Aspiring you will ever see.

Walk up the road to Lake Diamond, which is attractively fringed by willows and raupo. There's a circuit track around the lake, but otherwise follow the steep track under rock slabs to the lake lookout. Just past here the track divides, and a map signboard shows how the tracks follow a figure-of-eight pattern through the tussock.

Keep to the outer curves as the track climbs up through various rock bluffs, passing the link track, and then (and this is the best bit) sidling around the side of the tussock platforms to expose a stunning view of Mount Aspiring.

Then there is just a short walk up to the high point of Rocky Mount at 775 metres, and Lake Diamond glitters a long way below.

It's well worth enjoying lunch on top with all the hard work behind you, for easy trails descend past the nonchalant sheep back to the lake lookout and carpark.

The top of the hill and the view to Mount Aspiring, Lake Diamond walk.

187. ROB ROY GLACIER
Adventurous walk to ice and spectacle

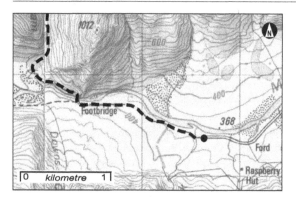

TRACK
A good walking track across the bridge and round to Rob Roy Stream, then it gradually gets rougher as it goes upvalley, degenerating into a tramping trail. A steady climb. There are several notable slips, which will probably not improve, and will freak out some people.

WALK TIME AND DISTANCE
3–4 hours (10 km) return.

ONE-HOUR WALK
Seat lookout by Rob Roy Stream return.

ACCESS AND FACILITIES
The Matukituki Valley road is an adventure in itself; good up to the Treble Cone skifield turn-off, it gradually becomes more basic. After a while the road seems to lose most of its gravel, and some parts can get heavily rutted or slick after rain. The major ford is at Niger Stream, by Mount Aspiring Station, and if you do not like the look of this then it might be wise to turn back. Beyond here there are four or five more fords before the road ends at the Raspberry Creek carpark. Heavy rain can make any of these fords tricky. It is 55 km from Wanaka and, as they say, half the fun is getting there.

The compensations for tackling the Matukituki River road are obvious. This is one of the finest mountain valleys in New Zealand, and you are not yet out of the car. Sharp slabs of mountains bracket either side of the valley, with snowfields suspended in the hanging basins. Waterfalls cut down the valley walls, and the sheer scale of the mountain scenery makes your neck ache. The Rob Roy track leads to a glacier and rock cirque, accessible and awesome.

From the large carpark the track skirts the riverbank to a swingbridge across the Matukituki River. There is a short section sidling through bush to a seat and lookout over the valley.

The track now climbs steadily up beside the Rob Roy gorge, and there are several slips where the track has disappeared and people have improvised trails across the wet mud and gravel slopes.

A seat marks the halfway point, then the track climbs less steeply, sliding past ribbonwood groves on old slips, and eventually up an old streambed of the creek into the alpine zone. It is not much further to a lookout with information panels — but really the view is language enough.

Sharks Tooth, Matukituki Valley, on the Rob Roy Glacier walk.

188. QUEENSTOWN CITY WALK — QUEENSTOWN HILL
Steady hill to a solitary sculpture and great views

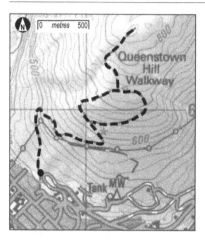

TRACK
Gravelled path, then tussock trails higher up. Total of 400 metres climb.

WALK TIME AND DISTANCE
2 hours (3 km) return.

ACCESS AND FACILITIES
Access is easiest (that is, highest) off Belfast Terrace which can be reached via Edinburgh Drive or Dublin Street. There is a carpark and information signs.

Queenstown Hill is a large, flattish, domelike peak on the eastern side of the town. Most visitors would not notice it, for it can hardly compete with the likes of Walter Peak and the Remarkables. But there is an excellent walk up it, plus a 'time walk', a sequence of information panels. The views anywhere above the treeline are tremendous, and this track is much less busy than Ben Lomond.

The walk is well signposted, and follows a 4WD track through pine forest up to a stylish wrought-iron gate. The information panels start here, and tell the history of Queenstown from early Maori to the present day.

At the first track junction turn right if you want to keep to the sequence of panels. There is a belt of dark forest of Douglas fir, then a rock lookout, then the track breaks out of the pine trees and into the broad tussock country up to a dainty tarn and a track junction. There is an alternative track back from the tarn.

On the left is a big metal sculpture, like a Maori kete (called 'the basket of dreams'), and a soothing view. For the high point, at 841 metres, continue past the tarn for about 20 minutes to the rock cairn. Every time I've been to the top there's been no one else around, so enjoy this breathing space above the hustle and bustle of Queenstown.

The cairn atop Queenstown Hill.

189. QUEENSTOWN CITY WALK — BEN LOMOND
A classic jaunt to the dominant peak behind Queenstown

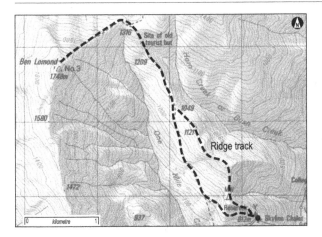

TRACK
Graded gravel path up to the saddle, then a solid foot-trail through the tussock and up to the peak. If you come back via the alternative Ridge Track this is well marked but has some steep drop-offs.

WALK TIME AND DISTANCE
From the gondola complex to Ben Lomond 4–5 hours (8 km) return; from town to Ben Lomond 6–7 hours (10 km) return. Total climb from gondola of 900 metres. Total climb from town of over 1300 metres.

ONE-HOUR WALK
Skyline Circuit and paragliding launch pad. This track is well signposted from the gondola over the luge. Roughly halfway around, take the paragliding track up to the launch site for excellent views.

ACCESS AND FACILITIES
Most people will go up the gondola and start from there, where the track is well signposted. If you want to save the cost of the gondola you can follow the access road from Lomond Crescent up some zigzags; at a junction, a foot-track links with the main Ben Lomond track.

Another alternative (particularly as a return route) is to go up through the attractive beech forest of One Mile Creek track, which links up with the main Ben Lomond track. This track starts about 1 km west of Queenstown, just past the youth hostel.

Lastly, from the gondola complex there is the Ridge Track, which climbs up past the paragliding launch area and onto a sharp crested ridge with rock outcrops, meeting the main Ben Lomond track 1.5 km at a saddle. This can be used as an alternative on the return, but it is suited to experienced walkers.

This is a classic hill walk to a 1748-metre peak behind Queenstown. There is a range of alternative routes and shorter options at the start, but they all coalesce near the saddle and there is no escaping the final heart-pumper to the rocky summit. It should be treated as a full-day tramp in fine weather. Take plenty of water.

Once you can tear yourself away from the cappuccinos and souvenirs of the gondola complex there is a good track that (somewhat surprisingly) sidles across the hill and even a little bit down.

Once through the pines it meets the historic packtrack, which went across to Moke Creek and the Moonlight goldfields in the 1860s. Already there are good views of Ben Lomond, and the route becomes obvious as the track climbs steadily past the Ridge Track junction and onwards to the main saddle at 1316 metres.

The saddle is a good lunch stop and turnaround place for those who do not fancy the last climb; allow 2–3 hours from the gondola complex.

The foot-trail to Ben Lomond is well worn, and negotiates around rock outcrops and tussock faces some 500 metres to the summit. There are no particularly steep parts, and it is easier and quicker than it looks from the saddle. An all-round vista of course. You have well and truly earned your cappuccino.

Nearing the top of Ben Lomond.

190. LAKE ALTA
Crystal alpine tarn deep in a circle of mountains

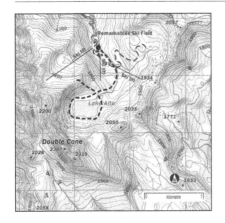

TRACK
Gravel trails and information boards. Before December there will still be patches of snow on the track, and the lake might well be frozen.

WALK TIME AND DISTANCE
1 hour return to Lake Alta (2 km).

ACCESS AND FACILITIES
From Queenstown drive to Frankton and then down Highway 6 to the turn-off to the Remarkables Ski Field and Rastus Burn Recreation Reserve (9 km). This road is kept open in summer and climbs up 6 km to just over 1500 metres, to the main carpark by the facilities base. Although it is a wide and well graded road, washouts and slips can occur, and drivers should take care at all times. Downhill traffic traditionally gives way to uphill.

At the carpark there is a public toilet (open in summer), information signs in the outside foyer of the base, and an intentions book beside the ski-patrol rooms.

There are few places in New Zealand where you can drive with such ease to such a magnificent setting. At the carpark there are impressive views of the rival skifield of Coronet Peak, and double-peaked Mount Earnslaw (2830 metres) on the left and Mount Aspiring (3033 metres) on the right.

From the carpark take the access road beside the ski-patrol room, as it curls around the back of the base and climbs into the basin. Ignore the first road on the right, but take the second after about 500 m. Footprints and the occasional yellow marker poles lead the way.

This road curves around to the top of the tow, and the nature trail starts here. There's a good worn track, and DOC usually replaces the information signs by early December.

This alpine wetland is fragile, and one hefty footprint can damage a lot of plants. Get down to the plants' eye level and marvel at the complexity of alpine mosses and flowers just in a single square metre. Some of the cushion plant flowers are only a millimetre across!

The track wanders up through rocks to a viewpoint that overlooks the unblinking eye-blue of the lake, trapped in a cirque of splintered mountains. Double Cone is 2307 metres high but you are standing at an altitude of 1800 metres, so the view does take your breath away.

OTHER WALKS
In fine weather you can scramble easily around this alpine basin, even up to the radio masts on a side peak at 2200 metres.

191. SAWPIT GULLY & THE MINERS TRAIL
Wandering water races and rollicking packtracks

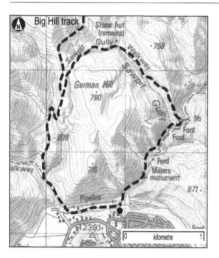

TRACK

A gravel track and tussock trails on the Sawpit Gully circuit, and steeper bush track on the Miners Trail. Good information boards at the carpark.

WALK TIME AND DISTANCE

2–3 hours (6 km) return for the Sawpit Gully circuit. Miners Trail add another 1–2 hours (3 km) for this longer loop.

ACCESS AND FACILITIES

Arrowtown is 20 km north of Queenstown via the Arthurs Point road, or via Lake Hayes. The town bustles with activity. The track to Sawpit Gully starts by the Chinese settlement carpark and information sign. Toilets, and good cafés in Arrowtown.

This is a walk steeped in gold history, as complex as the numerous water races that were constructed by the diggers of the 1860s. These gold-diggers made the track you walk on, supped grog in the ruined stone hut you rest by, and broke their bodies looking for the gold that you will more effectively capture in your photograph of the glorious evening light.

From the carpark, cross the small, pretty Bush Creek and follow the pipeline upriver past a multitude of 4WD tracks. There are steps over the pipeline, and the track wanders through maple and pine forest to a junction.

From here it climbs steadily out of the scrub and winds through a gully onto German Hill or Eichardts Flat. Wide-ranging views at the signposted junction of the Big Hill track.

The Sawpit Gully track follows past a ruined stone hut, then sidles down the creek to the lovely Arrow River gorge. The Miners Trail starts slightly upriver from here.

The river track cuts around schist bluffs, passes the monument to William Fox (the loudest discoverer of the goldfield) and returns to the Arrowtown carpark.

THE MINERS TRAIL

This newish track offers a longer walk back to Arrowtown. It starts from the footbridge, just upriver from where the Sawpit Gully track arrives at the gorge. Then it climbs steeply into, over and out of New Chums Creek, and picks up an old water race for a while.

The track climbs onto a wide broad ridge, and follows this with good views for 1 km. Then a short track drops down to meet Tobins Track. This broad easy road descends to Arrowtown, completing the longer loop.

Top: Water races over the hillsides on the Big Hill packtrack.
Above: Walkers on the Sawpit Gully circuit.

192. INVINCIBLE MINE
Golden views

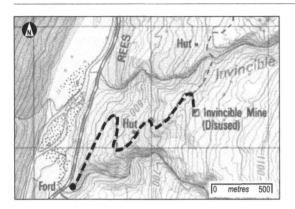

TRACK
An old vehicle and packtrack climbs steeply through beech forest and scrublands. Good track on a hot day as it is mostly shaded by beech forest.

WALK TIME AND DISTANCE
3–4 hours (3 km) return, which allows for some exploring. Total climb 500 metres.

ACCESS AND FACILITIES
From Glenorchy take the Glenorchy–Paradise road, and then the Rees Valley road some 15 km to the sign. One biggish ford to cross, wretched parking space. Access to the circular buddle is about 1 km further. This is an extraordinary shallow metal cone, some 10 metres in diameter, that separated the various ore materials. It looks quite unreal in the beech forest.

Heavy metal bands of the nineteenth century were rather different from those of today. They were groups of miners following the gold, or the antimony, or the serpentine, or whatever made a dollar, and it led them into spectacular locations.

The Invincible Mine has one of the best views anywhere. It looks down on the clean crystal waters of the Rees River, and across to the ramparts of snow underneath Mount Earnslaw, although one wonders if the miners had the luxury to enjoy the view.

From the roadside follow the track past the ruined tin hut and into the beech forest. The track was built in the 1880s so that heavy machinery could be hauled up to the mine, so it is a good easy surface.

About halfway up there is a derelict log cabin, then quite a few zigzags to the mine site. On the left there are seven berdans — revolving metal drums with heavy weights in them that ground the ore down. There is not much left of the battery, and the mine shaft is along a short track to the right. A grill blocks the entrance. The most notable things about this site (apart from the raw silence and solitude) are the mullock heaps, or tailings.

The Invincible was a going concern by 1882, with 10 stamps in the battery driven by an overshot waterwheel. Yields were good, and in 1884 another company processed the tailings, building a 679-metre chute (think about that for a minute — that is over 2000 feet!) to the valley floor. The material was sent down to a circular buddle for refining. By 1887, however, the quartz reef was 'lost'. The old brochure struck this little epitaph:

> Several other syndicates have tried to work the mine — notably in 1902, 1912 and 1922 — but all efforts to strike the reef came to nothing. In the long run it may be said that it was the reef which remained invincible.

And the view.

OTHER WALKS

The Glenorchy Wetland track is a flat, easy, magical gem. It starts right in Glenorchy and crisp boardwalks take about an hour for the circuit. Balmful and beautiful.

The historic scheelite mines area at the Whakaari Conservation Area (carpark 1 km before Glenorchy) is a magnificent mountain place to explore, with many track options leading to historic huts and scheelite workings. Half-day and full-day walks.

Ruined berdans, remnants of the Invincible Mine.

193. CHINAMANS BLUFF
Big mountain spaces and solitude, and the chance to see a mohua

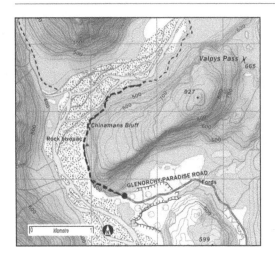

TRACK
Good track then open grass flats.

WALK TIME AND DISTANCE
2–3 hours (3–4 km) return.

ONE-HOUR WALK
1 hour return to rock bivs.

ACCESS AND FACILITIES
From Glenorchy take the Glenorchy–Paradise road and, once over the Rees River bridge, keep on Paradise Road (don't go to the Routeburn). This road is unsealed for about 16 km, with about six fords to the shelter and toilets beside the Dart River.

What a name to conjure with — 'paradise'. Well, this is not far off it, and this is the Southern Alps at its rawest. The striated faces of Mount Earnslaw loom over the carpark, while on the far side of the Dart River peaks like Mount Nox and

Mount Chaos stab into the clear air. In strong winds mini-tornados can skittle about the dusty gravel beds of the Dart River, and any cold southerly change can bring fresh snow to sprinkle on the mountains like icing sugar.

From the carpark cross the footbridge and follow the well graded track along the edge of the rock bluffs. There is a profusion of fern species along this section of the track, kept in perfect condition by the runnels of water draining from the rocks. It's quite an unexpected and lush fernery.

Once across a gantry, the track leaves the beech forest and turns onto a wide grassy flat beside the Dart River. It's like a door opening, with stunning mountains views into the Beans Burn valley.

There's a short walk across the flats and on the fringe of beech forest some informal trails lead up to two secretive rock bivouacs. Will you see a mohua?

These charming endemic bush birds, also called yellowheads, are now becoming very rare in the South Island, and this is one of the few places left they have been seen. Both male and female have bold yellow heads, and are gregarious, foraging in the canopy. The nest is usually in a hole high in an old or dead tree, with 2–4 eggs laid from October to December.

Beyond the rock bivouacs, the track winds up the Dart valley through beech and river flats as part of the five-day Rees–Dart circuit. It's certainly pleasant continuing for another hour or so, which gives you time to absorb the sheer scale of this mountain country.

Facing page: Mount Earnslaw provides an imposing backdrop to the carpark.

194. GERTRUDE SADDLE
An awesome alpine tramp

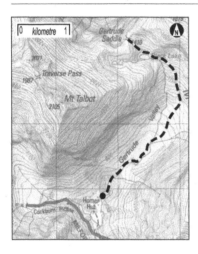

TRACK
A worn trail through tussock and rock, cairned but unclear in places. Near Black Lake there is a wire to hold onto. You need calm, clear weather to get to Gertrude Saddle itself, although the valley walk is straightforward in most conditions. Suited to experienced walkers and trampers.

WALK TIME AND DISTANCE
6–7 hours (6 km) return, total climb 700 metres.

TWO-HOUR WALK
To top forks return.

ACCESS AND FACILITIES
From Highway 94 to Milford Sound, turn off down the short gravel road before the Homer Tunnel to Homer Hut.

Fiordland is the most rugged part of New Zealand, the valleys so deeply incised it reminded the Maori of their facial moko, and they called it Te Rua-o-te-moko

— 'the pit of the tattooing'. In Gertrude Valley the glaciers carved painfully deep, with severe granite on every side, except for the goat path that climbs up to the saddle. This is a tramp rather than a walk.

From the Homer Hut carpark, take the signposted trail as it winds through boulders and crosses the (usually) dry streambed once, then trots along the west bank. You can move quickly through the beech forest and into open tussock with large boulders that sometimes attract rock wrens.

The sheer walls of the Gertrude Valley are awesome as the well defined trail reaches the top forks. The trail still sticks to the west bank, and climbs vigorously

Black Lake, on the Gertrude Saddle walk.

and crosses the Gertrude stream before sidling around towards the head of the valley.

Just before Black Lake there is a very short, steep section on rock and wire (which sounds worse than it actually is). The cable is well secured by DOC. The lake has a magical mirror effect on a good day. Less experienced or less confident walkers should consider stopping here.

Another thick cable has been bolted up the smooth rock slabs above Black Lake, but on a dry day the steep rock gives a good grip. At the top of the cable, sidle across easier slabs, then scramble up through the cairned rock piles onto the obvious low point that is Gertrude Saddle.

Stupendous views. A remarkable place.

195. MARIAN CASCADES & LAKE MARIAN
Dashing waters and an alpine lake in a Fiordland cirque

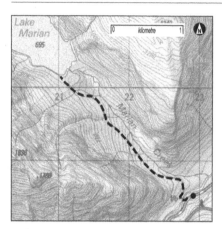

TRACK
Good at first, with boardwalks alongside the cascades, then getting much rougher towards the lake.

WALK TIME AND DISTANCE
1–2 hours (2 km) return for Cascades; 3–4 hours (6 km) return for Lake Marian. Total climb 400 metres.

ONE-HOUR WALK
Marian Creek cascades return.

ACCESS AND FACILITIES
From Highway 94 to Milford Sound, turn off 4 km down the Hollyford Road.

The cascades are a noisy, bubbling, frenzied collision of waters, quite in contrast to Lake Marian. This alpine lake lies in a deep trench, hemmed in by granite walls. Gulls sometimes penetrate here, but there is not much other sound to diminish the serious silence.

From the carpark, cross the swingbridge over the Hollyford River and follow the well gravelled track as it wanders through the thick rainforest. Moss literally drips from the trees.

After 15 minutes the track gets up on cantilevered boardwalks and verandahs bolted into the rock face, and overlooks the mossy boulders choking Marian Creek, with the water seething underneath. A fine and popular lookout.

It is much less popular to carry on to Lake Marian, and the track gets rougher as it climbs away from the creek. It crosses fern gullies, where there may be a bit of scrambling, and climbs almost 400 metres from the Hollyford road to the lake outlet.

There is a sheltered grass clearing on top of the rockfall that shuts the lake in, and a short track down to the lakeside itself. After heavy rainfall you cannot get near the foreshore, but usually the lake level is low enough to walk around. Rocks provide a backrest for lunch, and you are almost above sandfly level. It is like another world.

OTHER WALKS IN THE MILFORD AREA
The Chasm, 20 minutes return; Homer Tunnel nature walk, 15 minutes return.

196. KEY SUMMIT
One of the best

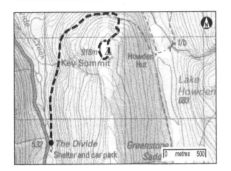

TRACK
A well graded track and boardwalks.

WALK TIME AND DISTANCE
3–4 hours (5 km) return.

1.5-HOUR WALK
Track junction.

ACCESS AND FACILITIES
From Te Anau drive north on Highway 94 to the start of the Routeburn Track at the Divide Saddle. Shelter, toilets and carpark.

There is a dainty sprinkling of tarns on this alpine wetland, which overlooks three great valleys — the Hollyford, the Greenstone and the Eglinton. Maori on war parties to the West Coast and carrying greenstone out of it; early settlers looking for cattle country; and goldminers looking for gold all traipsed this way. Now it is walkers and tourists who make the trek up to Key Summit and admire the rugged panorama.

From The Divide carpark the well graded track (which is also the start of the Routeburn Track) climbs up through silver beech forest with ribbonwood and tree fuchsia. The fuchsia has distinctive bell-shaped red flowers in summer. There are several streams to cross, bubbling over pretty waterfalls.

It is about an hour of gradual climb to the turn-off to Key Summit itself, and there are reasonable views here. It is quite a crossroads on a busy summer's day, with walkers and trampers stopping for a breather and a gossip.

From the junction the track climbs up through open slopes of flax and tussock, and there is an easy circuit with plastic information sheets that you can pick up then deposit on the way down.

Tarns and walkers on the trek up to Key Summit.

The main track reaches a boardwalk around a beautiful tarn with bog cushion plants, mosses and the alpine sundew. A plane table helps you identify the mountains.

The little circuit track goes through pockets of beech forest shaggy with hanging lichen, and continuously enjoys a panorama of mountain scenery that is breathtaking — the Darran Mountains, a bit of Lake Marian and the great elongated valley of the Hollyford River.

197. LUXMORE HUT
Garden path up to tussock downlands

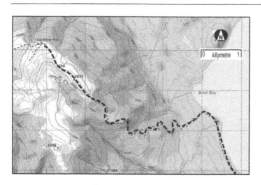

TRACK
An extremely well made, graded track on a steady climb up through the bush, then some boardwalk on the tussock tops.

WALK TIME AND DISTANCE
7–8 hours (18 km) return.

ONE-HOUR WALK
Dock Bay return.

ACCESS AND FACILITIES
From Te Anau take the Manapouri Road for 5 km, turning off to the signposted Control Gates. These are a little removed from the carpark and you have to walk down to them.

If walking from the Fiordland National Park Visitor Centre in Te Anau, there is a lakeside path that goes past Te Anau Wildlife Centre and continues around to the Control Gates. About 45 minutes (4 km) one way.

Note: You can get water-taxis and pick-ups from Te Anau to Brod Bay, saving an hour's walk each way.

This track is a veritable garden path, climbing from the glistening Lake Te Anau to the undulating tussock hills around Luxmore Hut. Despite the 1000-metre climb, and the altitude (1200 metres above sea level), the quality of the track enables many people to visit this alpine region in a day return. The views of the lake and the remote Murchison Mountains are certainly worth the effort.

Cross the Control Gates and follow the gentle lakeside track as it wanders through tall red beech forest. There are occasional footbridges and plenty of birdlife as you pass the Dock Bay picnic and camping area and go on to Brod Bay beach and shelter. This is a sparkling little bay, slightly spoilt by the hungry sandflies.

Now the climbing starts, in gentle lazy zigzags up the thick-forested hillsides. Not many views, but about two-thirds of the way up you reach a limestone bluff, with some fossils in the rock. It is about 100 vertical metres now to the bush edge, and the track has got squelchier and the forest has changed.

It is a wonderful moment when you burst out onto the rolling downlands, and the slopes are gentle as the track follows boardwalks and tarns another kilometre to the palatial Luxmore Hut.

With 60 bunks it is rather a wart on the landscape, but there are fine views from the verandah and lounge. A good place for lunch and a brew-up before the long lollop downhill.

198. SHALLOW BAY

Sphagnum moss swamps, dragonfly heaven and an enchanted lake

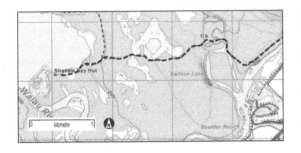

TRACK
Well made tracks.

WALK TIME AND DISTANCE
3–4 hours (8 km) return to Shallow Bay.

ACCESS AND FACILITIES,
From Te Anau drive south on Highway 95 for about 12 km to the Rainbow Reach carpark and footbridge. This is also one end of the Kepler Track.

Manapouri is the fifth largest lake in New Zealand, called originally by Maori Roto-ua (the rainy lake) and Moturau (many islands). The eastern end of the lake was a favoured food-gathering area for Maori, and with its inlets, scattered bush islands and rain-filled mists, Manapouri has a degree of enchantment about it. It is many people's favourite lake.

From the Rainbow Reach carpark the track (which is the main Kepler Track) crosses the swingbridge and follows the Waiau River downstream in the fertile river terraces. Red beech and mountain beech with a thick carpet of crown ferns make up the forest here, as the track wanders around Balloon Loop, a side channel of the Waiau.

The track crosses the Forest Burn and climbs slightly to an attractive sphagnum moss swamp and lake, which is a piece of dragonfly heaven. The lake is called a 'kettle lake', and was formed when a large block of ice from a glacier was isolated and trapped on the glacial moraine.

Sphagnum is a plant with peculiar properties. It can absorb up to 20 times its own weight of water, so it is useful for the flower and potting market. It is also sterile, and was used for bandages in the First World War, and has now found a modern use in sanitary pads. Sphagnum has no root system, and comes in many species, textures and colours.

After the moss swamp the track reaches a signposted junction, and the Shallow Bay track drops down to the lakeside and follows along the gravel beach to the battered and well used six-bunk hut.

Bush birds can be plentiful: tui, bellbirds, rifleman, grey warblers, fantails, tomtits, native pigeons, fernbirds and parakeets can often be heard and frequently seen. But it's the rippling vistas across the lake waters that catch the eye and soothe the senses.

199. BLUE CLIFFS BEACH
Remote Fiordland coast with old-time cribs on the driftwood shore

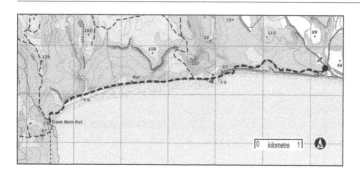

TRACK
Good track at first, then beach walking to the Track Burn. A low tide is useful, though you can walk along the old road at high tide.

WALK TIME AND DISTANCE
3–4 hours (12 km) return along coast to Track Burn and 'smoko' shelter. This is the main access route to the Hump Ridge Track and Port Craig with many tramping options.

ONE-HOUR WALK
To Waikoau seaside cribs.

ACCESS AND FACILITIES
From Tuatapere township turn onto the Papatotara Coast Road, and drive 14 km to the Rowallan Burn to reach Blue Cliffs Beach Road. Drive 4 km up onto the terrace to the large carpark and signboards.

It feels a bit like the end of the world on the Blue Cliffs beach, and it practically is. There is only Rakiura/Stewart Island between you and Antarctica. The sea has been gnawing away at the beach for a long time, and quite successfully, for parts of the old road have been swallowed up, leaving the shore even more wild and remote.

Initially the well constructed track stays on the high terrace, before dropping down to a long footbridge over the Waikoau River. There are several old fishermen's cribs on this small spit, and some of them look as if they have been washed up by the tide itself.

From here you can follow the old gravel road, but at low tide it's much more enjoyable on the beach. Driftwood has been twisted into sculptures, and the golden sands have dark channels where the occasional side-creek runs down through the coastal forest. You'd stop and linger, if it wasn't for the murderous sandflies.

After an hour you reach the Hump Burn, and cross via another footbridge. By following the road briefly for 10 minutes you reach a private crib, with a public 'smoko' room and logbook. Another footbridge crosses the Track Burn here.

OTHER WALKS

There's a wealth of landscape to explore if you have more time. Thirty minutes on is the junction to the main Hump Ridge Track, and the boardwalk leads you through some superb lowland rimu forest.

Or you could head on another 30 minutes from Hump Ridge junction to the next bay, cross the short headland and arrive at a magnificent beach called the Blowholes. If you reach here don't forget about the tides!

Port Craig can be reached by fit people in a very long day tramp, about 10–12 hours (22 km) return from Blue Cliffs carpark.

Walkway on Blue Cliffs Beach.

200. ACKERS POINT
A historic cottage on the way to a lighthouse peninsula

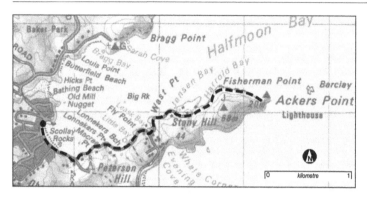

TRACK
Road walk then gravelled path. Some seats.

WALK TIME AND DISTANCE
1–2 hours (6 km) return.

ACCESS AND FACILITIES
Stewart Island/Rakiura can be reached by ferry (slow and rough) or plane (fast and not so rough). People with good stomachs or motion-sickness pills will enjoy going over one way and returning the other.

Halfmoon Bay is a beautiful languid settlement, softly tucked into the bush hillsides. Most of New Zealand's best bush birds are perched about the houses as if they own the place, which is probably half right. Not too many cars, with only 25 km of roads, and electricity has quietened the generators.

From the settlement foreshore, follow the coastal road around the south edge of Halfmoon Bay as it wanders in and out of small bays. In one eucalyptus grove there is a loud colony of kaka, and it is quite likely you will see individual birds up close as they tear at the tree bark for grubs. Tui and kereru (native pigeons) are equally abundant.

The coastal road climbs up and ends at a stile and signpost, after which an excellent gravel track continues, sidling past Ackers stone cottage. This historic cottage, built in 1834, is worth the short detour.

The main track cuts around Fishermans Point (good seat here) then out to the lighthouse at Ackers Point, where there are information boards about the little blue penguins and sooty shearwaters, which return to their burrows here at dusk. The views towards Bluff are sometimes sharp, sometimes hazy.

201. MAORI BEACH
Coastal bridle path to a bonny bay

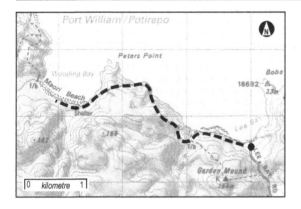

TRACK
Mostly flat walking with some mud.

WALK TIME AND DISTANCE
2–3 hours (6 km) return to Maori Beach.

ONE-HOUR WALK
Little River beach return.

ACCESS AND FACILITIES
From Oban walk/drive over to Horseshoe Bay, then take the road to Lee Bay to the start of the Rakiura Track (5 km).

This far south the sky has a luminosity you do not find anywhere else. Maori called Stewart Island Rakiura — 'land of the glowing skies' — which is poetic and appropriate, and this walk along an old bridle path takes you out of the scant settlement of Halfmoon Bay into a wilderness of beaches and light.

The Rakiura Track to Maori Beach starts from Lee Bay (through the *Anchor* sculpture). The track is well graded, as it was once the main land route to the sawmill settlement at Maori Beach. Birdlife is usually vocal, with bellbirds, native pigeons, chattering parakeets and kaka.

After a kilometre, southern rata is particularly evident around the pretty Little River estuary. There is a footbridge, but at low tide the track skirts the sand. Upstream from the bridge there is a pleasant picnic area and a toilet.

Now the track climbs steeply, and there are glimpses of the bouldery coastline as it wanders across the headland at Peters Point and drops abruptly to Maori Beach. At a lower tide you can cross directly to the beach, but there is a very muddy high-tide alternative track.

Maori Beach, 1 km long, is elegant between its headlands. Behind the beach a massive boiler remains from the days of the sawmill.

OTHER WALKS

It is 2 km on to Port William, with a 150-metre climb on the way. Port William was the site of a failed government-sponsored settlement in the 1870s, but today gum trees are the only reminder. There is a hut, jetty and picnic areas. Add another 2 hours return.

Top: Taking a rest on Maori Beach.
Above: Sydney Cove, Ulva Island (see facing page).

202. ULVA ISLAND
Birds on paradise

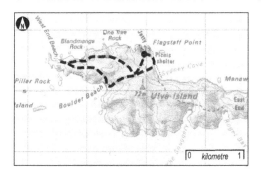

TRACK
Well maintained bush tracks.

WALK TIME AND DISTANCE
Boulder Beach return 1 hour (1 km); West End Beach 2 hours (2 km) return.

ONE-HOUR WALK
Nature walk via Sydney Cove and lookout.

ACCESS AND FACILITIES
You need a water-taxi. Check at the DOC information office for times and prices. Obviously the amount of time you spend on the island depends on your arrangement with the water-taxi, but if the weather is fine you should take lunch and make it a 3–4 hour session. Information panels, toilets and shelter on the island.

In the middle of the moody, atmospheric, inland sea of Paterson Inlet, Ulva Island has been turned into a sanctuary for birds and plants. Predators such as rats and stoats have been eliminated from the island, and when the sudden Stewart Island squalls break and illuminate the forest in gold, you feel that this is a suitable place for a refuge.

The water-taxi drops you at the wharf, and past the information signs you can wander at will on the tracks. Dense podocarps go down to the water's edge and mingle with bright strips of sand. The birds flourish and sing at this lonely outpost, as they might have sung thousands of years before. And the birds take absolutely no notice of you.

I watched baby bellbirds chasing their mum for food, brown creepers doing exactly what their name suggests only a metre from my nose, and kaka hacking pleasantly away at the old tree bark. Tui, parakeets, fantails, all are here, sometimes even a kakapo.

So for those few people who make this long journey down to the near conclusion of New Zealand — and to the end of this book — the rewards are immense.

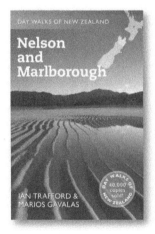

THE
OLD WAYS OF
CUMBRIA

HISTORY & LANDSCAPE

BETH & STEVE PIPE

AMBERLEY

Every attempt has been made to seek permission for copyright material used in this book. However if we have inadvertently used copyright material without permission or acknowledgement, we apologise and will make the necessary correction at the first opportunity.

First published 2019

Amberley Publishing, The Hill, Stroud
Gloucestershire GL5 4EP

www.amberley-books.com

British Library Cataloguing in Publication Data.
A catalogue record for this book is available from the British Library.

ISBN 978 1 4456 8678 3 (print)
ISBN 978 1 4456 8679 0 (ebook)

Typesetting by Aura Technology and Software Services, India.
Printed in Great Britain.

CONTENTS

INTRODUCTION AND ACKNOWLEDGEMENTS

This book has been several years in the planning. We initially had the idea back in 2014, but it's taken a bit of refining to get it to what you're holding now. The journey of this book is almost as interesting as some of the routes within it. When we were researching an earlier book, we came across a small book from 1996 by Jack Woods titled *The North Road*, which describes in detail the route of the old road from Kendal to Shap. In the introduction he mentions that he sent an early draft to Alfred Wainwright, who replied with a very complimentary note and mentioned how it inspired him to publish a small book he'd been working on for some time, *Old Roads of Eastern Lakeland*.

As big fans of ancient routes we tracked down a copy of Wainwright's book and, as we began exploring the routes, we realised that more people would be interested in what we were discovering. The original book was, as the title suggests, very focused on the eastern part of the county, so we combined a few of his routes and added a few extras of our own – The Cistercian Way, Ambleside to Ravenglass and Carlisle to Bowness-on-Solway were our additions.

We have walked all of the routes described and, although this isn't strictly speaking a walking book, the routes we took should be easily identifiable from an OS map. We've added large-scale maps to give you a rough idea where the routes are but do please take your own. When exploring the old routes, we were struck by how practical they were; this wasn't a time of walking for pleasure, this was about getting from A to B in the most efficient manner, so the routes tend to stay low as long as possible, before nipping up and over the high parts.

There was also a lot of incredibly interesting history to be found along each and every route that it's been a challenge to cram it all in. While we've mentioned the better-known stories and events, we've tried hard to dig out lesser-known facts and focus on activities that we can still see evidence of today.

As well as thanks to Jack Woods for his original book, and, of course, to Wainwright, a huge debt of gratitude is owed to the many local history groups who conduct valuable research and make it freely available online, particularly Patterdale Today, who were immensely helpful when it came to my unhealthy obsession with Chapel-in-the-Hause! Enormous thanks are also due to Cumbria Libraries who are under-resourced but are an absolute treasure trove of information, help and support.

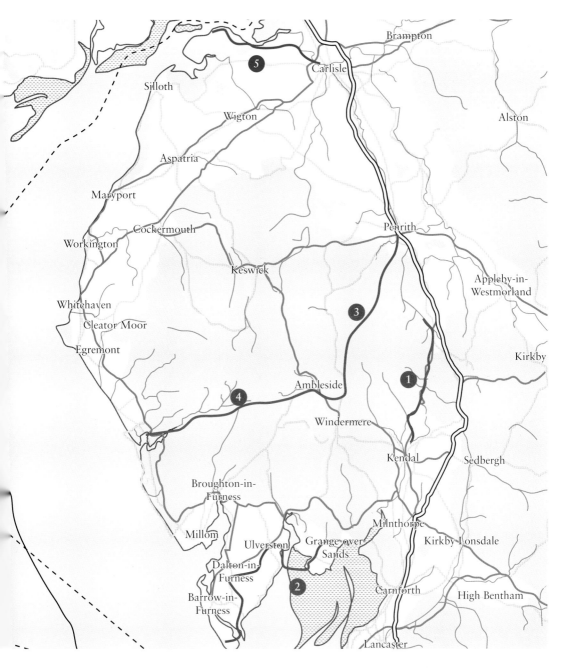

Key

1. The Old North Road
2. The Cistercian Way
3. Roman Road Part I – Penrith to Ambleside
4. Roman Road Part II – Ambleside to Ravenglass
5. Carlisle to Bowness-on-Solway

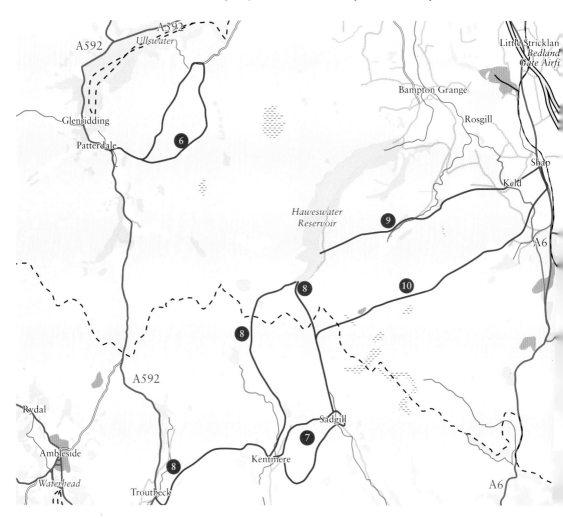

Key

6. Martindale and Patterdale
7. Kentmere and Longsleddale
8. The Three Passes – Garburn, Nan Bield and Gatescarth
9. Haweswater to Shap – Old Corpse Road
10. Longsleddale to Wet Sleddale – The Old Quarrying Routes

1. THE OLD NORTH ROAD

Introduction

We have long been fascinated with this route and it's fairly easy to pick it out on an OS map, as it winds back and forth across the present-day A6. Pretty much all of it is still accessible to walkers, and regular buses run between Shap and Kendal if you only fancy doing 12 miles one way or don't want to juggle cars. We walked it from Kendal to Shap but there's a lot more downhill if you walk it the other way around...

The Route

We started at Otter Bank where there's a large layby and a clearly signed path leading off parallel to the A6. Wainwright's account begins just to the south of Plough Farm, and the buildings there can be seen on Ogilby's Britannia Map from 1675, although it wasn't a farm

Bannisdale.

back then; it was an inn providing much needed refreshment for the weary traveller. Today the modern road turns sharply left while the old road continues straight on, through open fields, to Bannisdale and the site of another old coaching inn, The Bay Horse. According to one source, Bannisdale got its name from an early Nordic settler who was somewhat feisty and regularly invoked the gods to curse anyone he fell out with. His nickname was 'Bannandi', meaning 'the man who curses', and the area became known as 'Bannandi's Dale' and later Bannisdale.

From there, the route takes a sharp left at Thorn Cottage, before rejoining the A6 near Kids Howe, and continuing north over High Borrow Bridge to Hause Foot.

After heading up to the TV Repeater Station and crossing the A6 again, the Old Road throws up a few reminders of life before the petrol engine. Half buried in the grass on the right of the track is an ancient mile marker; Wainwright mentions that it's possible to make out the number '10' on it but although we found the stone, we struggled to decipher anything legible. Then there's Packhorse Hill on the left, where the horses, having slogged all the way up the valley, would have been allowed to take a short break before a nice downhill stretch to the beautiful Wasdale Old Bridge.

After rejoining the A6, the last stretch of the Old Road forks off right, before looping down through the site of Shap Granite Works and continuing north under the new A6. Our route ended in the centre of Shap, where there's a decent car park, a bus stop and an award-winning chippy.

Ancient mile marker.

The History

Sometime during the thirteenth century, a landowner in Shap provided land for a road to be built southwards towards Kendal. This was no easy undertaking, as much of the area it needed to cross was either boggy, rocky or both. As with many old routes, it evolved from a combination of farm tracks and communications routes between local communities, which all joined together to create a long distance road, though we can't think of it in the same terms as a modern road.

'Roads' were originally meant for feet, packhorses and sleds – before carts became common place flat wooden sleds were the preferred mode of transport for peat, hay, mineral ores and slate. Outside of the towns, the responsibility for maintaining these roads fell to the local landowners who would be pressurised into keeping them in some sort of acceptable condition by the people who used them. Of course, they weren't always keen to maintain a route that they personally didn't often use, and records show regular court orders were made forcing them to resolve a particular issue or face a substantial fine. In 1669, the Kendal Quarter Sessions ordered the owners of land on either side of the North Road to '... cut and flash their hedges hanging into the way under pain of 10 shillings each'. They obviously didn't learn their lesson as the same order was made again in 1703.

There were no nice smooth surfaces either, meaning that in anything other than warm, dry weather the going would be difficult, however you were travelling. Back in the days before rubber wellington boots and raincoats, the lucky well-to-do folks would wear heavy woollen long coats with leather boots and the labourers would have to make do with wooden clogs bound with iron. Those travelling by coach would have had it a little easier but if the coach got bogged down in mud or snow, the passengers could often be called upon to help dig it out.

Old North Road and modern A6 near Huck's Bridge.

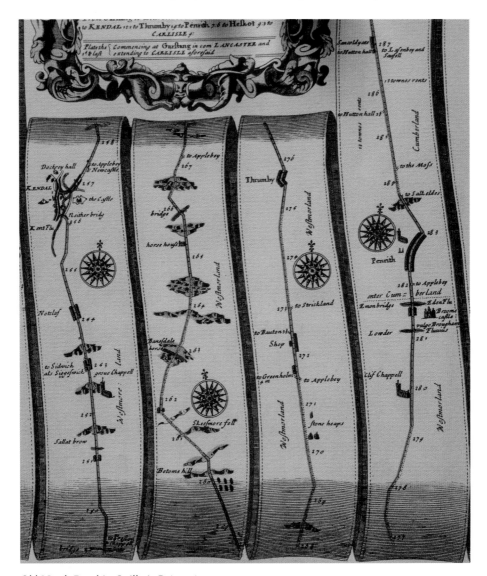

Old North Road in Ogilby's *Britannia*.

The route of the Old North Road was recorded in 1675 by John Ogilby in his spectacular book *Britannia*, the first map of all the major roads in England, and many of the landmarks he identifies are still visible today. It would be very easy at this point to get sidetracked into telling you a lot more about Ogilby and his fascinating past, which included using lottery winnings as a child to begin a career as a dance instructor in order to bail his father out of prison for debt, founding the first theatre in Ireland, narrowly avoiding getting blown up in the Irish Rebellion, getting shipwrecked, moving to London, and having his house burnt down in the Great Fire. All before being appointed 'His Majesty's Cosmographer and Geographic Printer' and producing *Britannia* in 1675. It was meant to be the first of three volumes but sadly he died the following year. Safe to say he had an interesting life and is well worth learning more about. But back to the Old North Road ...

Today we might walk from Shap to Kendal for pleasure or fitness, or to see wildlife, but that is a modern phenomenon. In the past walking was the only option for the majority of the population; coach fares were too high for regular working-class folks and carts, etc. were for transporting goods, not people.

Not that those journeys were always easy. The poor state of the Old Road has its place in British history, as it was used by the army of Bonnie Prince Charlie, fleeing the Duke of Cumberland's forces in 1745. The weather and heavy going caused a lot of problems for their carriages, and a number of them were bogged down overnight. Some lightened their load by dumping cannonballs into local lakes or paying 'sixpence to every man who could carry cannon balls'. It's said that some local farms still have cannon balls serving as ornaments and door stops.

In the late 1700s, the Turnpike Trusts were formed across England so the money raised from tolls would address these issues and pay for the upkeep of the roads. In 1815, the Heron Syke Trust, responsible for the Old North Road, borrowed £17,000 (over £1.4 million in today's money) to improve the road. There were two major roadbuilders to choose from at that time: Telford and McAdam. The trust selected McAdam on the grounds that he was the most cost-effective. He redesigned the route all the way from Heron Syke (near Burton, south of Kendal) through to Shap, and his key aims were to reduce the gradient of the road and improve the drainage, both of which he achieved.

Travel was very much improved and toll records show that traffic doubled in the years after the road was finished. The new road (now the A6) also cost a lot less to look after with maintenance costs falling by a third. It wasn't all good news though. For a start, speed wars broke out when, in 1823, the North Mail (a popular coach of the time) shaved forty-five minutes off the journey time from Kendal to Carlisle, reducing it to just five hours fifteen minutes. In 1831, it was reported that £2 10s had been collected from 'fines for furious driving'.

As the roads improved so more people used them, both tradespeople and visitors alike as, for the first time, it became easy for people from towns and cities to access more remote communities, and vice versa. New influences were seen in buildings, furniture, fashion and literature and, as is human nature, many people were resistant and suspicious of such

Near Plough Farm.

Above: Looking along old road towards the steep gradient at Hause Foot, and the gentle gradient of the new road along the hill on the right.

Below: High Borrow Bridge.

changes. On 17 April 1819, the *Westmorland Gazette* reported that 'We have not less than 60 arrivals and departures of coaches to and from this town in a week' and there's no denying that the increased visitor numbers were a benefit to the local economy in the same way then as they are today.

In an effort to boost the local economy still further some trades, such as those involved in the wool industry, were exempt from toll charges but the tolls were still not popular and some farmers preferred taking detours via Nan Bield or Gatesgarth Pass to paying the fees.

The heyday of the toll roads couldn't last forever, and in 1846 the Preston to Carlisle railway opened, providing a quicker and easier mode of transport. As a consequence, toll takings plummeted, although the A6 remained the main route from the north-west into Scotland until the M6 opened in the 1970s. People who travelled along it back then remember colossal traffic jams from Shap to Kendal caused by poor weather in the winter and visitor numbers in the summer.

Throughout its history it's been a hotspot for accidents with many coaching accidents occurring in the eighteenth and nineteenth centuries due to the poor conditions of the Old North Road. Even its modern replacement has been the site of a number of notorious incidents, including the worst road accident in the region, which occurred in August 1953 when a coach plummeted down the rocky hillside near to Huck's Brow, sadly killing seven people and injuring many more.

These days, with the majority of traffic now racing along the nearby M6, the A6 from Kendal to Shap is usually a pleasant and uneventful drive. If you don't fancy exploring the whole route, there are plenty of laybys where you can park up and wander along the quiet valleys on either side of the route. Near to the highest point on the road is a large layby on the right (as you're travelling north), with a lovely stone as a fitting memorial to all the people who helped make the route possible.

Wasdale Old Bridge.

Above: Steep embankment near Huck's Brow.

Below: Memorial to those who created the new road.

THIS MEMORIAL PAYS TRIBUTE TO
THE DRIVERS AND CREWS OF VEHICLES
THAT MADE POSSIBLE THE SOCIAL
AND COMMERCIAL LINKS BETWEEN
NORTH AND SOUTH ON THIS OLD AND
DIFFICULT ROUTE OVER SHAP FELL
BEFORE THE OPENING OF THE M6
MOTORWAY.
REMEMBERED TOO ARE THOSE WHO BUILT
AND MAINTAINED THE ROAD AND THE
GENERATIONS OF LOCAL PEOPLE WHO
GAVE FREELY OF FOOD AND SHELTER
TO STRANDED TRAVELLERS IN BAD
WEATHER.

2. THE CISTERCIAN WAY

Introduction

The Cistercian Way is a 33-mile (53-km) route that winds along the south coast of Cumbria from Walney Island to Grange-over-Sands. It was once signposted throughout and featured on a series of promotional leaflets and materials produced by Cumbria County Council to attract visitors. However, the route fell out of favour, it is no longer marked on an OS map, many of the signposts have disappeared, and the route is no longer endorsed by the council, all of which is a huge shame because it offers miles of glorious views and plenty of natural and historical interest.

The Route

We took our version of the route from Ian Brodie's 1989 official guide, *The Cistercian Way*, except we didn't complete all of it and we did it back to front.

We began our journey on Walney Island but as the original route called for us to cross the sands, we opted to stick to dry land and instead headed around to Roa Island. From there,

Furness Abbey.

we followed the route described past Furness Abbey and on to the wonderful surprise that is Dalton Castle. Leaving Dalton, we wove our way through Little and Great Urswick and on, via Swarthmoor Hall, into Ulverston where we visited Conishead Priory before, again, sticking to the land and driving around to pick the route up again at Lenibrick Point near Cark. We did manage to nip over to Chapel Island as part of a guided tour though, which was well worth the effort and definitely recommended.

From Cark, we journeyed on past Holker Hall through the woods around and down into Cartmel. Much of the land the Cistercian Way passes over is owned by the Holker Estate, who are very keen to bring the route back into regular usage.

After pausing at Cartmel, it was a short push up over Hampsfell and back home to Grange-over-Sands. The route officially starts or ends at the railway station and, if you prefer to be based in one place, we found most of it to be easily accessible as day hikes, hopping on the train for the outward journey and walking back a couple of stations each time.

We've seen the route described as 'challenging' but most of it is low level with only a few small hills, and there are plenty of places along the way for provisions if you prefer a lighter backpack. A couple of small sections were a little trickier to navigate, but this is only because it has fallen out of use.

The History

It makes most sense to start with who the Cistercians were, as they give their name to the route and had a huge influence on the history of this area of Cumbria. The Cistercian Order was formed in 1908 at Cîteaux in Burgundy. The monks who initiated the order wanted to return to a life of simplicity and austerity, which is interesting to bear in mind when we see later how the monks of Furness Abbey operated. The Cistercians sited their abbeys 'far from the concourse of man' and they committed to spending their days in solitude, prayer and the study of the scriptures. The impact of the order on the region was so strong that even today there are many visual reminders of their existence.

Sheep Island, right at the start of our route, is, as Wikipedia informs us, 'an uninhabited grassy island of around 15 acres located ¼ mile from the shores of Walney Island'. Fair enough, there's not a lot there these days. In the past, it would have been used as a stopping off point on the walk across the sands from Walney to Roa Island and the mainland beyond. It was also once home to an isolation hospital, where sailors with nasty diseases were dropped off on their way in to Barrow, although this building has long since disappeared.

The next island over, Piel Island, is home to Piel Castle. At the time of the Spanish Armada (1588), the harbour was considered to be the finest between Milford Haven in South Wales and the Scottish Borders. The monks of nearby Furness Abbey owned the island and used it as a base for their lucrative import/export business. The castle was fortified in 1327 to protect it from the many Scottish raids occurring at that time, and the monks maintained the island and traded extensively through the port, becoming wealthy, influential and owning substantial areas of land across much of the region, somewhat removed from their original goals of austerity and simplicity.

Next up for us was Roa Island and it would be a shame to visit without also including a detour to Foulney Island. Roa Island was once a proper island before being bought by

Above: Sheep Island.

Below: Piel Castle.

John Abel Smith in the 1840s. He envisioned creating a Harbour Company that he hoped would one day dominate the world and he got as far as building the permanent causeway to the island. In 1846, the Furness Railway Company (FRC) completed a rail connection to the island but they struggled to negotiate an acceptable deal with John Smith and it was not a happy relationship. In December 1852, a severe storm damaged the causeway that Abel could not afford to repair and the FRC happily bought him out for £15,000 (the equivalent of around £2 million today).

Nowadays Foulney Island is owned by Cumbria Wildlife Trust and is a haven for migrating birds and rare marine shingle plant life. It is regularly cut off by high tides and I can thoroughly recommend getting stranded there on a warm sunny afternoon with a good picnic and a pair of binoculars for a spot of very peaceful birdwatching.

Moving inland towards Furness Abbey, there is a spectacular viewpoint to be had from the stile just behind Bowesfield Farm (easy to spot on an OS map). From this vantage point, you can see both Furness Abbey and Bow Bridge nestled among the trees and it is particularly pretty during the autumn.

Approaching the abbey across Bow Bridge is an excellent way to get a feel for the site. The bridge was built in the fifteenth century with locally sourced sandstone and limestone and is a beautiful example of an old packhorse bridge. Although connected to the trading monks of the abbey, it also sits on one of the most important medieval trading routes in the North West and would have been a popular and much used crossing point for local traders.

When the abbey was constructed, the site would have been remote and untouched but with a ready supply of fresh water and timber nearby. There were no major towns in the area, and the easiest way to access the region would have been from the sea or the sands. The abbey was

Roa Island Causeway.

Above: Cut off by the tide on Foulney Island.

Below: Bow Bridge.

originally part of the Order of Savigny and was absorbed by the Cistercian Order in 1147. Although parts of the abbey existed at this time much more was added during the twelfth and thirteenth centuries. The abbey initially prospered before a series of crises (plague, famine and war with France) badly affected the Cistercian Order. During the fifteenth century the abbey was in decline with reduced land holdings, fewer monks and deteriorating relationships with local landowners. One local landowner took the abbot to court charging that 'the said Abbot and more than 22 of his monks behaved in a riotous manner'.

On 9 April 1537, Furness Abbey became the first of the major monasteries to be dissolved when the abbey was stripped of its assets and much of the building was dismantled. Over

Dalton Castle.

the intervening years, it passed through numerous hands before arriving, by marriage, into the Cavendish family. In 1847, the railway was built right through the middle of the site, much to the consternation of many people, including William Wordsworth. The upside was that a lot of archaeological research was carried out during the construction of the railway, which in turn brought in many visitors and stimulated an interest to protect and preserve what remained. In 1923, Lord Richard Cavendish handed the remains of the abbey to the guardianship of the state, with the present car park and museum opening in 1982.

From Furness Abbey, it's a relatively short walk to Dalton-in-Furness and the castle tucked away at the top of the town. It's not open every day, so it's best to check ahead if you're keen to see inside. It's 45 feet high and 30 feet wide with walls up to 6 feet thick and was most likely built to defend the town from raiders from the north. It also served as the local courts of justice and prison and was overseen by the Abbot of Furness. It ceased holding prisoners in 1774 but the court leet (local court of record) was held there until 1924. These days, it's in the safe hands of the National Trust.

Having passed through Little and Great Urswick the route winds over a beautiful hill with far-reaching views before dropping down to Ulverston via the sixteenth-century Swarthmoor Hall, regarded as the birthplace of the Quaker movement. The hall was built by local lawyer George Fell in 1568 then passed to his son Thomas, a travelling judge. Thomas' wife Margaret was interested in the teachings of George Fox, one of the founders of the Quaker movement, and she persuaded Thomas to allow George to stay with them and hold meetings in the hall. Thomas died in 1658 and eleven years later Margaret married George and they lived in the hall for the remainder of their lives.

Down on the shores of the estuary is Conishead Priory, founded as a hospital in 1160 by the Order of Augustine and raised to a priory in 1188. It was seized and dismantled in 1537 then gifted by Henry VIII to William Stanley, who built a large private residence on the site. Having gone through several changes of ownership and been demolished and rebuilt, in 1878 it was bought by a Scottish syndicate who turned it into a Hyrdopathic Hotel, which was so popular it merited its own branch line, the remains of which can still be seen in the gardens.

From 1928 to 1972 it was owned by Durham County Miners Welfare Committee, where it provided a welcome retreat for miners and their families, apart from during the Second World War when it served as the largest military hospital in the North West. After that, the site remained empty for a number of years and it fell into disrepair. Some work was carried out in the 1980s before £500,000 was raised in 1991 to fully repair and restore the site. It is now owned and maintained by the Manjurshi Buddhist community, who host a number of international festivals and worship at the impressive golden temple now in the grounds.

Looking across the estuary you can't fail to spot the Levens Viaduct, originally built in 1857 and rebuilt in 1880. On 27 February 1903 it was the scene of a frightening train derailment, when an early morning mail train became stranded on the bridge and blown over in an almighty gale. Luckily the carriages all remained on the bridge and all of the passengers managed to crawl across the bridge to safety.

Holker Hall in nearby Cark is the present-day home to the Cavendish family. The first hall was built on the site in the sixteenth century and the hall we see today is the result of a

Conishead Priory.

Above: Levens Viaduct.

Below: Cartmel Priory.

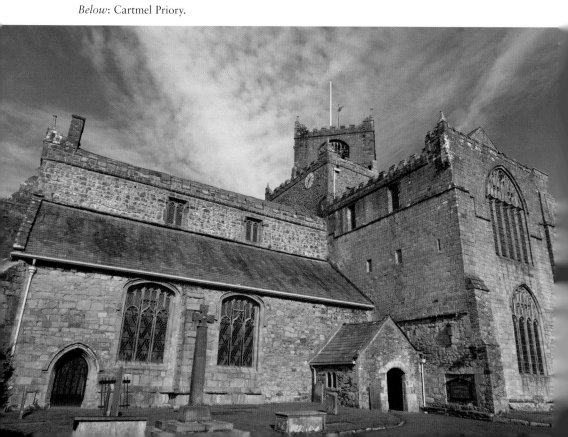

rebuild, following a disastrous fire in 1871. The grounds and hall are open throughout the year with a wide variety of fairs and festivals taking place.

The last major site of historic interest on the walk is Cartmel Priory. The priory was founded in 1189 by William Marshal, 1st Earl of Pembroke, and it was saved from the dissolution because he had been granted an altar in one of the chapels, allowing the locals to successfully argue that it was their parish church. It didn't escape unscathed though: the monks were expelled and the assets, including the lead roof, were stripped and ten laymen were hung, drawn and quartered at Lancaster for treason. The site has remained a place of worship throughout the centuries, ringing in the changes with electric lights being introduced in 1934, and is still the focal point of the beautiful village of Cartmel.

3. ROMAN ROAD PART I — PENRITH TO AMBLESIDE

Introduction

When we set out to walk this route, we planned it around the well-known old Roman road up and over High Street, but as we researched it, we quickly realised that the Romans were only a small part of the story. There were people here long before the Romans arrived and the landscape has continued to evolve thanks to all the people who came after. To be perfectly honest, we could have written an entire chapter just about Penrith but seeing as we'd gone to all the trouble of planning a route and booking accommodation, we thought we'd best crack on.

The Route

Although the Roman route starts from Brougham Castle, we travelled by train so started from the station. We wound down through the town passing St Andrew's Church and Dockray Hall, before picking up the A6 south and passing the old Plague Stone in the housing association grounds on our left. We carried on over Eamont Bridge

Brougham Castle.

where we cheated and turned right past King Arthur's Round Table rather than head back to start at the castle (we'd already been there and had a long walk ahead of us!).

We continued on through Yanwath and Tirril, before picking up the road past Winder Hall and out onto the fell. We broke our journey at Pooley Bridge for the night before continuing up over High Street proper where, despite it being August, we were pelted by hail and strong winds, an apt reminder to always be prepared for anything on the high fells. Dropping down into Troutbeck via Beatrix Potter's old farm, we picked up Robin's Lane and followed it around the base of Wansfell and down into Ambleside.

On the whole the route is fairly easy to follow but there are sections up on top of the fell where the road becomes indistinct and later footpaths have taken precedence.

The History

This area is swathed in layer upon layer of history and rather than try to recount it chronologically we will, instead, piece it together as we follow the route.

First up is Penrith Castle, bang opposite the station. The castle was originally built in the fourteenth century by Ralph Neville on a site once occupied by a Roman fort and formed part of the defence of the Scottish border. His son, Richard, made it his headquarters and fortified it further. Following his death, the castle was granted to Richard, Duke of Gloucester and future Richard III, who lived there for several years making further extensive renovations. After he became king, the castle was no longer used as his residence and, barring a brief period of use during the Civil War, fell into disrepair. Parts of it were dismantled and, as was the custom at the time, the stones were put to good use in surrounding buildings.

Richard III is also involved in the second interesting site, Dockray Hall in the centre of town, where he lived while the castle was undergoing restoration work. For over 150 years, the hall was an inn known as the Duke of Gloucester in his honour and his coat of arms

Richard III's coat of arms on Dockray Hall.

can still be seen above the doorway. It is said that the castle was linked to the hall by means of an underground tunnel over 300 yards long, which was used both as a means of escape if the castle came under attack and as a way to bring goods in and out away from watchful eyes.

A short walk from Dockray Hall is St Andrew's Church where you'll find an intriguing spot of Cumbrian folklore in the form of the Giant's Grave. The grave is marked by two large pillars with four smaller 'headstones' between them and early drawings show them to have originally been ornately decorated. It is most likely an early Christian burial site for a family or connected group of people but the folklore is far more entertaining. The story goes that the grave marked the final resting spot of Ewan/Owen/Hugh (depending which version you read) Caesarius, who towered over 17 feet tall and was renowned for hunting, fighting and killing wild boar.

Down along the A6 is the Plague Stone, a reminder of a turbulent time in Penrith's past. Between September 1597 and January 1599, 2,260 people in the town were wiped out by the plague, accounting for around one-third of the population. When towns were known to have the plague they were put into isolation, which made things like food difficult to come by so, on the outskirts of the towns, plague stones were placed where traders could leave food at a safe distance and the locals would drop their money into a hollow filled with vinegar to disinfect it. Penrith's stone survives and is now in the grounds of a housing association but easily visible and accessible from the road.

Eamont Bridge crosses what was once the boundary between Cumberland and Westmorland. The bridge itself is one of the oldest in the country still in regular use and it's thought that it was constructed during the fifteenth century before being widened in the nineteenth and twentieth centuries.

Brougham Castle stands on what were the remains of the ancient Roman fort of Brocavum and there are the remains of a small marching camp on the other side of the A66 (which broadly follows the route of another Roman road). Roman legionnaires were expected to be able to march 20 Roman miles (18.4 miles or 30 km) in a day and this fort sits 22 miles south of Carlisle and 20 miles north of Brougham Castle, with Ambleside fort 20 miles to the south-west.

Giant's Grave.

Plague Stone.

Marching 20 odd miles a day wouldn't have been much fun for them. The typical legionnaire would have worn underwear, tunic, hobnailed boots, sandals, armour padding, armour, two belts, a sword, a dagger, padded cap, helmet, shield and javelin. Then there would have been the yolk they had to carry with all their bedding, pots and food on it, with the whole lot weighing in at around 5 stone – and we were commenting that our backpacks were feeling a little heavy...

Around 1214, Robert de Vieuxpont acquired the land on which Brougham Castle is now built with the aim of protecting King John's land against raiders from the north, and stones from the old Roman fort were used in the construction of the castle. As with many castles in the region, it played many important roles in British history, including the Wars of the Roses. The castle fell into disrepair but was briefly revived in the seventeenth century when Lady Anne Clifford, an important figure in the history of the region, resided there and upgraded and improved the building. She was such a strong character that when it was suggested to Oliver Cromwell that he should stop her building, he replied, 'Let her build what she will, she shall not be hindered by me.' There is also reputed to be a skull hidden in the walls that keeps the ghosts at bay. Apparently, any time that a previous resident tried to remove the skull from the hall, the ghostly goings on increased dramatically until the skull was returned, so one resident buried it deep in the walls and they've had no trouble since.

Heading out towards High Street the road passes two sites that remind us of man's presence in the region long before the Romans: King Arthur's Round Table and Mayburgh Henge, both thought to be of Neolithic origin. Although the exact purpose of these sites will never be fully known, they were both clearly of huge significance and it's thought that jousting may have taken place at King Arthur's Round Table. Originally there were a series

Mayburgh Henge.

of standing stones at Mayburgh Henge but now only the central stone remains with the raised bank surrounding it creating an ethereal amphitheatre.

Travelling out through Tirril and on to Celleron the Roman road finally leaves tarmac and climbs up past Winder Hall (an imposing seventeenth-century hall that is now a dreamy but expensive holiday let) and out onto Heugh Scar where there are some glorious views out over Ullswater. The poet Thomas Gray visited the area in 1769 and his descriptions were so vivid that artist Joseph Farringdon followed in his footsteps five years later to paint the views originally described. There is a peace and tranquillity to this spot that Farringdon captures beautifully, and although the local town of Pooley Bridge has grown, the view has lost none of its magic.

Soon the route passes through another Neolithic site, known as The Cockpit, on Moor Divock. Being broad and flat with rich soil and a good supply of running water, this would have made a great place for an early settlement. Numerous hut circles have been found together with a small stone circle and a number of tumuli. Some of the tumuli were opened during excavations in the early twentieth century and were found to contain Bronze Age remains and relics.

Apart from admiring the stunning views and wondering how on earth anyone could have ever considered turning Ullswater into a reservoir (which happened in the 1960s and was successfully defeated by Lord Birkett who sadly died two days after his victory and now has Birkett fell named in his honour), there's not a lot of other remains to explore up on the top of the fell. It's a fairly straightforward walk (apart from when you're getting hammered by hail) so there is plenty of time to enjoy your surroundings.

Above: Ullswater.

Below: 'The Cockpit' on Moor Divock.

Racecourse Hill is so named because it really did hold horse races and fairs on its summit until the mid-nineteenth century. The site would have been a central meeting point and a vital catalyst for communication and trade in the days when valley communities were very remote.

As the Roman road drops down to the valley floor it passes Troutbeck Farm, which, in 1923, was bought by Beatrix Potter to protect it from development. From here, she successfully bred Herdwick sheep and became well respected in local farming circles, becoming the first female elected president of the Herdwick Sheep Breeders' Association in 1943. The house is not open to the public but there are plenty of gorgeous 'Herdies' grazing in the nearby fields.

Further along the valley is the beautiful Townend House. The house was built in 1623 by George Browne, who was an enthusiastic woodcarver, and it's well worth a visit to the house to see the many fantastic items he left his mark on. The house remained in the same family right the way through to 1923 when it was handed over to the National Trust – beautifully preserved and kept exactly as the Brownes left it. The distinctive Westmorland chimneys give it an imposing feel but inside its cosy and homely and the guided tours give a fascinating glimpse in everyday life in the house and surrounding valley.

The final section of the walk into Ambleside is a gentle leg-stretcher along a nice broad path. We've walked that way many times and have always wondered about a random stone pillar in a nearby field and have finally discovered what it is: it's apparently one of twenty-one viewing stations that were essential for all Victorians to visit. They were popularised in a guidebook of the era and those undertaking the 'grand tour' were required to visit each pillar and admire the views.

Racecourse Hill.

Above: Troutbeck Farm with High Street in the far background.

Below: Townend House.

4. ROMAN ROAD PART II — AMBLESIDE TO RAVENGLASS

Introduction

This route is obviously the continuation of the route started in the previous chapter, but there's so much going on that we needed to split it into two. The local area is overflowing with fascinating history and sadly we can't cram it all in so these are our highlights. As with the previous chapter, although this is primarily known as a Roman route, if that was all we focussed on we'd be missing out on a whole pile of fascinating historical nuggets.

The Route

I'll be honest up front, we deviated from the original Roman road for a couple of main reasons – firstly because it poured with rain for the whole of the first day of our walk. We'd have loved to have the luxury of rescheduling but sadly that wasn't an option so we hauled

Wrynose Bottom.

on the waterproofs and cracked on, avoiding a section of the walk at Hardknott Pass, which looked somewhat swampy, and stuck to the road instead. The other reason we deviated was that the original route passed over a stream and there was no footbridge. Given the pounding rain, the stream was in spate so we thought it unwise to attempt a crossing.

The actual route runs out of Ambleside through Clappersgate, then along the main road through Skelwith Bridge to Colwith Brow. From there it drops down to wind through High Park and Stang End into Little Langdale, where it gets a whole lot easier as it pretty much follows Wrynose Pass to Wrynose Bottom. Here the Roman road is clearly marked on the OS map but we stuck to the road for the reasons above.

The original road loops around the fort at Hardknott Pass, before following the modern-day road down to Eskdale Green. From there it winds along the base of Muncaster Fell and was still the main road in use through the eighteenth century. The road then passes through Muncaster Castle grounds and up through Dovecote Wood, dropping into Ravenglass via the Roman Bath House.

The History

Although this route isn't all about the Romans, the Roman fort in Ambleside is obviously a good place to start. It originally began as a small wooden fort in the first century but by the second century the stone fort was built and was in use through to the fourth century. Although marked on maps as Galava, it's not completely certain that this is the correct name for it.

Roman maps were rudimentary at best and there are several accounts of Romans getting lost as they generally relied on local information to find their way around. That said, they did produce basic maps but these were generally of a highly practical nature for military use, featuring the important roads and forts, and bore only a passing resemblance to the actual geography. The Peutinger Table, a thirteenth-century copy of an original Roman map, is fascinating to study but tricky to match up to present-day locations.

Ambleside Roman Fort.

There is still plenty to see at the Ambleside site and there are lots of information boards that give a real feel for what life must have been like at that time. It is known that they used Windermere in some form, possibly for food and to move men and materials around the shores.

It's pretty hairy these days walking along the A593 with cars whizzing past, especially on the narrow sections, but it got us pondering how Romans built their roads and just how they got them to last so long, especially in such inhospitable places as the top of High Street and Hardknott Pass. Well, it turns out there were several stages to the building of the roads, which went something like this:

- Firstly army builders would clear the ground of rocks and trees – roads were always as straight as possible as it was the quickest route between two points.
- Next a large trench would be dug and filled with stones, pebbles and rudimentary cement on top. This would have been packed down as firmly as possible.
- Then would come a layer of more cement, possibly mixed with broken tiles.
- On top of this would sit paving stones, fitted together as tightly as possible and with a small camber to improve drainage.
- Lastly keystones would be slotted in onto either side to keep everything in place and a drainage channel cleared for water runoff.

You have to be impressed with how long their roads lasted, especially given the volume of roadworks constantly needed on today's roads. Though, to be fair, the Romans generally travelled by horseback, on foot or with oxen-drawn carts so the roads didn't have to contend with the volumes we see today.

Wrynose Pass leading up from Little Langdale.

The stretch through Little Langdale was wonderfully peaceful and it's always been a quiet little valley with blissfully little mobile phone signal. Telephones first reached the valley in 1923 but a year or two later all the lines were brought down with snow; the reports from that time all focus on the problems of the wires all across the road with no mention made of the inconvenience of having no phones.

The route was also popular with Victorian visitors on charabanc tours who would journey up and over past Blea Tarn to the Old Dungeon Ghyll for lunch. The driver of the charabanc would stop at the top of the pass and blow his horn to let the inn know they were coming, with the number of blasts informing staff as to how many passengers to expect. The inn has always been popular with those drawn to the outdoors with many famous rock climbers staying there over the years, but surely the most intriguing guest was the future emperor of Japan, who stayed there as a prince and enjoyed a little rock climbing in September 1915.

At the end of the valley, just before the road climbs up to Wrynose Pass, there's small mound in a field behind the farm. This is the Ting Mound, thought to have been the site of an ancient Viking assembly and situated here to take advantage of the road already put in place by the Romans. There's not a lot to see there today but it was clearly a site of some importance in the past.

The iconic Three Shires Stone at the top of Wrynose Pass was sadly missing when we visited, having been knocked over and damaged, possibly deliberately, in August 2017. It marked the historic point where the boundaries of Cumberland, Westmorland and Lancashire met and was made from limestone quarried near Cartmel. The National Trust is repairing it and hopefully it will soon be back where it belongs.

The route along Wrynose Bottom has an other-worldly feel of isolation and loneliness, despite the ever-present cars. It's a remote valley, high in the fells, and I wonder what the Romans made of it when they arrived for the first time. During the Roman occupation there was an era of climate warming known as the Roman Warm Period, so temperatures may have been a little warmer than today and less of a shock to those more familiar with a sunnier climate. Having waded through the surrounding fields, it seems appropriate that Hardknott Fort was known to the Romans as Mediobogdum.

Ting Mound.

Remains of Three Shires Stone.

The current road route over Hardknott Pass deviates from the original Roman road, which stayed on the valley floor past Black Hall before climbing up the fell. We noticed this as a common feature when following the old routes; they often stay lower longer before shooting up and over the fells, whereas modern roads follow a more gentle gradient. I'll be honest, I haven't found any data on why this is, but I'm guessing it's to do with the fact that the valley floors were less exposed to the weather so time 'on top' was kept to a minimum.

The fort there is magnificent. The day we visited for the walk, the weather was foul but we've been lucky to be there completely alone on a warm, sunny evening and the views are immense. It was built in the second century during the reign of Hadrian and housed a cohort of 500 men. The layout of the fort is still very easy to see including the commanding officer's house, the granaries and the nearby parade ground.

Dropping down through the Eskdale Valley was an absolute treat, and although it's popular with visitors today, that wasn't always the case. In Maxwell Fraser's *Companion into Lakeland* he states, 'Those who avoid the Lake District because they fear it is overrun with tourists would do well to visit Eskdale.' In the 1959 journal of the Fell and Rock Climbing Club one report reads that 'Eskdale has never had much attraction for rock climbers', adding 'If you fancy climbing somewhere new, on unscratched routes, relatively free from vegetation ... Eskdale is the place for you.'

Above: Top of Hardknott Pass.

Below: Hardknott Roman Fort.

Eskdale Valley.

Of course in such a remote place there are a number of stories of hauntings and odd goings on. A long-deserted farmhouse in Eskdale Green is reputedly haunted by a man who posed as a gypsy woman to gain entry to the farmhouse where a woman lived alone with her baby. When she discovered the ruse, she waited until he fell asleep then poured boiling tallow down his throat and he still haunts the ruins. There's also the tale of a horse that ran away coming over the old corpse road with a dead body strapped to its back. It was never found and now still haunts the valley.

The most popular attraction in the valley these days is the Ravenglass & Eskdale Railway, known as La'al Ratty. The route dates back to 1873 but the present railway has been running since 1915, originally moving passengers and goods along the remote valley. Today it is a popular, and rather wonderful, visitor attraction with the journey from Ravenglass to Dalegarth, taking around forty minutes.

On the walk to Ravenglass you'll soon pass the King George Inn, which was originally named the King of Prussia Inn, before being retitled during the First World War. Further down, the route passes straight through the grounds of Muncaster Castle, which has been owned by the Pennington family for over 800 years and is home to a broad variety of events throughout the year.

The approach into Ravenglass passes the Roman Bath House, which was built alongside the fort that once occupied the field opposite. There are plenty of walls still left to admire at the bath house – in remarkable conditions considering they're over 2,000 years old – but nothing remains of the fort, although there have been many interesting pottery and jewellery finds over the years.

If this seems a convoluted way to approach Ravenglass then spare a thought for the folks who tried to get there via the coast road over the years. When John Wesley (one of the founders of Methodism) visited in 1759, it took him from 8 a.m. until midnight to travel from Bootle to Whitehaven, causing him to remark, 'I can advise no traveller to go this way, he may go round by Kendal and Keswick, often in less time, always with less expense and far less trial of his patience'.

In 1824 help was sought to improve the roads but ten years later there were still problems, highlighted by specific complaints about the inability of mail coaches to reach the area. When a new county road surveyor was appointed in the 1870s he said they were 'the worst kept roads I have yet examined', with problems of upkeep and flooding, especially around

Ravenglass Roman Bath House.

Eskmeals Dunes and Ravenglass.

Eskmeals Dunes. By the late 1800s the railways arrived and changed everything, reducing the cost of travel and improving travelling conditions.

Despite the challenges, Ravenglass was still a popular place to visit, having been granted a market by King John in 1208, although when the plague hit in the 1500s the advice was clear: 'It will not do to buy at the Ravenglass Fair as "the sickness" is rife in Walney and dealings with any man in Cumberland must be avoided'.

Thankfully that was all cleared up a long time ago and now Ravenglass is the perfect place to start, end, or stop off on any journey.

5. CARLISLE TO BOWNESS-ON-SOLWAY

Introduction

This is the last of our trilogy of Roman walks, and for a county so full of Roman history, it's impressive they only make up three of the routes explored in this book. Again, there's a lot more to the history of this region than the Romans, even if it does include Hadrian's Wall. Although it's low level throughout, this walk is exposed in many sections; when I read that in a book, I imagined the issue of the exposure will be the wind and the rain but, in this case, it was the sun. We undertook this walk during the very hot spell of June 2018 and even though we broke it into smaller sections we still struggled with the relentless heat.

The Route

This one's easy as we followed Hadrian's Wall Path from Carlisle through to Bowness-on-Solway. Starting on the banks of the River Eden, the path leaves the city and passes through a series of very pretty villages including Burgh-by Sands (which also has an excellent pub) and Drumburgh with its fascinating castle. (We found the very exposed stretch between these two by far the most challenging with no shade whatsoever.)

After looping inland slightly towards Drumburgh Moss the path returns to the coast, passing through the fascinating hamlet of Port Carlisle before ending in Bowness-on-Solway, where there are plenty of facilities to greet the weary walker.

Exposed route across salt marsh.

The History

Volumes of books have been written about Carlisle, and rightly so as the town is relentlessly interesting with glorious nuggets of history lurking around every corner. I would love to give you a potted history of Carlisle but even an abridged version would easily fill an entire book, so I will restrict myself to just the bits that relate to this route and strongly recommend that you visit the Tullie House Museum for a full history of the city. Tullie House is a fine Jacobean house built in 1689 and was a family home until the 1840s when it became a cloth warehouse. It was saved from demolition in the late 1800s and opened as a museum in 1893. You'll find everything you need to know about Carlisle in there, plus some fine cakes in the café too.

Clearly the Romans are famed for being in the city, although they were far from the first. There's evidence of land management in the region dating back to the Mesolithic Period (9600 BC–4000 BC) as well as Bronze Age and Iron Age finds. It's likely that when the Romans arrived they built on a pre-existing habitation as the region had a lot going for it; plentiful water supply surrounded by dense woodlands and right on a main thoroughfare to the north.

The first fort was built in AD 72, occupying a site roughly where the castle is today, with a later fort built at nearby Stanwix. The timber forts were demolished around AD 150 and replaced with a stone fort, which served throughout the rest of the Roman occupation. In Bitts Park near Stanwix you'll find the Sauceries where football has been played for at least 500 years; it's even said that Mary, Queen of Scots watched a game when she was ensconced in the castle.

Hadrian's Wall was built around AD 120 and ran for 80 Roman miles (73 imperial miles or 117 km) from Bowness-on-Solway to Wallsend on the River Tyne and was originally planned to be constructed of turf for the first 30 miles and stone for the rest. Prior to that the forts in the region had been linked by a road known as the Stanegate and when travelling along the road, if they were not staying at a fort, Roman soldiers would have camped under animal skin tents and dug defensive ditches each night as protection.

Rather like an ancient episode of Grand Designs the original plan for the wall was altered, with the Romans adding both a *vallum* (defensive ditch and mound) and another

Carlisle Castle.

Carlisle Castle, with the route of Hadrian's Wall on the left and the Sauceries in the foreground.

road to the original plans as well as upgrading the entire wall to stone. Kevin McCloud would, no doubt, have been 'deeply worried' by how this would affect their budget.

A castle was first built in Carlisle in 1092 by King William Rufus. It was largely made of wood and built partly over the site of the old Roman fort. In 1122 Henry I of England ordered the fortification of the castle and, although ownership regularly changed hands, over the following century successive kings continued fortifying the structure. The castle has seen plenty of action, with invasions, battles, five sieges and the imprisonment of Mary, Queen of Scots. In the nineteenth century, things calmed down and today the castle is managed by English Heritage and houses an interesting military museum.

Carlisle has long been a vital transportation hub and during the late 1700s, eight mail coaches and seven stagecoaches entered and left the city every day, with eighty horses stabled in the city to support them. During the nineteenth century, steps were taken to turn Carlisle into a port and the plan was to create a canal from a village called Fisher's Cove along the coast to move people and goods into the city from the coast. From 1819 to 1823 a canal was cut at a cost of over £90,000 (the equivalent of over £7.5 million in today's terms) and the village renamed Port Carlisle.

This may seem extreme but travel by sea was far cheaper than coach travel back then. For example, to travel from Whitehaven to Liverpool by sea was 15s for first class and 10s 6d for second, whereas the coach fare for the same journey was 24s for 'inside' and 17s for 'outside'. To take advantage of this, in 1826 a company was set up to establish a steamship route from the newly named Port Carlisle to Liverpool.

Sadly, despite all of this, the canal never managed to pay its way. The Liverpool steamer service was diverted to Silloth and the canal was eventually filled in and, ironically, turned into a railway. To convert the canal the locks were removed and the bridges raised before the track was laid on the drained canal bed. Between Drumburgh and Port Carlisle the 'trains' were horse-drawn coaches with converted wheels known as 'Horse Drawn Dandys', which ran until 14 April 1914; after that steam took over and the line remained open until 1932.

Carlisle's population boomed during the early nineteenth century, rising from 10,221 in 1801 to 29,417 in 1861, thanks to this improved access and growing industries. In 1847, a large gasworks was built and by 1851 it had eleven spinning mills, but in my opinion

Above: Port Carlisle.

Below: St Mary's Church, Beaumont.

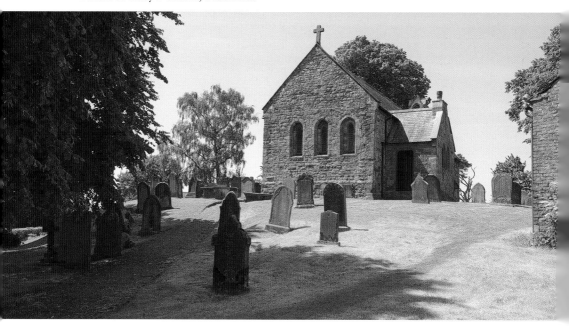

the most important development was the opening of the Carr's Biscuit Factory in 1831. In the 1840s, it was the biggest biscuit manufacturer in Britain on account of the fact that dry biscuits stayed fresh for longer and so could be transported further. Now owned by McVitie's, the site still produces many of our favourites. The nation held its breath when the factory was flooded following Storm Desmond in December 2015 but thankfully by April 2016 our beloved Bourbon Creams were back on the shelves again!

The Solway coast is a magical place full of fascinating history and folklore. Although our route follows Hadrian's Wall, the wall itself is not visible, at least not in wall form, as the stones have been robbed out and used in the creation of other buildings. Many of the buildings we now see are a result of the activities of the monks at Holme Cultram Abbey, who managed the land during the twelfth and thirteenth centuries.

Even if you are not of a religious nature, there are three fine churches to explore along the route: St Mary's Church in Beaumont, St Michael's Church in Burgh-by-Sands and St Michael's Church in Bowness-on-Solway. St Mary's is the only church built directly on the line of Hadrian's Wall and stands on the site of an old Roman fort and subsequent Norman motte. The small hill it stands on was known as Beau Mont, or 'Beautiful Hill', and gave the village its name.

St Michael's Church, Burgh-by-Sands.

King Edward I Monument.

St Michael's in Burgh-by-Sands was built with stones from the wall and houses a wonderful array of mythological creatures carved into the stonework, probably of Anglo-Saxon origin. In 1307, Edward I visited the church on his way to tackle Robert the Bruce but died out on the marshes and his monument out on the sands (and clearly marked on the OS map) is certainly worth a visit. His body was brought back to the church to lie in state before being transported back to London for burial. The unusual church tower doubled up as a place of refuge from the regular Scots raids, hence its squat shape and barred gated entry.

In the middle of Drumburgh stands Drumburgh Castle, though it's a lot less castle-like than you might expect. Originally built as a defensive pele tower in 1307 and constructed with stones from Hadrian's Wall, the site fell into decay before being restored during the sixteenth century by Lord Tomas Dacre. Over the following centuries it passed through a number of hands and in the 1970s the castle was fully restored and became a private home.

Many of the other more humble homes in this region were built as 'clay dabbin cottages'. Materials could not be brought in from great distances so inhabitants had to make the

Drumburgh Castle.

St Michael's Church, Bowness-on-Solway.

Hadrian's Wall Path.

most of what they had around them, in this case clay, cobbles and boulders for the walls, wood for the roof frame and turf, reeds, straw and bracken for the roof itself. At the turn of the twentieth century, there were over 1,300 'dabbins' in the area but today there are fewer than 300.

St Michael's Church in Bowness-on-Solway stands at the end of one of the ancient crossing points of the Solway Firth and is also built with stones from Hadrian's Wall. The original church bells were stolen by Scots raiders from Annan in 1626 but, as they were escaping, they dumped them into the Solway in attempt to lighten their load and the bells were lost forever in the sands. In retaliation a group of local men mounted a raid into Scotland and stole bells from churches in Dornock and Middlebie. Tradition has it that each time the parish of Annan (which includes Dornock and Middlebie) receives a new vicar, they request the return of the bells from Bowness but, for four centuries, all these requests have been ignored and the bells still sit at the back of St Michael's.

6. MARTINDALE AND PATTERDALE

Introduction

Ullswater is regularly voted as one of the prettiest lakes in the Lake District, and I'm not going to disagree; it is absolutely stunning. Perhaps because of that it is very popular with visitors throughout the year and many of the homes in the region are now holiday homes rather than permanent dwellings, but obviously that wasn't always the case. Before the advent of modern roads and technology, if people wanted (or needed) to visit each other there was only one way to do it – on foot and up over the fell. What we now see today as a rather lovely circular walking route from Patterdale was once a vital link between remote communities.

The Route

This really is a lovely route and even sitting here writing about it makes me want to grab my walking boots and head back out there. The directions are simple: from Patterdale

View over Patterdale and Glenridding.

head up to Chapel-in-the-Hause then drop down along Boredale and back along the Howe Grain valley. There's a sharp climb at the start and a long gentle ascent back to the Hause at the end.

We've wandered around here many times and if you want to add on a little extra or try something different the top of Place Fell is a short(ish) sharp climb that will reward you with a spectacular panorama of the Lake District fells. Alternatively you could explore the top of Beda Fell, which is less of a climb and also has wonderful views.

The History

The starting point, Patterdale, takes its name from St Patrick's Church in the valley (St Patrick's Dale becoming Patterdale) and the saint is said to have visited the valley around AD 450. There's been a church on the site since the fourteenth century but the one we see today dates back to 1853 and was designed by Anthony Salvin who, when he wasn't designing churches, specialised in restoring collapsing castles; during his illustrious career, he worked on Norwich, Newark, Carisbrooke, Caernarvon, Warwick and even Windsor Castle.

St Patrick's Well is a little closer to the lake but, according to an account from 1797, it was once the site of some impressive St Patrick's Day celebrations: 'There is annually a ceremony observed here on St Patrick's Day of drinking a bottle of rum over the spring and on that day dancing and all sorts of merriment go on with great spirit' (*A Tour in the Lakes*, William Gell).

St Patrick's Church, Patterdale.

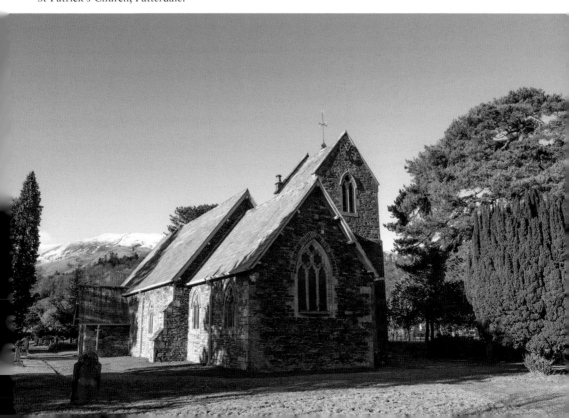

St Patrick's Well.

What we now see as a rural farming community was, until around 1960, a nationally renowned mining area. The Greenside Lead Mine just along the valley from Glenridding originally began production in the late eighteenth century and was famous for its production of lead and silver – the communion plate in the church is made of silver from the mine. These mines made an indelible mark on the landscape in several ways. Apart from the still visible mine fifty-two cottages were built in the area to house mine workers, and when the mine closed and the workers left many of these became the holiday homes we see today.

However, it wasn't just the housing that the mines affected, it was also the transportation routes; the ore from the mines needed to be shipped away and was sent by cart over to Carlisle where it could be moved more swiftly initially by canal and later by rail. This meant that the road route from Patterdale to Carlisle was much improved compared to other 'less important' routes.

Patterdale also gave its name to the Patterdale Terrier, a hardy short-haired terrier descended from Fell Terriers. Such dogs were regularly used to control the local vermin. The Fell Terriers were renowned for their toughness and persistence as this story from 1779 illustrates. A farmer went out at 2 p.m. on a Saturday afternoon and his dog took off after a fox. The dog was not seen again until the following evening when it returned, still

Old mine cottages.

in pursuit of the fox. Apparently both animals were so exhausted that they collapsed and lay down together under a gooseberry bush. After making enquiries, the farmer discovered that the dog had been seen chasing the fox in Wythburn (9 miles away) and Legberthwaite (13 miles away)!

From Patterdale, the path climbs to Chapel-in-the-Hause and the remains of what is reputed to have been a chapel. In his book Wainwright confidently states that the route 'also served as an approach to a chapel on the top of the pass', but having done a lot of digging around, I can't find any definite confirmation that the ruins there were ever an actual church. Trust me, I've investigated the records of the Anglicans, the Methodists and the Quakers, but there's no hard evidence.

The word 'hause' (or 'hawse') most likely comes from our Viking ancestors and means 'mountain pass', although interestingly what is now known as Hause Crag is listed as Horse Crag on the 1863 OS map. Differing snippets of folklore say that the chapel was either built by St Patrick himself in the fifth century or built later and dedicated to St Martin of Tours (*see* later), but there is no evidence for either of these. In Baddeley's thorough guide to the Lake District in the late 1800s, he clearly marks a shelter at that point, so perhaps there were more of the ruins left back then.

The first map I could find that mentioned 'Chapel in the Hause' was from 1863 but a map of the region from 1760 by Bowles, Sayer and Bowles clearly marks Martindale Chapel in Martindale and St Patrick's Well in Patterdale, but makes no mention at all of a chapel on the pass so, whatever it was, either didn't exist then or wasn't important enough to merit inclusion.

Chapel-in-the-Hause.

If you do decide to take the detour up onto Place Fell (historically known as Martindale Fell) then take heed of these words from 1778 when Thomas West described it as 'the most romantic, pleasing and terrible situation upon the lake, especially if the wind blows'. On one particularly parky visit we were lucky enough to find a series of frozen tarns full of frozen bubbles. I'd never seen anything quite like it before and it really was rather beautiful.

The route then follows Boredale Valley, which has also undergone a name transformation over the years from Boardale. You're unlikely to bump into any boars along there these days but, if you're quiet and don't have a dog with you, there's a great chance of spotting the red deer who have roamed these valleys for over 300 years. There's also a fantastic selection of birdlife to watch out for and buzzards and skylarks will accompany you on most summer walks.

Down in Martindale, there are another two churches to explore. The 'new' church of St Peter is on the top of Martindale Hause, was built in the 1880s and has a glorious collection of stained-glass windows designed by modern stained-glass artist Jane Gray, who also worked on the magnificent windows in the nave of the new Coventry Cathedral.

The 'old' church of St Martin of Tours is next to the road along Howe Grain. Records show that there has been a church on the site of over 700 years but there's also a yew tree near the church that is over 1,300 years old. Yew trees have long been associated with churches so it's possible there was some sort of place of worship here as far back as the

Above: Boredale Valley.

Below: Martindale 'old' Church.

ninth century. The present church was built during the sixteenth century and was visited by William and Dorothy Wordsworth. William used his visit to the church as inspiration for his second book, *The Excursion* (1814):

> Till, chancing by yon lofty ridge to pass
> A heap of ruin, almost without walls
> And wholly without roof (in ancient time
> It was a Chapel, a small Edifice
> In which the Peasants of these lonely Dells
> For worship met upon that central height).

In his guide to the Lake District, written *c.* 1880, Baddeley states that 'Martindale parish church stands on How Grain about 1,000 feet about sea level and is one of the most remote and inaccessible churches in Britain'. His accompanying map, however, shows the two churches in Martindale, both well below 1,000 feet and no church marked up on Boredale Hause (for the record Martindale Parish Church is 636 feet (190 metres) above sea level and Chapel-in-the-Hause is 1259.9 feet (384 metres) above sea level).

While the parish church is in a remote valley, it is along the main village road and couldn't be described as inaccessible. According to the 1881 census there were thirty-four families living in the village at that time. Baddeley's guides were the go-to guides for the period and were incredibly popular, so much so that following his death a clock tower was built in his honour along the road from Bowness-on-Windermere to Windermere where it still stands today marking the boundary between the two parishes.

View of Chapel-in-the-Hause.

The parish church of St Martin fell into disrepair and would have been roofless when Wordsworth and Baddeley made their separate visits (the church was restored and reroofed in 1882). Our ancestors were a practical bunch and wouldn't have ventured up onto a fell top to attend chapel unless there was a very good reason for it. In the absence of hard evidence either way my theory is that the building referred to as the 'chapel' on Boredale Hause was a temporary solution that functioned as a church while the valleys either side were without a place of worship, and once the churches in the Martindale and Patterdale were restored, the chapel on the hause was no longer required.

Before I leave the subject alone once and for all, it's also worth adding that it was St Martin who gave us the word 'chapel' in the first place. Before he was a saint, Martin was a Roman soldier stationed in France. One day he found a shivering beggar so tore his cloak in half, giving the other half to the beggar. Following his death, St Martin's half of the cloak, known as '*cappa Saincti Martini*', was preserved and watched over by priests known as 'cappellani', which evolved into 'chaplain'. The small churches built to house the cloak were called 'capella', which then evolved into 'chapel'.

Heading back along the valley towards Dale Head, the red roof of 'The Bungalow' is very easy to spot away in the distance. These days it's a luxurious holiday villa but it was originally built in 1910 by the Earl of Lonsdale as a hunting lodge for a visit by Kaiser Wilhelm II who, despite having a very anti-British stance, was grandson of Queen Victoria and remained very close to much of the royal family. The kaiser also took a ride on the Ullswater steamer *Raven*, whose decks were painted yellow for the occasion (yellow being the Earl of Lonsdale's favourite colour).

'The Bungalow'.

While we're on the subject of the lake, Donald Campbell set a water speed record there on 23 July 1955. The average speed of the two runs (and official record) was 202.32 mph (325.6 kph) but on the first leg he reached 215.08 mph (343.13 kph). These days most of us prefer to explore the lake at a rather more sedate pace, thanks to the Ullswater Steam Navigation Company, which was formed in 1855 to offer pleasure cruises along the lake. Prior to that it was reported that 'the navigators of this lake find much amusement by discharging guns or small cannon' (*A Guide to the Lakes*, Timothy West, 1778). Good job they didn't try that when the kaiser was around.

Red stag.

7. KENTMERE AND LONGSLEDDALE

Introduction

The final four routes all interlink around a cluster of eastern fells and are clear evidence that what we now see as quiet, dead-end valleys were once busy thoroughfares carrying people and goods. Today it's a 29-mile (47-km) drive from Sadgill in Longsleddale around via the A6 to the head of Haweswater, but it's only 3 miles (5 km) up and over Gatescarth Pass. Similarly it's 14 miles (23 km) from Kentmere around to Sadgill but only 2 miles (4 km) up and over the fell. If you were on foot, which route would you choose?

The Route

Starting and ending at Kentmere church, this is a very lovely 6.6-mile (10.6-km) circular route. Please note that parking at the church is very limited and there is an honesty box there so please do make a contribution. Plenty of people still live in the village so please park considerately.

Longsleddale Valley.

The easiest way round to walk it is to head out from Kentmere following the path that loops south towards Skeggles Water before returning back north towards Sadgill. This first part of the walk is less distinct probably because it was less used as it wasn't a direct path. The return journey up and over the bridleway is very clear and easy to follow.

The History

One of the most obvious landmarks in the village is St Cuthbert's Church. The church is named in honour of St Cuthbert, who lived on Lindisfarne and was originally buried there before the Danes invaded in AD 875 and local monks removed his body for safety and took it on a tour of the north of England. Kentmere lies on what was once an important route between Shap Abbey and Furness Abbey so, although there is no evidence, it is possible that St Cuthbert's body may have rested in the village.

Despite its size and the considerable cost involved in its construction, very little is known about its origins. It is thought that it was built during the sixteenth century and recent renovation works have identified that it was built well, with very little settling or other movement occurring over the centuries. Dendrochronology tests on the roof beams confirmed that the trees used were felled around 1514 and once supported a lead roof. Much more of its history was uncovered during the renovation work and it's well worth visiting the Kentmere.org website for more detailed information.

A lovely insight into life in the valley comes from a curious old book: *The Annals of a Quiet Valley*, edited by John Watson. It is purported to be the edited diary of a country parson from the eighteenth century and, although it may not quite be all that it seems, there

St Cuthbert's Church, Kentmere.

The Old Church.

Drawing of St Cuthbert's from *Annals of a Quiet Valley*.

are plenty of interesting stories in there that give a feel for what life must have been like. He tells of shearing festivals when all the sheep were brought down from the fells for clipping. Everyone in the village would have been involved in one way or another and a shearing feast was laid on at the end by the farmer with 'tobacco, ale, spirits and a series of most inspiriting ballads'. There were also athletic events associated with it, with the best wrestler being rewarded with the finest fleece clipped. Then there was the Auld Wives' Hake, usually held on Christmas Eve and 'observed by matrons only', which appears to be an evening of tea drinking and gossiping.

My favourite of them all has to be 'Nut Monday', which occurred on the first Monday in September, when the whole village would go out 'nutting'. There are some wonderful old photos of dozens of people crammed into open horse-drawn coaches heading out in their 'nutting party' – obviously all dressed in their finest clothes. They were off to gather the hazelnuts along the valley, much to the dismay of the local squirrels. The hazel has long been thought of as having mystical powers, but from a purely pragmatic perspective, the nuts would have been an important source of food during the winter months.

In these remote valleys, fresh food through the winter was generally confined to eggs, poultry and geese, but thanks to the rivers, salmon was very popular; in fact it was so popular that local schools and employers often had to write into their contracts that fish would be served no more than three times a week. A pamphlet from 1827 ('Manners and

River Sprint.

Customs in Westmorland') describes the food as being primarily 'oaten bread, dressed barley and a few onions' and any animals killed were salted and smoked to preserve them with nothing wasted: 'The briny liquor in which the beef had been cooked, thickened with a little meal, was taken as broth, and this meal was helped down with pickled red cabbage'.

Potatoes weren't really eaten until around 1730 and even then there weren't many of them. Tea arrived at much the same time and was a popular drink with the ladies, but not everyone warmed to it. One elderly lady received a pound of tea from her son in London and proceeded to smoke it as she was under the impression it was tobacco. She complained that it wasn't as good as her usual Virginia!

For many years the church in Longsleddale was without a door and to prevent the cattle wandering in, a large thorn bush was dragged into the doorway. The responsibility for putting the thorn bush in place rested with the last person to leave but the parson would often have to intervene if someone had skipped their duties. In the winter months, the congregations would dwindle during periods of poor weather when people just couldn't get there, which meant there was more communion wine to go around and the clergyman was often heard to whisper 'drink gayley deep; there's not many o' us this morning'. There was also one notable occasion when the communion wine ran out and the vicar replaced it with rum thinking that no one would notice.

This part of the world is 'Herdy Central' and a walk around here simply would not be complete without the smiling face of a Herdwick sheep brightening up the day. They've been on the fells for hundreds of years and are so well adapted that they can be left on the high fells all-year round. During heavy snow, Herdies will generally not follow the other sheep and shelter alongside walls, where they are likely to get caught in drifts; instead they

Herdwick sheep.

will instinctively make their way to higher, open areas to avoid getting buried. Even if they do get buried, they still don't give up and will eat their own fleeces to keep them going until the farmer comes to dig them out.

One of Kentmere's most famous residents was Bernard Gilpin (1517–83), whose many acts of kindness earned him the name 'The Apostle of the North'. As well as feeding and clothing the poor, he would also support poor boys in their education. Whenever he met one on the road he would chat to them and if they were intelligent, he would pay for them to attend university; one young boy went on to be provost of Queen's College, Oxford, and another became the Bishop of Chichester.

The main section of the route is part of an ancient road linking Shap to Barrow and is still very well used, although the presence of 4×4s on the route is contentious and often makes the local news as campaigners make their feelings known. Transport in the valley has long been an emotive issue and locals were amazed and horrified when the first horse-drawn chaise arrived in the valley. People had generally moved between the valleys on foot or horseback, with women riding pillion behind the men, and few people travelled further than they absolutely had to.

Even in the 1940s, a trip to Kendal was considered a big day out. In *School in the Fells*, Olwen Harris recounts how she left her home in Dudley in the West Midlands to spend fifteen months working as the schoolmistress of Longsleddale School from 1940. She describes the scene on a Saturday afternoon in Kendal when everyone was getting ready to board the bus back from town with the farmers' wives 'laden with their huge market baskets'. They had sold all their eggs and butter and the baskets were now filled with food, sewing materials and clothes, plus they had batteries for their wirelesses, which had been taken to town for charging.

Above: Kentmere Valley and ancient linked routes.

Below: Cyclists in Kentmere.

During her time in the valley, Ms Harris lodged at Beech Hill Farm, very near to the church and school. She describes an idyllic scene teaching eighteen pupils between the ages of five and fourteen, spending plenty of time in the outdoors and connecting with the nature around them. Books and other literature came from Kendal Education Office, and a box of books from the library would be delivered and collected by the local bus driver.

Many of the scenes she describes are still familiar today. She talks about trying to get the train back from the West Midlands and not being able to get a seat because of all the visitors coming up for their holidays or the day Mr Dixon was knocked off his bicycle by a lorry that didn't stop and she had to bandage him up. She also describes the deprivation of some of the children; how pencils and a penknife were quickly stolen from her desk and how her own family would regularly send gifts of toys for the children.

At least there was electricity in the 1940s. Prior to that winter evenings in the village would have been very long and very dark. People rose and slept with the sun and, in the winter, the only light would have come from candles made of rushes and mutton fat. Despite the lack of light, Longsleddale Valley still produced a famous botanist by the name of John Wilson. He started off as a shoemaker, then became a baker to make more money and turned to botany as he recuperated from severe asthma attacks. In 1744, he published a *Synopsis of British Plants in Mr Ray's Method*, which was the first systematic account of British plants in English (Carl Linnaeus had published his *Systema Naturae* in 1735 but that was in Latin).

Remote as they valleys were, and tough as life undoubtedly was, they still knew how to celebrate and weddings were a great excuse for the villagers to have fun. In the 1700s, the bride would have been decked in a brightly coloured home-made outfit decorated with

Signpost for all forms of transport.

Above: Longsleddale Barn.

Opposite: Foxgloves.

large ribbons and following the ceremony an unusual custom took place. Once outside the church, the young men would pull off their shoes and stockings to show a ribbon wrapped around each leg. The bride would then start them off on the 'race of kisses' and they would run, barefoot, to her house and back with the winner being rewarded with a kiss and another ribbon from the bride. The parties generally lasted through the night with people finally dispersing as day broke. It was probably a good job the whole village was invited.

8. THE THREE PASSES — GARBURN, NAN BIELD AND GATESCARTH

Introduction

These are three of the most popular walking passes in the Lake District and connect remote valleys with busy trade routes. The scenery is magnificent, but if you're planning to do the Nan Bield to Haweswater then back via Gatescarth route then heed the words of Wainwright who warns 'This walk is rather too arduous to be done "there and back" by walkers of only average ability.' He does have a rather lovely solution to long linear walks though. He suggests making arrangements with another walking party, each parking at one end, and swapping car keys when you meet in the middle. Cheaper than a taxi but I feel sure the insurance companies would have something to say about it.

The Routes

Garburn Pass is still shown as Garburn Road on OS maps and starts down in Troutbeck as an offshoot of the old Roman High Street road. It's a long steady climb but the views of Troutbeck Valley provide a picturesque distraction as you gain height. Keep your eyes

Hikers on Garburn Pass.

and ears open, as the route is very popular with mountain bikers but, since June 2011, it has been designated as a 'restricted byway' meaning it is now off limits for 4×4s and motorbikes. There was a proposal many years ago to fully upgrade it to a proper road, but this met with strong opposition and never came to fruition.

Nan Bield Pass is a little like Ravel's Bolero; it begins sedately with a long gently rising climb along the very pretty valley, but be ready for the final stretch, which is a very steep hairpin hike up onto the col between Mardale Ill Bell and Harter Fell. If you're doing the there and back route then this is where you have a choice: you can either drop down to Haweswater then climb back up Gatescarth Pass or nip up and over Harter Fell and enjoy magnificent views over Haweswater.

Gatescarth Pass also has a long steady lead in along the valley but the up isn't quite so sharp and nasty at the end. It's also a much broader and well-laid track but, again, you need to be aware of bikes and 4×4s, which also use the route.

The History

Garburn Pass – Maximum Height 447 metres (1,467 feet)

Troutbeck Valley, like many other parts of the Lake District, was once heavily wooded and Troutbeck Park was a popular place for pig farming, with the pigs happily snuffling around in the woodland undergrowth. Even back in the twelfth and thirteenth centuries, the woodlands were under threat and local lords were doing what they could to preserve them. 'Pannage' is the practice of allowing commoners to release pigs into woodlands to feast on the fallen nuts and in 1423 this was worth £6 15s to the Countess of Richmond

Troutbeck Church.

(who owned the land) but, almost ten years later, this value had dropped to 60s 10d. By 1454 she was receiving nothing, most likely indicating that the woods, and the pigs, were no longer present.

By the late fifteenth century, woodlands were being damaged by cattle and sheep trampling or munching the saplings, and pig ownership was restricted to one per family, which had to be ringed and kept at the door and away from the woods.

The lords owned the woods but they were looked after by tenants who didn't always abide by the rules. The tenants were only allowed to take wood to meet the necessities – repairs, fencing, etc. – as well as being allowed to take dead wood for burning, but they often felled more trees than were required, and records show the manorial court regularly imposed fines on those overstepping the mark. The woods were also being depleted for making charcoal, which we mainly use today for relaxing summer barbeques, but back in the eighteenth century it was a highly valuable product much in demand from the various ironworks in the region and supplies were tightly guarded.

The route is very easy to follow and drops down into Kentmere just behind Kentmere Hall, a beautiful fourteenth-century pele tower. The tower, and farmhouse it now forms part of, were rebuilt during the sixteenth century, and it's said that the workmen were helped by a local lad named Hugh Hird (also referred to as Cork Lad of Kentmere or Hugh Gilpin in different texts) who was renowned for his strength and gigantic size. Allegedly he lifted a beam 'thirty feet in length and thirteen inches by twelve and a half in thickness' into place in the hall, without help from anyone else.

It is also said that he lived with his mother in Troutbeck Park, where they basically squatted in a house until the owner came to remove them. Hugh was then sent to London and, while he was there, took part in a wrestling competition attended by Edward VI.

Garburn Pass.

After winning the competition, the king asked what he would like as a prize and Hugh asked for the right to continue living in the house where they had squatted as well as modest rights to cut peat and wood. The king immediately granted this and Hugh returned to the house and lived there until he died pulling a tree up by its routes, aged forty-two.

Badger Rock or Brock Stone is an enormous boulder sitting in a field as you approach Kentmere church, most likely a huge glacial 'erratic' left behind when the ice sheets melted. These days it's a very popular with climbers and is well known among the bouldering community with thirty-two different logged routes to the summit.

Badger Rock.

Nan Bield Pass – Maximum Height 640 metres (2,100 feet)

I'm always intrigued by unusual names and 'Nan Bield' is a curious name. The best I can come up with is that 'bield' means shelter and 'nan' is old English for 'none' so it could be that this was known as the pass with no shelter or shelters, although now there are a couple at the Haweswater end. When we tackled the route it was a surprisingly hot October day, which caught us out a little bit, and I can vouch for the fact that there was nowhere to shelter (and very few places to sit and have lunch) on the entire first section of the route.

What I sadly didn't discover until afterwards is that Toadhowe Well, which we splashed through on our way to the head of the valley, was once 'famed for being the best water in Westmorland' according to Harriet Martineau's guide from 1855. Harriet was a British novelist and journalist who, as well as travel guides, also wrote extensively on politics and religion. Born in Norwich, she moved to Ambleside in 1845, where she lived until her death, writing about her garden, her explorations of the area and her autobiography. I also love a tenuous link and it turns out that Harriet's great nephew, Francis Martineau Lupton, is the great-great-grandfather of Catherine, Duchess of Cambridge.

As the path climbs along Hallow Bank, look down into the valley and just below Tongue Scar you may spot the remains of a Romano-British settlement. This is an excellent example of these small farmsteads and consists of an enclosure containing the remains of ten stone huts, some of which are thought to be dwellings while others were most likely used for storage or as guards huts. The site is a Scheduled Ancient Monument so if you do decide to go down and pay it a visit, don't move anything.

Up above you on the right is the distinctive shape of Drygrove Gill, which, despite its name, is the source of a spring but its curious cigar shape had me reaching for my

Ullstone Gill.

Above: Looking down Nan Bield Pass to Haweswater.

Below: Kentmere Reservoir and 'Gillespie Gill' on the far right.

geology textbooks. All of the rocks on this section are Ordovician volcanic (around 461 million years old) but the rocks in Drygrove Gill are tuffs and therefore slightly softer than the surrounding andesite. In the short term this doesn't really matter but after 450 million years the differences will begin to show as the water erodes more quickly into the softer rocks.

Lastly for Nan Bield is a little bit of forgotten history, rediscovered thanks again to Harriet Martineau. In her book she mentions Gladgove Gill, which is the gill dropping down in between Wander Scar and Gavel Crag. She describes how it has recently changed name to Gillespie Gill in honour of a group of men who had recently died there. It turns out to be a very sad story from 1838 where two men, John Huddlestone and Thomas Gillespie, plus Thomas's fourteen-year-old son, perished on their return from a fishing trip to Hayes Water. The weather was 'very boisterous' and it is presumed they died of exhaustion and hunger.

Gatescarth Pass – Maximum Height 572 metres (1,877 feet)

The road to Gatescarth Pass starts at Sadgill Bridge, most famous for being 'the Postman Pat bridge'. John Cunliffe, who wrote the *Postman Pat* books, lived in Kendal and based

Sadgill Bridge with remnants of original bridge.

the village of Greendale in the books on Longsleddale and Sadgill Bridge is the bridge Pat drives over at the start of each episode. The local postmen must be famous as many visitors (us included!) have lain in wait to snap them as they drive over the bridge. The original bridge was built in 1717 and if you look closely at the sides of the bridge you can still see the remnants of the original, much lower, bridge.

Although the pass is open to 4×4s, they can only drive over there with a permit and usually only twenty to thirty permits are issued each year, so your chances of meeting one are fairly low. Plus they are restricted as far as Wrengill Quarry.

Deep under your feet as you make your way over the pass is the Haweswater Aqueduct. I am an unashamed geek of huge engineering projects, and have a very soft spot for both the Thirlmere and the Haweswater aqueducts. The survey posts from the building of the aqueduct can still be found on the fells in the area (marked as 'pillar' on the OS maps) and are the only indication of the lifeline running beneath them. The aqueduct carries over 570 million litres of water a day. It was completed in 1955 and in recent years current owners United Utilities conducted a thorough cleaning and upgrading of the pipes using specially designed vehicles and a team of 'aquanauts'.

Gatescarth Pass winding down to Haweswater.

Gatescarth Pass in winter conditions.

Gatescarth Pass used to be famous for ending at the Dun Bull in Mardale Green but this is sadly no longer the case as the remains of the Dun Bull lie at the bottom of the Haweswater Reservoir along with the rest of the village. Instead the pass now ends at the car park at the head of the reservoir, which is very useful for parking but a decent pint would be nice...

9. HAWESWATER TO SHAP – OLD CORPSE ROAD

Introduction

We first walked this road in the middle of winter when there was snow on the frozen ground and the wind was stinging our faces and making our eyes water. Despite being well wrapped up in windproof down jackets with thick waterproof boots and socks, plus thermal woolly hats, we were still pleased to curtail the walk and get down to the Haweswater Hotel for a warming bowl of soup and a hot coffee in front of the fire. Imagine what it must have been like when none of those luxuries were available, and you had to transport your recently departed relative, strapped to a pony, over the unforgiving fells.

The Route

Obviously the Old Corpse Road used to start down in Mardale Green but, unless you have scuba gear, the starting point is now at the southern end of the lake opposite The Rigg.

Old Corpse Road sign.

From there, it zigzags up and over Mardale Common, then down through Swindale. After following the road for a short way, cross the footbridge by the ford and follow the path as it skirts the lower edge of Ralfland Forest, then down through Keld and into Shap.

The History

Haweswater valley was very popular with visitors during the eighteenth and nineteenth centuries and is described in most of the guidebooks written at that time in the most glowing of terms: 'One of the loveliest of the lesser lakes and not nearly so well known as it deserves to be' (Martineau, 1876).

Where today we now see a large reservoir there was once a smaller lake. Although it's hard to picture what that lake would have looked like, Arthur Young's account from 1770 gives us some idea: 'The lake is a small one, about three miles long, half a mile over in some places; almost divided by a promontory of enclosures, joined only by a strait, so that it consists of two sheets of water.'

Thomas West (1778) tells us that at its narrowest part (below Sandhill Knotts) a man could throw a stone across it but he's not that impressed with Riggindale: 'Above the chapel all is hopeless waste and desolation. The little vale contracts into a glen, strewed with the precipitated ruins of mouldering mountains.'

There are numerous maps, images and accounts in existence which describe the village of Mardale Green, all of which help us to understand why there are so many important passes in the region, because what we see today as a dead-end valley was once a busy and important thoroughfare.

Haweswater Reservoir.

The dam to create the reservoir was built in the 1930s to provide water for the good people of Manchester, who were in desperate need of a clean, reliable water supply at that time. The settlement of Burnbanks was created at the northern end of the valley to house the workers but it was only ever intended to provide temporary accommodation. One guidebook of the time noted that the trees surrounding the village had been thoughtfully planted in order to hide the scars left once the temporary houses were dismantled. Although some houses were removed and the settlement fell into disrepair, it's still there today and makes for a very pretty and interesting stop on a walk around the lake.

The church in Mardale is believed to be medieval but the grounds weren't consecrated until 1729, so the dead had to be transported up and over the fell to be buried at Shap church. Post-1729 burials took place there but when the village was flooded for the reservoir these bodies were exhumed and reinterred in Shap.

As with all good coffin routes, there are a number of folklore and ghost stories associated with it. Hugh's Laithes Pike, just to the north, is said to be the final resting place of Jimmie Lowther, who apparently led 'a riotous life'. He died after falling from his horse while racing it when he was drunk. Because he died too suddenly to have time to repent, his ghost haunted the village so they reburied him on the top of the fell, safely out of the way.

The valley was a popular retreat for writers and artists, and a popular novelist of the time, Hall Caine (a vocal opponent of the reservoir), based his novel *Shadow of a Crime* around another piece of local folklore. A man from the village died and was being transported over the fell for burial but, unknown to the villagers, he had committed a serious crime (possibly

The Old Corpse Road, wild and remote.

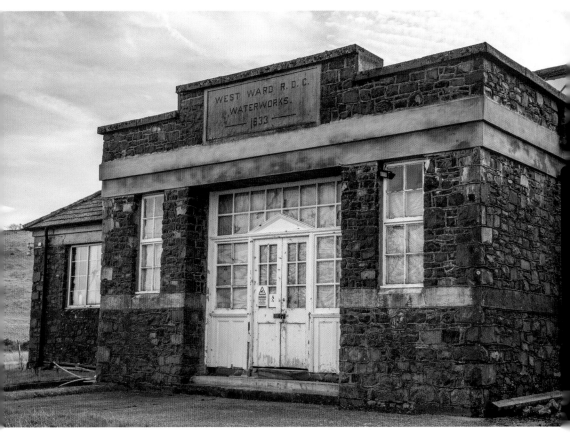

Old waterworks building.

murder). During the journey, there was a big storm and the horse carrying his body bolted, only returning three months later with the grisly remains of the body still attached. By now his crimes had been discovered, and the villagers deemed that this was a fitting punishment for his wicked doings.

The corpse road follows what would have been an old peat cutters track and drops down into the very pretty and very tiny village of Swindale, which Wainwright observes has been 'plundered unobtrusively for water'. The only evidence of this is a rather lovely old waterworks, dated 1833, at the edge of village, which, at the time of writing, is undergoing transformation into a self-catering holiday cottage.

What there is evidence of is a water intake structure, which at first sight sticks out like a sore thumb but on investigation was created for very good reason. During 2016, following extensive research, a project was undertaken to address flooding issues in the valley by 're-meandering' Swindale Beck. It had been artificially straightened over 160 years ago and had developed large levees along the banks as a result of generations of dredging. The result was that the river raced through the valley with no means of escape and, when it did overflow, the levees prevented this water from draining back into the beck.

By re-meandering the river and introducing gravel bars the flow has been slowed and, as a consequence, habitats for local wildlife have improved. Future plans include

Swindale Beck.

further managing of the land, a controlled amount of replanting and introducing fencing along some sections of the channel, thus restoring it to how it would have been before it was straightened. The building around the water intake also allows for safe fish and eel migration.

The route from Swindale to Keld near Shap can be boggy and tricky to follow. It's a wonderfully remote valley missed by most visitors so the footpaths are not as well trodden as elsewhere in the county. On the approach to Keld, the Old Corpse Road is crossed by the more recent concrete road, which was built to link the A6 to Burnbanks and allow deliveries of the materials for the construction of the dam. Technically it's not open to traffic, but keep your wits about you, as it's still a popular cut through for locals.

Keld derives from the ancient Viking word 'kelda', which either means 'spring' or 'the still part of the water in a river' and the River Lowther does slow here as it navigates Keld Dub. Keld Chapel is a wonderful place to visit for a real step back in time. It's owned by the National Trust and although it is always locked, the key is kept on the doorpost of the house opposite and in a world of high-tech entry passes, it is a wonderfully huge, thick, 'proper' key.

Inside the chapel you'll find a series of reproduced letters exchanged in 1917 between Lord Lonsdale, his solicitor and Cardinal Rawnsley, where Lord Lonsdale argues that it was a barn not a chapel, and its location made it 'impossible for a full load of hay' to pass. He offered the cardinal £25 (equivalent to just over £1,600 today) to buy it so he could pull it down. Thankfully his offer was rejected and the chapel still stands.

It is thought (though it is not certain) that it may have originally been built as a chantry – a special chapel built for saying prayers for the dead – by the monks of nearby Shap Abbey. Sometime before 1698 it changed from a religious building to a private dwelling and

Above: Keld Chapel.

Below: Shap Abbey.

remained as such until the late nineteenth century when Revd J. Whiteside repaired the collapsed roof and reinstated it as a place of worship.

Shap Abbey is just a short diversion from the route, and although there's not much other than the church tower remaining, it's still an interesting site to explore. The abbey was founded in the twelfth century and holds the distinction of being the last abbey to fall during Henry VIII's Dissolution of the Monasteries, before it was finally dissolved on 14 January 1540.

The last point of interest on the route is Goggleby Stone, large and unmissable and adjacent to the footpath as you approach Shap. This is one of the final reminders of a once great and widely renowned 'Avenue of Stones' that existed here. It was described as being 'the Stonehenge or Avebury of the north of England' by Professor J. Y. Simpson MD (who, when he wasn't studying antiquities, introduced the use of both chloroform and forceps to the world of medicine). The avenue was nearly 2 miles long and, on an OS map, the line of stones marked across the fields to the east of the town is still visible. The original structure is believed to be Neolithic and stood for centuries before being demolished and removed as the region developed.

A painting from 1775, credited to Lady Lowther, shows a stone circle at the top and a broad avenue of stones sweeping away into the distance. The lack of preservation of the stones and their destruction without documentation, in large part by the rail company literally railroading their way through the centre of the stone circle, means that definite evidence for dating the stones or understanding what their function was is frustratingly absent. If you're interested in finding out more about them, there is a

Goggleby Stone.

The Avenue of Stones, Lady Lowther.

fascinating paper on the Modern Antiquarian website (referenced in the bibliography), where the authors have tracked down many of the original stones, now incorporated into walls and gateposts.

Once you arrive in Shap, there are many historical places of note to visit. Wikipedia names over thirty listed buildings in the parish, including the Greyhound Inn, an old coaching inn, which dates back to the early eighteenth century and is reputedly where Bonnie Prince Charlie stayed. He was less than complimentary about the experience, but I'm sure it's now under new management.

The end of the Corpse Road is St Michael's Church, which predates the abbey by a hundred years or so, although it's thought there has been a place of worship on the site since AD 750. There's a monument in the churchyard to the men who lost their lives building the Lancaster to Carlisle railway, which is a sobering reminder that perhaps the introduction of health and safety regulations aren't an entirely bad idea.

Inside the church the only reminder of its ancient past are the Norman columns, the rest of the original building having been lost in a restoration in 1898. The Millennium Window depicts local scenes and land uses and was installed and dedicated in September 2000. It was designed by Adam Goodyear, who involved the local community to design something that reflected life in the parish.

St Michael's Church, Shap.

In 2011 there were concerns that the church may have to close after thieves stole the lead from the roof and the insurance payment fell far short of what was needed to complete the work. The story was picked up by the national press and people from all over the country generously donated money, with United Utilities also adding a £6,000 grant to the funds, thus allowing the repairs to be carried out and the church to return to full use once again.

10. LONGSLEDDALE TO WET SLEDDALE — THE OLD QUARRYING ROUTES

Introduction

This is a combination of old quarrying routes and bridleways. As well as the main Longsleddale to Wet Sleddale route, we'll also take a short diversion along a track back to Swindale as it holds a wonderful surprise. Once you leave Gatescarth Pass, just after Wrengill Quarry the scenery changes dramatically from jagged soaring fells to a more rounded landscape, which is both beautiful and boggy. There are plenty of sheep around and you'll find plenty of Swaledales, Rough Fell sheep and Texels. Rough Fell and Swaledales look a lot alike but Rough Fell sheep have longer, more luxuriant fleeces, while Texels look like they might mug you.

The Route

The main route starts at Sadgill bridge and follows Gatescarth Pass up to Wrengill Quarry where you'll find a clearly signed path leading off to Mosedale and Swindale. At the fork,

View over Wet Sleddale Reservoir.

the left-hand route drops down to Swindale and if you don't fancy a there and back detour, it can be made into a looped route using the Corpse Road back to Haweswater. The right-hand route climbs a little to Scam Mathew where, if you turn around, there are lovely views back along Mosedale Valley. As you approach Wet Sleddale, the original track continues along Stackhouse Brow, but we opted to drop down via Sleddale Hall because it was more interesting and less boggy. You can then continue on to Shap, either along the nice solid A6 or via Steps Hall, where the going underfoot is generally swampy.

The History

First up, let me get contentious by taking Mr Wainwright and Miss Martineau to task. They both describe Mosedale Valley in less than glowing terms. Wainwright states that it is 'one of six upland valleys of that name in Lakeland, all being desolate wastes of marshy ground', while Martineau calls it 'the most desolate and dreary of all the vales'. Now there is no getting away from the fact that it is somewhat moist underfoot here and definitely one to avoid after prolonged rain, but desolate and dreary is just being plain mean. We walked it in November and February, and both times it looked absolutely lovely. For desolate read peaceful, deserted and tranquil, and for dreary read spacious, rolling and gentle on the eye. Lakeland beauty isn't just about the high fells; it's also about hidden away gems like this.

It wasn't always peaceful, quiet and deserted though. When both Wrengill and Mosedale quarries were in action, there was plenty of activity in the valley, and the presence of the quarries resulted in the hard tracks we see along the valleys.

Much-maligned Mosedale Valley.

The approach to Wrengill Quarry passes over a small bridge with a dedication etched into the stone under it. The dedication simply reads 'Denys Beddard 1917 – 1985'. Denys, I discovered from a footnote on a blog by the 'Boot Boys', retired to the Lake District with his wife. He was the chairman of the Westmorland Geological Society, worked in medical administration and is cited in a book titled *Food Poisoning, Policy and Politics* (2005), which analysed the responses to the numerous food health scares of the 1980s. Remember that when you're sitting there tucking into a warm ham sandwich that has rattled around your rucksack for a few hours.

Wrengill Quarry must, like all disused quarries, come with a health warning: there is old machinery lying around and lots of sudden unfenced-off drops, so if you are going to explore, do be careful. Slate was mined there from 1729 to around 1847. Back then it was known as 'Rangle Quarry' and produced large quantities of 'fine blue slate', which was used in equally fine buildings of the period. The slabs of slate had to be removed from the quarry by pony all the way back down into the valley, where they could be loaded onto carts and carried away for distribution. This explains why the upper sections of the route up from Longsleddale are unusually metalled; it was to prevent the ponies slipping.

The quarry reopened briefly in the mid-nineteenth century and was allegedly worked by Italian prisoners of war during the Second World War. When they were sent home they put down their tools and left and the quarry was never worked again. Although this is hard to confirm, there was a POW camp called Merrythought near to Penrith (the site is now owned by DEFRA) and local landowners and farmers would regularly use prisoners as labourers, so it's not beyond the realms of possibility.

Opposite: Metalled track.

Below: Denys Beddard Bridge.

By far the finest image of the quarry is the one from 1835 drawn by Thomas Allom and engraved by J. W. Lowry. I love it because it captures an image of goings on there long before photography and also because it's exaggerated in the way artists of that time tended to do. The quarry is spectacular in a brutal, industrial way, but even though we've visited several times, we've not spotted the huge ravines or soaring packhorse bridges shown in the painting.

Mosedale Quarry mined exactly the same blue slate, but it's likely that rather than removing it down through Longsleddale, it was instead moved out of Swindale to the old road/A6. That section of the route is peppered with the remains of old buildings and, where it hasn't been lost, the track is broad and was clearly well laid initially. The spoil heaps still scar the landscape but slowly Mother Nature is claiming them back, and it won't be many years before they have vanished completely.

Mosedale Cottage, at the head of the valley, was once a permanent dwelling but was last inhabited in 1930. Previous census reports show a shepherd and his family living there but they were gone by 1861. Today the bothy is owned and looked after by the Mountaineering Bothies Association, and is free to stay in with no prior booking required. Although bothies can vary widely in their standards, this one is warm, cosy and has a decent sofa, which could be due to the fact that some of the outbuildings are locked and still used by the local shepherd who most likely still keeps a watchful eye on the place.

If you take the offshoot path to Swindale, be sure to loop back to see Forces Falls marked on the map. There is an excellent footbridge there now and the field opposite is part of the re-meandering project described in Chapter 9. The falls are one of Cumbria's glorious surprises and even Wainwright describes them as 'a spectacular ravine'. He was wrong about Mosedale but spot on about the forces; they are spectacular and were they to be anywhere more accessible, they would surely be swamped with visitors throughout the year.

Back on the main route to Wet Sleddale, the track passes by the curiously named Scam Matthew. The word 'scam' in its modern sense only came into use in the 1960s, but there's a map of the region from 1960 with Scam Matthew marked on. It's unlikely to have become a widely enough used term to have had a landmark named after it by then, so it's more probable that it's after the local dialect word 'scamb' meaning 'crack' or 'injury'. Sadly I've not been able to track down who Matthew was.

As you approach Sleddale Hall, on the opposite side of the valley is an old deer park, two oddly shaped fields immediately adjacent to the River Lowther. Anecdotal local history suggests that the monks at Shap Abbey used to fatten their deer here for venison, but there's not a lot of supporting evidence for that. Although many of the typically high walls of the old deer park remain, the last deer in the park were put there as an experiment by the 2nd Earl of Lonsdale in the 1860s.

These days Sleddale Hall is the stuff of local legend since it was used in the cult film *Withnail and I*, where it featured as Uncle Monty's cottage Crow Crag. Its early history is hard to pin down but as with many old local buildings, it may once also have been associated with the monks at Shap Abbey. In 1802 it was noted that although it had land covering around 250 acres, most of it was 'poorish meadow' or 'barren mountains' and was not highly valued. According to another source, the hall was the Sleddale family home, one of whom went on to become the first mayor of Kendal. The title was first given by Charles I in 1636, and the first mayor on the roll of honour is Thomas Sleddall, who had previously served as an alderman in 1617 and 1634, so if that's the case this could date the hall to at least the seventeenth century.

Waterfall, Wrengill Quarry.

Above: Wrengill Quarry, Thomas Allom and J. S. Lowry.

Below: Mosedale Cottage.

Sleddale Hall ('Crow Crag').

Only the downstairs rooms and the exterior of the hall were used during filming – the bedroom and staircase shots were filmed elsewhere. Despite its remoteness, the hall has long attracted fans of the film, many of whom have left graffiti on the outside of the building. The house was owned by United Utilities but the ownership of the hall hung in the balance for a while before it was eventually sold in 2009 to an architect and fan of the film, who vowed to restore it 'in a way that other fans of the film would approve of'. Certainly from the outside it looks much as it did in the film, although somewhat tidier.

Wet Sleddale Reservoir is another of the local reservoirs built to supply Manchester. It was completed in 1966 and the water is moved via tunnels to Haweswater and then on to Manchester. The dam wall is 21 metres (69 feet) high and is very impressive to see, especially when the water overflows down the front. If you don't fancy a long hike, there is ample public parking near to the dam wall and a lovely footpath circling the reservoir. One year while we were enjoying a walk there we heard the first cuckoo of the year calling in the nearby woods.

The building of all the reservoirs in the region may have been one thing that spurred the Friends of the Lake District into existence. They first met in Keswick in July 1934 (the national park wasn't formed until May 1951) and early members were required to pay 2s 6d per year. The original press release stated that (among other things) they aimed to 'mobilise local and national opinion' and create a fund to assist local authorities. The initial signatories to this press release included Eleanor Rawnsley (wife of Canon Rawnsley), Gordon G. Wordsworth (grandson of William) and Geoffrey Winthrop Young, climber, poet and mentor to George Mallory, whose attempt to summit Everest left the world with an enduring mystery that may never be solved.

Above: Wet Sleddale Reservoir.

Below: Red deer.

BIBLIOGRAPHY

Books

Baddeley, M. J. B., *The Lake District* (Ward, Lock & Co., 1940)
Brodie, Ian O., *The Cistercian Way* (Carnegie Press, 1989)
Budworth, Joseph, *A Fortnight's Ramble to the Lakes* (Cadell and Davies, 1810)
Burnett, T. R., *Friends of the Lake District* (Journal of Fell and Rock Climbing Club, 1934)
Cappelli, Tim, *The Thirlmere Way* (Sigma Leisure, 1992)
Collingwood, W. G., *Lake District History* (Titus Wilson & Sons, 1928)
Cooper, D. G., *The Crummock Water Aureole* (Journal of the Geology Society of London V145, 1988)
Dickinson, J. C., *The Land of Cartmel* (Titus Wilson, 1980)
Edmonds, Mark, *The Langdales* (Tempus Publishing, 2010)
Fletcher Buntin, Tom, *Life in Langdale* (Titus Wilson, 1993)
Fraser, Maxwell, *Companion into Lakeland* (London, Methuen and Co., 1937)
Gell, William, *A Tour in the Lakes Made in 1797*, ed. by William Rollinson (Frank Graham, 1968)
Harper, Charles G., *The Manchester and Glasgow Road* (Cecil Palmer, London, 1924)
Harris, Olwen, *The School in the Fells* (Mitre Press, London, 1969)
Hodge, E. W., *Old Maps* (Journal of Fell and Rock Climbing Club, 1934)
Honeyman, Neil, *Old Mardale* (Stenlake Publishing, 2012)
Howorth, Billy F. K., *Carlisle History Tour* (Amberley, 2018)
Hunt, Irvine, *Old Lakeland Transport* (Rusland Press, 1978)
Hurst, John, *Lakeland Reporter* (Sutton Publishing, 1996)
Lofthouse, Jessica, *Lancashire and Westmorland Highway* (Robert Hale, London, 1953)
Logan Thompson, Bruce, *A Deer Park in Wet Sleddale* (Transactions of the Cumberland and Westmorland Antiquarian and Archaeological Society, 1934)
Logoe, John, *Some Eskdale Rock Climbs* (Journal of Fell and Rock Climbing Club, 1959)
Martineau, Harriet, *The English Lake District* (Simpkin Marshall, London, 1876)
Murray, John, *A Tour in the English Lakes with Thomas Gray and Joseph Farington* (Frances Lincoln, 2012)
Nicholson, Joseph, *The History and Antiquities of the Counties of Westmorland and Cumberland* (Joseph Nicholson, 1777)
Ogilby, John, *Britannia* (1675)
Ramshaw, David, *The English Lakes* (Amadeus Press, 1996)
Richard, Guthrie, *A Tour Through Old Lakeland* (Stenlake Publishing, 1996)
Spence, Dr J. E., *An Early Settlement on Moor Divock* (Transactions of the Cumberland and Archaeological Society)

Wainwright, Alfred, *Old Roads of Eastern Lakeland* (Westmorland Gazette, 1985)
Walker, Peter N., *Folk Stories from the Lake District* (Robert Hale, London, 1993)
Watson, John, *The Annals of a Quiet Valley* (J. M. Dent & Co., 1894)
West, Timothy, *A Guide to the Lakes* (Richardson and Urguhart, London, 1778)
Williams L. A., *Road Transport in Cumbria in the Nineteenth Century* (Allen & Unwin, London, 1975)
Wilson Parker, John, *An Atlas of The English Lakes* (Cicerone, 2002)
Woods, Jack, *The North Road* (J. Woods, 1996)

Miscellaneous

Cumberland Official Guide 1962–1963
English Heritage Guidebooks: Hadrian's Wall, Carlisle Castle, Brougham and Brough Castles, Furness Abbey
Guide to Dalton Castle by Barrow Borough Council
Shap Abbey in Westmorland and the Chapel at Keld by Ronald Wentworth Taylor
Solway's Built Heritage by Solway Wetlands
Solway's Churches – leaflets by East Solway Churches
St Cuthbert's Parish Church, Kentmere by Staveley and District History Society
The Shap Fell Story by Shap Local History Society
Ulverston Leaflets (assorted) by Choose Ulverston

Websites

Archaeology UK, www.archaeologyuk.org
Archive, www.archive.org
BBC, www.bbc.co.uk
British History Online, www.british-history.ac.uk
English Lakes, www.English-lakes.com
Fell and Rock Climbing Club, www.frcc.co.uk
Historic Population, www.histpop.org
Kentmere Village, www.kentmere.org
Lakes Guides, www.lakesguides.co.uk
Modern Antiquarian Shap Avenue, http://www.themodernantiquarian.com/post/29979/weblog/british_isles.html
Patterdale Today, www.patterdaletoday.co.uk/history